THE LITTLE WARS OF THE UNITED STATES

THE LITTLE WARS OF THE UNITED STATES

Colonel R. Ernest Dupuy

and Major General William H. Baumer

With a Foreword by
General Harold K. Johnson, U.S.A., Ret.

Maps by Jean A. Brown

Hawthorn Books, Inc. Publishers New York

 This book was manufactured in the United States of America and published simultaneously in Canada by Prentice-Hall of Canada, Ltd., 1870 Birchmount Road, Scarborough, Ontario. Library of Congress Catalogue Card Number: 68-28130.

First Edition: 1968

Design by: Gene Gordon

To Laura and Alice

Foreword

We live in a dynamic age. Time and distance have long since ceased to be major obstacles to the further advance of man; paradoxically, they have also ceased to provide man any measure of safety from his enemies. Yet, in spite of the demands placed upon us by the accelerated tempo of the present, we have not forgotten that the past holds valuable lessons for us.

The authors of this splendid book have explored in depth a series of "little," but significant, wars in United States history, in order to glean for us any lessons they may hold. Each reader must judge for himself whether the authors have accomplished their purpose; I believe they have. For me, not only have they described these lesser known episodes interestingly, they have succeeded in bringing into sharp focus the striking resemblances between the past and the present.

HAROLD K. JOHNSON
General, United States Army,
Retired
Former Chief of Staff, U.S.A.

Preface

Twice since 1950, the American people, groping in the fog of war, have discovered what many of them apparently believe to be phenomena new to the national experience. The first of these is "little" war, the second is "limited" war and the third is "guerrilla" war. A fourth newly coined label is "cold" war, but that expression, in this atomic age, needs no clarification.

What is a "little" war? How does it differ from a "big" war? Is there any justification for today's common practice of classing "guerrilla" war and "jungle" war as synonyms? Or for the frequently expressed argument that the Korean War was the first "limited" war in which the United States has engaged?

These are interesting questions. The authors propose to show that prior to the Korean War the United States has engaged, on foreign soil, in no less than seven wars, all "little" in that they laid no serious strain on the economic resources and stability of the nation, and all "limited" in political objective.*

One may point out, parenthetically, that the War of 1812, the War with Mexico, and the Spanish-American War were also each limited in their respective objectives. Unlike the Civil War, these conflicts were not "total"; not aimed at the destruction of the adversary's national existence. But all three of these were "big" in that they necessitated an appreciable strain upon

*Our century of Indian wars, although coming within this category, is not touched upon here. Interested readers are referred to *The Compact History of the Indian Wars*, John Tebbel, Hawthorn Books, New York, 1966.

the national economic resources, and are, therefore, aside from this study, except to note that each of them included "guerrilla" warfare.

All the wars discussed here included guerrilla operations, *i.e.,* combat on land or sea against irregular or partisan forces. One of our examples was a matter of sea warefare in its entirety. Another, with the exception of one extraordinary land expedition, was also a matter of sea wartare, while sea power played a more or less definitive supporting role in the other five. One of our case histories included Arctic warfare; jungle warfare played a part in three; and in one case fledgling wings flapped in air warfare.

From this two conclusions may be drawn: first, that guerrilla warfare may be, and frequently is, concomitant to any war; and second, that climate and terrain affect only strategy and tactics.

So much for semantics. Far more important is the fact that by 1950 the United States government and its armed forces had been exposed to a century and a half of limited little wars on both hemispheres, and in a wide variety of climate, terrain and international relationships.

Important also is the vociferous and at times violent opposition displayed at home to these wars, with the single exception of the China Relief Expedition. In some instances this dissent flamed far beyond the norm of debate and of the free speech so highly prized by Americans as the cornerstone of our democracy. The motivation of such dissenters might have been moot; but in each case the objective was the same: to thwart national policy by multiplying the burdens on fellow Americans in uniform, who were at the time staking their lives in support of that policy. This opposition at times approached dangerously that gift of "aid and comfort to the enemy" which is our national definition of treason.

The authors, presenting history here, also desire to emphasize the devotion to duty of American armed forces in situations little remembered today, but in striking resemblance to the present political-military situation of the United States. The record is clear. If the nation is not now utilizing the wealth of past experience narrated here, it is not the fault of the

American soldiers, sailors and airmen whose sagas are sung in these pages.

R. ERNEST DUPUY
WILLIAM H. BAUMER

Washington, D.C.

This narrative is based upon a wide variety of source material, primary and secondary, both official and private. The opinions expressed and the conclusions drawn are those of the authors and cannot be attributed either to the Department of Defense or to the services at large.

Contents

List of Maps

1

The Quasi War with France, 1798-1801

When Crew and Captain understand each other to the core,
It takes a gale and more than a gale to put their ship ashore;
For the one will do what the other commands, although they are chilled to the bone,
And both together can live through weather that neither could face alone.

—From "Together" by Rudyard Kipling

Captain Thomas Truxtun, USN, looked down at the blue water of the Caribbean as his frigate, USS *Constellation,* thirty-six, knifed through the sea at a fast twelve-knot clip. Under full sail, this new ship of the United States Navy, 175 feet long and 1265 tons, was a delight to her severe commanding officer. From the keel laying to commissioning a year and a half earlier, in 1797, he had observed the cedar and live oak which went into it. He had recruited his 268 sailors and forty-one Marines and had pounded into them obedience and competence, for "Terrible Tom" Truxtun was a strict disciplinarian. He alternately hounded, harassed, bullied, coaxed, and lauded officers and men. His rigid ways and tempestuous proclamations caused lifted eyebrows in Congress and the Navy alike. But he made men—bold seamen and capable gunners—as he was soon to prove.

The *Constellation*, on this morning of February 9, 1799, was a beautiful example of Joshua Humphreys' art of shipbuilding.

Toward the sky towered three great masts, as many clouds of sail. Rated as a thirty-six-gun frigate, she actually carried more—twenty-eight long eighteen-pounders on her gun deck, ten squatty twenty-four-pounder carronades on spar deck, quarterdeck, and forecastle.

The squat, red-faced Captain Truxtun knew what was expected of him. The United States was involved in an undeclared or quasi war with France. His frigate was as ready for action as a strong-willed captain could make it. His instructions from the Commander in Chief, President John Adams, was to cruise West Indies waters in search of French privateers and warships while giving protection to American trading vessels.

Adams' orders to the Navy were crystal clear: "You are hereby authorized, instructed and directed to subdue, seize and take any armed vessels of the French Republic."

So when from the foretop came the bellow "Sail ho!" this breezy morning, captain and crew both tensed. It was noon; eight bells had just been made and the ship's position recorded; *Constellation* was about five leagues (fifteen miles) off the northeastern point of the island of Nevis.

Truxtun's peering eyes made the stranger to be a full-rigged ship—definitely a man-o'-war. There seemed to be something wrong with her top-hamper for she carried no sail on her main-topmast. Was she British? Apparently not, for as the *Constellation* bore down on her, the flutter of Truxtun's signal bunting making the recognition signals then agreed upon between the American and Royal Navies went unanswered.

Then French she must be, and rolling drums beat to quarters as *Constellation*'s crew scampered to battle stations, and the Stars and Stripes broke out. The stranger, her own crew at quarters too, fired one gun to windward—a challenge to combat, and the French tricolor was mast-headed. She was *L'Insurgente,* forty, Captain Barreaut, an extremely fast frigate. However, a heavy squall had cracked her main-topmast that morning, so she lacked maneuverability.

Sensing his own superiority in speed and maneuverability, and since firing the guns to leeward in a stiff breeze and a rough sea would be troublesome, Truxtun deliberately gave his opponent the weather gauge and approached her lee beam. With both ships heeling from the wind, *L'Insurgente*'s gunners would thus be hampered. Moreover, *Constellation* was a cranky ship, and she handled better on the wind, it seems.

Constellation, her loaded guns run out and matches burning, her Marines in the tops, on forecastle, and quarterdeck, crept abreast of her adversary.

This would be the young American Navy's first major battle since the Revolution. How would it stand up in battle with French warships? The French Navy had already been strong at the time it had helped the American revolutionists beat the English. It had been fighting continuously since 1793 in the war between France and England. If the English Navy could not defeat the French, how could we? French naval officers, previously noblemen, had been replaced by the citizen sailors of the new French Republic. How good was their leadership? That was an uncertain factor, but what was known was that ships and guns were first class. Now was the moment of truth, as gunners blew on their glowing matches.

Constellation's broadside flamed. It neatly swept the Frenchman's quarterdeck where her carronades were mounted. But Barreaut was brave and like most Gallic ships *L'Insurgente* carried a huge crew. The French ship came rushing down upon the *Constellation*, Captain Barreaut shouting, "Stand by to board!"

Truxtun caught the indication of this move before it was fairly begun. Though the ships were only fifty yards apart, he clapped on more sail quickly enough to draw ahead, raking *L'Insurgente* on a diagonal as he did so; then suddenly the *Constellation* swung her bows and administered another diagonal rake from the opposite beam.

Things were now going all to pieces aboard the French frigate, but just at this juncture a ball from one of the long eighteen-pounders on her forecastle struck *Constellation*'s foremast just below the cap, damaging it so badly that the topmast threatened to topple at the next severe strain.

With the pitching sea, press of sail, and quick maneuvering, this would not be long in coming. Young David Porter, midshipman of the foretop, hailed the deck to report the damage, could get no answer through the din of cannon and shouting, so without orders clambered up himself to cut the slings and lower the fore-topsail yard, thus relieving the pressure. His quick thinking was to be echoed by later Porters who won fame in serving their country in other wars.

All this time the forty-one American Marines under First Lieutenant Bartholomew Clinch, USMC, used their muskets with terrible effect on the Frenchmen.

The American frigate's fire was meanwhile dismantling *L'Insurgente.* Her mizzen-topmast came down. All her forward braces were shot away; she could no longer maneuver. The *Constellation* tacked back and forth across her bows, pouring in raking broadsides. Finally, Barreaut struck his colors after an action of about two and a half hours, about an hour of which was at close quarters.

On the gun deck Truxtun had long eighteens to shoot against the long twelves of the French ship. Despite short weight of the American shot and the overweight of the French, including the heavy carronades on *L'Insurgente*'s decks, the proportion in weight of broadside metal was 369 pounds for the Americans to 338 for the French. But what was most impressive was the brilliance of Truxtun's tactics and the accuracy of the gunners he had trained, who inflicted seventy casualties while taking only four themselves and who completely wrecked the French ship.

Captain Barreaut was bitter in defeat, asking how the Americans could attack his ship when the countries were "not at war." In his anger he had completely forgotten that he challenged the *Constellation* and that he himself had made captive the United States schooner *Retaliation* the previous November.

Lieutenant John Rodgers, another "first" of a line of American naval heroes, was sent to take possession of *L'Insurgente.* With him went twenty-three seamen and a midshipman. For the latter he chose the young Porter, who "seems to be able to get out of his own way," and boats began bringing the prisoners over.

There was not much daylight left when the process started, and as night began to fall, the wind rose, making transit between the two ships flatly impossible. French sailors to the number of 170 were still aboard *L'Insurgente;* they were now without officers and in a nasty mood of defeat.

As Rodgers soon discovered, the French crew had thrown overboard all the handcuffs and shackles in the ship as well as the hatch gratings by which they could have been kept below decks.

Most of *L'Insurgente*'s running rigging was gone. Her decks were cluttered with dead men, and a storm was rising. The two American officers placed a man with a blunderbuss and a pile of loaded muskets at each hatch and tipped a loaded carronade to point down the main one. Then with their tiny work force they rushed back and forth madly throughout the night, setting a jury rig on the frigate. Dawn found them on a sea roughened by the storm, with the *Constellation* nowhere in sight. Now began a prodigious struggle with wind, sea, and the malevolence of men. It lasted for three days and two nights more, during which the French doubtless could have retaken the ship had there been among them a couple of suicidal heroes, willing to accept the first bullets in their chests so that the rest could rush up before a reload. But there were none such. Rodgers and Porter brought their prize frigate safely to harbor on St. Kitts.

The day after the battle Captain Truxtun thanked the "officers, seamen, ordinary seamen, and Marines" for their "zeal, activity and bravery." In a letter to Major William Ward Burrows, first Commandant of the Marine Corps, he highly praised the actions of Lieutenant Clinch. He also presented to him a sword captured from the French officers. President John Adams later thanked the officers and crew for their "good conduct, exact discipline and bravery."

On February 14, from St. Kitts, Truxtun reported that after great exertions both ships had been brought to that port and anchored safely. He added: "I shall proceed to repair the damages sustained by both ships as speedily as possible, and until the pleasure of the President of the United States is known, I intend to give Lieutenant John Rodgers an order to command the *Insurgente*."[1]

[1] After refitting, *L'Insurgente,* a United States frigate now, was sent off on an unproductive cruise to Lisbon under Captain Alexander Murray. Homeward bound a year later, Captain Patrick Fletcher, her new commander, reported himself on August 10, 1800, off Cape Henry. Then she disappeared. An equinoctial gale, it is assumed, swallowed ship and crew.

The President was delighted with this first major victory over the French. Victory had been long in coming but it was sweet to John Adams, the man who was fighting political battles at home to keep the nation committed to the undeclared war with France.

The war had grown out of years of friction during George Washington's second administration and the first two years of John Adams' presidency. France, at war with England, called upon the United States to fulfill its treaty obligations to assist her in the West Indies. This treaty, the first approved by the Congress, became the subject of bitter debate between the Jeffersonian Republicans who favored France, and the Hamiltonian Federalists who sided with the English.

The treaty with France had been negotiated by Benjamin Franklin during the dark days of the Revolution. France provided us with money, arms, artillery, and ammunition, and in return Franklin signed a treaty with the French in 1778 guaranteeing that the United States would protect any French possession in the West Indies which might be threatened by any other nation.

Later, when England went to war against Revolutionary France, she set out to gobble up all the French Islands in the West Indies. The French, invoking the treaty, called on the United States for help. Congress refused to live up to the treaty, declaring that this country wished to remain neutral. The French government retaliated by ordering American ships and cargoes to be seized on any pretext, taken to French ports, condemned and sold.

Typical was the case of Captain John B. Thurston, of the brig *Commerce*. He reported that he had sailed from Gibraltar "and a French privateer came up and gave us a gun." Captain Thurston broke out the United States colors. The captain of the French privateer—*La Revanche*, sixteen, from Bordeaux—ordered Captain Thurston aboard and immediately sent a boarding party to the *Commerce*. His men returned after a minor bit of plundering of food supplies. The French captain then ordered a search of the different officers as well as of the ship. After two hours of digging in the salt bin, the search party discovered twenty-two jars in which were $11,000, the property of the shipowners in New York. In the privateer's cabin Captain Thurston was stripped to his shirt and robbed of $160, which also belonged to the shipowner. The French threatened to sink or burn the vessel if Thurston withheld any money which on search they should afterwards discover. After a while the French captain ordered five Americans to remain on board his vessel and let the *Commerce* take off.

Captain Neil MacNeal of the ship *Eliza* appeared in Madrid in July, 1798, to report how his ship had been treated by a French privateer. The French ship coming close up under the *Eliza*'s quarter fired a nine-pound shot and a volley of musketry into the American. The *Eliza,* armed, returned the fire. Then after subsequent close action within pistol shot for an hour and a half, the American ship was obliged to haul down its colors to *L'Heureux Décidé,* privateer of Bordeaux mounting eighteen nine-pounders and with a crew of 185 men.

The schooner *Lemmon,* commanded by Thomas Smith, was taken by a French privateer, *Le Requin National,* in the West Indies. Gunshot was brought to bear on the *Lemmon* and she was obliged to surrender, having neither ammunition nor fire-arms on board to defend herself. When Captain Smith was brought aboard the French ship, which was out of Curaçao, he was told that he was a damned liar, struck in the face, and confronted by a loaded pistol. Captain Smith declared, "They came on board of us like savages, driving captain, mate, and people below, making use of their cutlasses and handspikes in such a manner that we were obliged to ask for quarter."

The initial policy of the United States had been to obtain damages for the loss of our merchant ships and to stop further depredations upon our merchant shipping. However, negotiations were to no avail. France thumbed her nose at our efforts. The insulating "X. Y. Z. Affair" was followed by Talleyrand's suggestion that were the United States to bribe certain members of the French government with liberal sums of money—$250,000—the attacks on our shipping would be stopped, to which Charles

G. Pinckney, one of our envoys to Paris, made his famous rejoinder: "Millions for defence, sir, but not one cent for tribute!"[2]

By early May, 1798, the revulsion of the American people toward France had become evident to Congress. Adams, with popular sentiment now behind him, as Commander in Chief had only neglible forces with which to carry on a conflict with France. What fighting forces were available were operating under a Secretary of War who now found himself overburdened with the demands to prepare to fight a naval war.

Urged on by the administration and by the American people, Congress adopted a number of warlike measures in the spring and summer of 1798. An increase in the size of our tiny Army was ordered. Some eighty thousand militia were called out, and the aging George Washington was persuaded to assume command, as "Lieutenant General and Commander in Chief." The Army, however, was to take no part, as it turned out. The source of trouble was in the Caribbean, and sea power was needed. Unfortunately, as President Adams remarked, the United States was "a country Impotent at Sea tho Powerful by Land." His dual problem was to unify the country politically and create a Navy to cope with the French. The first step was to establish a Navy Department, taking maritime affairs from the War Department. Benjamin Stoddert, capable ex-Continental Army officer, was appointed Secretary.

Adams and Stoddert tackled the building of a Navy with great vigor. Fortunately, the country could thank George Washington for the fact that three fine frigates, built for possible action against the Barbary pirates, later were commissioned and were now available. They were the *Constitution* and *United States*, both forty-fours, and *Constellation,* thirty-six: all from the drawing board of master-craftsman Joshua Humphreys.

As President Adams had requested, a total of twelve new vessels were to be commissioned. It was obvious that the quickest way to recruit the fleet would be to buy ships. One of the first purchases was the *Hamburgh* packet, renamed the *Delaware,*

[2] John Bartlett, *Familiar Quotations,* 10th ed., Halcyon House, New York, 1919, 861. But *Oxford Dictionary of Quotations,* 2nd ed., London, 1913, 238:4, attributes the words to Robert Goodloe Harper.

twenty; Stephen Decatur, Sr., was appointed its first commander. Other ships purchased were the *Baltimore,* twenty; the *Ganges,* twenty-four; the *Herald,* eighteen; the *Montezuma,* twenty; the *George Washington,* twenty-four; and the *Richmond,* eighteen. Meanwhile, efforts were made to speed up construction, and the first vessel to be built was the *Diligence,* a twelve-gun sloop completed August 30, 1798.

Captain Richard Dale—he had been John Paul Jones's first lieutenant on the *Bonhomme Richard*—with his ship the *Ganges,* was at sea at about the time the new Navy Department was being established. He had written the Secretary of War on the twenty-fourth of June and received a reply from the Secretary of Navy on the twenty-seventh saying that while Dale's services had not been as brilliant as his wishes, they nonetheless had been meritorious and useful. "You have frightened the French cruisers from our coast and have relieved in a considerable degree our commerce from depredations on our own shores. Before long you will be permitted to return into port to prepare yourself better. Captain Decatur will join you for a few days in the *Delaware.*"

Stoddert's attack strategy was to dispose most of the infant Navy in the West Indies where he expected it to come to grips with French naval power. America's fighting ships were stationed along the chain of islands which formed a giant fishhook over sixteen hundred miles in length, from Cuba, some hundred miles south of the tip of Florida, eastward past the large islands of Haiti and Puerto Rico. As the fishhook bent southward the islands were smaller, but almost all provided safe harbor for privateers and French naval vessels. Secretary Stoddert's dispositions had Decatur, Sr., in the *Delaware,* at Havana. Dale's *Ganges,* a converted East Indiaman, guarded the Windward Passage between Cuba and Haiti. At the bend of the fishhook was Captain Truxtun's squadron—*Constellation, Baltimore, Richmond, Norfolk,* and the revenue cutter *South Carolina*—cruising between Puerto Rico and St. Kitts. Farther south in the Lesser Antilles stretching to the coast of South America, was Captain John Barry with the frigate *United States,* forty-four, and supporting ships. His station extended from St. Kitts to Tobago.

Instructions to Captain Samuel Nicholson of the frigate *Constitution* in the summer of 1798 were to secure the principal ports of New Hampshire, Massachusetts, and Rhode Island from depredations of French cruisers, and also to pay some attention to the port of New York. It was suggested that his cruising ground would extend ten or fifteen leagues eastward of Georges' Bank. Similarly, the cruising ground of Captain Dale was to extend from Cape Henry to Long Island.

The *Constellation* sailed in time to celebrate July 4, 1798, at sea, and her crew drank to "Admiral Adams, who throws out the signal for battle, and will never strike to the enemies of his country the Freedom of the seas; here we plough, and shall pirates take the harvest? The present rulers of France, may they soon be dismasted and lie keel uppermost."

The first naval action occurred on July 7, 1798, when Captain Stephen Decatur, Sr., in his twenty-gun sloop, the *Delaware*, captured *La Croyable*, a French privateer schooner of ten guns and fifty-three men.

At sea off the New Jersey coast, Captain Decatur fell in with the merchant ship *Alexander Hamilton*—bound from New York to Baltimore—which had been plundered by a French privateer schooner. Decatur immediately went in search of her, and soon sighted four schooners off Egg Harbor. Not knowing which was the culprit, he thought it best to stand off as if he were a merchantman alarmed at what might be armed vessels.

The maneuver had the intended effect, for one of the four, an armed schooner, gave chase until she discovered the *Delaware* to be a vessel of force, when she attempted to sheer off and get in close to shore where she supposed she would be safe. It was, in fact, *La Croyable*, which surrendered to the *Delaware* after a long chase and after several shots had been fired at her. The captured vessel, renamed the *Retaliation*, joined the U.S. Navy.

Later in 1798 came unexpected disaster. The refitted *Retaliation*, fourteen, under the command of Lieutenant William Bainbridge, was cruising off Guadeloupe on the twentieth of November, 1798, at 6 A.M., when three sails were sighted two leagues distant. USS *Montezuma*, twenty, commanded by Captain Alexander Murray, and the brig *Norfolk*, eighteen, commanded by

Captain Thomas Williams, were to the west, accompanying the *Retaliation*. Captain Murray hailed *Retaliation* and asked if the ships to windward had signaled their flag. He was answered in the negative, with an intimation that they were probably British.

When two other sails appeared in the west, the *Montezuma* and *Norfolk* took off in pursuit, leaving Bainbridge's *Retaliation* alone to cope with the three vessels sighted earlier. Bainbridge made the signals agreed upon by American and English commanders, by which they were to recognize each other. Although the strangers to the eastward did not answer his signals, he still believed them to be Englishmen. He did not discover his mistake until two of the ships, which proved to be French frigates, had approached so near that it was impossible for him to escape. One of them, *L'Insurgente*, thirty-six, hoisted French colors and fired into the *Retaliation*, while the other, the flagship *Volontaire*, forty-four, ordered Bainbridge on board. He had no alternative, so accordingly struck his colors, went on board the *Volontaire*, and surrendered to Commodore St. Laurent, the ranking French officer. Meanwhile, *L'Insurgente* had immediately sailed in pursuit of the *Montezuma* and the *Norfolk*. While watching the chase, St. Laurent inquired of Bainbridge the force of the American vessels. Without hesitation, Bainbridge greatly overstated the number and weight of their guns, thus inducing the Commodore to recall *L'Insurgente*. Before the deception was exposed, it was too late to renew the chase and the two American vessels escaped.

The officers of the *Retaliation* were held as prisoners on board the French frigates but the crew was confined in a loathsome prison at Basseterre on St. Kitts.

The *Constellation*'s capture of *L'Insurgente* had been, as we have noted, the one major American victory since the commencement of the war in 1798. However, the Navy was growing in strength as new ships were purchased or built. The ships in commission had gained sailing and cruising experience and their crews were becoming well trained, though the caliber of the seamen and officers was uneven due to the disparate characters of captains and the lack of a naval tradition. New experiences challenged the new American Navy. There was gradually emerging an *esprit de corps* and a more knowledgeable fighting fleet.

On the other hand, a running battle over seniority among the captains in this new Navy threatened both morale and discipline at its roots. Secretary Benjamin Stoddert summed it up feelingly: "The avarice of rank in the infancy of our Service is the Devil!" The matter rankled throughout 1798 and was only resolved by the President himself late in July 1799. The situation came about in this fashion:

When President Washington in 1794 had authorized construction of six frigates for possible war in the Mediterranean against the Algerian pirates, he had named six captains to them in order of rank from the date each keel was laid: John Barry, Samuel Nicholson, Silas Talbot, Joshua Barney, Richard Dale, and Thomas Truxtun. All had distinguished themselves in naval action during the Revolutionary War. Let's look them over.

John Barry had covered himself with glory in the Revolution. Still capable, he was now old, however, and probably had lost some of his daring. Nicholson, a wealthy Maryland planter, appears to have been a political appointee. Silas Talbot, who reveals himself in his letters as a courageous fighting man, was a trained leader. He had been in the Army during the Revolution, but because as a Rhode Islander he knew ships, he had been called upon to lead cutting-out expeditions—the kind of operations for which the Marines were later noted. He had fought wherever he was asked to fight and he fought well. Joshua Barney, a brilliant privateersman in the Revolution, deserved his rank. Richard Dale, who, like Nicholson, had long abandoned the sea, was a Southern squire. "Terrible Tom" Truxtun, of Jamaica on Long Island, had been a daring privateer during the Revolution. He had cruised with two privateers into the Channel and made a defense against superior English force so far beyond privateer standards that it won him a considerable reputation.

In 1795 an economy-minded Congress suspended construction on three of the original six vessels. It was the luck of the draw and the varying speed of the shipbuilding that now gave the three completed ships to Barry, Nicholson, and Truxtun, respectively first, second, and fifth in rank. For example, the *Constitution* (Talbot) and the *Constellation* (Truxtun) developed a number of faults. Talbot tried to correct those on the *Constitution* before it was launched and had more or less bad luck in timing. Truxtun got the *Constellation* out of the yards, but later had to correct the difficulties. Nevertheless, the *Constellation* was considered "complete" when the Navy was cut back in 1795, so the three captains chosen were the ones whose ships were complete.

This situation unfortunately left Talbot and Dale out of jobs. Unlike Barney, who, feeling he was unjustly rated behind "Colonel" Talbot, had at once resigned in 1796 to take service with the French Navy,[3] they stayed in uniform, harrying the Navy Department with their complaints that Truxtun had been jumped over their heads.

Secretary of the Navy Stoddert took official notice. Not only did he make his comment about the "avarice of rank in the infancy of our Service" but he wrote a letter in October 1798 to the President. He stated: "Talbot & Dale contend for the Rank given them by the first appointment in 1794: And without obtaining it, I fear will not continue in the Service. If they do obtain it, I fear Truxton (sic), a man of equal merit will not—In 1794 they were appointed to rank above Truxton; and have by no act of their own forfeited their right to such Rank.—On the other hand Truxton is in possession—his Commission, I understand is No. three."

When the seniority question boiled to fever pitch, President Adams laid down his decision in a masterly essay of many pages. On July 23, 1799, he wrote: "In the case of Captain Talbot, I am perfectly clear, in my own mind, that he has been a captain in the navy of the United States from the time of his appointment, in 1794, to this hour; that a legal title, and an estate in his office, was then vested in him; and that he has never been divested of either." Adams went on to recite in detail Talbot's unparalleled patriotic service during the Revolution.

With regard to Truxtun, the President concluded: "I respect, I esteem, and especially since his late glorious action (victory over *L'Insurgente*), I love the man . . . But this meritorious conduct makes no alteration in my judgment. . . ." Even though Truxtun now threatened to resign, Adams stuck by his guns. Talbot

[3] Barney played no part in the quasi war and would later come home to serve in the United States Navy during the War of 1812.

was to be continued in his proper rank.

The situation finally cleared up with time, as such things will. Nicholson proved himself to be incompetent, so Talbot succeeded him in command of the *Constitution* in May 1799. Dale took a furlough to command a fine merchantman in the China trade. Stoddert, taking the extraordinary step of refusing to accept the sulking Truxtun's resignation, instead ordered him to sea again in the refitted *Constellation*. On taking command, Truxtun as usual harangued the crew, promising them glory and profit from prize money. That glory came rather quickly, but it brought no prize money.

On the evening of February 1, 1800, the *Constellation* sighted the French frigate *Vengeance*, fifty-two, Captain Pitot, southwest of Guadeloupe. Truxtun hoisted English colors and cleared for action. The *Vengeance*, a bigger ship with more broadside fire power than *L'Insurgente*, attempted to run away. Her captain was avoiding action because he had a large cargo of gold specie aboard. Truxtun gave chase, pursuing through the night and the daylight of the second.

About eight in the evening, the *Constellation*, ignoring the Frenchman's stern and quarter guns, drew abeam and the two ships began a drumfire of broadsides which would last for five long hours. Truxtun's gunners, obeying his command, aimed for the enemy's hull, while *Vengeance*'s people, both because Pitot hoped to get away with his precious cargo, and because it was also normal French gunnery tactics, aimed for *Constellation*'s rigging.

The Frenchman was hulled 168 times, but Truxtun's top-hamper was a shambles when *Vengeance*'s fire died away. *Constellation*'s mainmast, all stays and shrouds cut, swayed dangerously, but little Midshipman Jarvis commanding the maintop refused to leave his post. Just then the *Vengeance* swung around into the wind, her mizzen-topmast pitching overboard as she did so. Truxtun ordered all hands from the guns to save his own mainmast, but too late. The next roll of the ship sent the tall spar splintering overside, throwing Jarvis to his death far out into the black water.

Toward the end of the engagement, the French captain ordered his crew to make ready to board the *Constellation*. The attempt came to nothing, thanks to the accurate musket fire from the Marines under the able command of the same Lieutenant Bartholomew Clinch who had commanded them in the battle against *L'Insurgente* a year before.

Pitot now took advantage of the lull to claw himself away, while the *Constellation*, her mainmast gone, was left rocking on the night sea, without the power to turn or tack after her vanishing enemy. Yet the *Vengeance* was even worse off. Twice in the last hour of battle the French frigate had struck her flag and hailed for quarter only to have the smoke and dark hide the signal. Half her crew were dead or wounded, and she was making water. However, not being under pursuit, she headed for Curaçao. En route her upper masts collapsed and her pumps were unable to hold out against the mounting water. She had to be beached at the mouth of the port, where she was condemned as beyond repair. The *Constellation*, with twenty killed and forty wounded, limped into port at Jamaica for repairs.

On March 29, 1800, Congress voted a medal to Captain Truxtun for his success on this occasion "wherein an example was exhibited by the Captain, officers, sailors and Marines honorable to the American name and instructive to its rising Navy." The Secretary of the Navy on March 20, 1800, wrote that "all officers and men" nobly performed their duty.

It was the smaller vessels that won distinction during the last two years of the war. The most fortunate were the twin schooner-rigged *Experiment* and *Enterprise*—built especially for the work of cruising in the shoal waters where pirates and privateers lurked. They were eighty-footers—light, swift, and of small draught. Each mounted twelve six-pounders. The *Experiment*, the first of the two ships to get into action, carried a crew of seventy, of whom fourteen were marines commanded by Second Lieutenant Nathan Sheredine. Her skipper was Lieutenant Commander William Maley and his first officer was Lieutenant David Porter.

Haitian affairs caused conditions in the West Indies to become very complex. In the battle area the Americans had to take extreme precautions not to encroach upon the possessions and rights of Spain, Great Britain, and Holland. In French Haiti, Toussaint l'Ouverture and General Hyacinth Rigaud dominated affairs. These two, the former a Negro and the latter a Mulatto, split forces and in the end Toussaint, who had declared himself against France, caused the flight of Rigaud, who had espoused the cause of France.

As early as March 16, 1799, Secretary Stoddert directed the *Ganges* to take the ship *Kingston,* carrying the American Consul General, Edward Stevens, "under convoy" to Cap François (now Cap Haïtien), Haiti. "Hover about for a day or two to give Doctor Stevens an opportunity to influence Toussaint to invite you in, in which case it may be useful," wrote the Secretary to her commander. "If you should have an interview with Toussaint, conduct yourself with your usual prudence and good sense. . . . It is our policy to conciliate the good opinion of that gentleman and his people."

Toussaint owed a considerable part of his success in ridding himself of Rigaud to the assistance of American naval forces and Marines. American vessels furnished Toussaint with munitions, and at times the Haitian general reciprocated, in kind, to the American Navy and Marines.

While operating in the West Indies the *Experiment* was given four merchantmen to convoy. On New Year's Day, 1800, a calm found the five in the Bight of Léogane, north of Gonaïve Island, off Haiti, a place of frequent calms. At this time all southern Haiti was in the hands of the ruffian Rigaud, the prototype of several future Caribbean dictators. He claimed the authority of France, but actually lived by piracy, his people being called Picaroons. As the *Experiment* and her convoy of four ships lay becalmed, about five hundred Picaroons came rowing out from Gonaive in ten barges, big enough so that each carried a four-pounder in its bow.

The sight so unnerved Lieutenant Commander Maley that he proposed making signals of surrender to save bloodshed. Porter pushed him aside and took command. Marines on the quarter deck and forecastle were hidden behind the bulwarks, guns double-shotted with grape, but ports remained closed. By this time the Picaroons were within musket shot, making for all the ships at once. Down came ports, out ran gun muzzles, to blaze away. Repulsed in their first offensive the freebooters attacked several times again with muskets, cannon fire, shrieks, and menaces, but were severely defeated. Consul General Edward Stevens, on board, reported that the guns of the *Experiment* were well served. "The fire of the Marines continued with great steadiness and activity, (and) we at length succeeded in driving them off after a smart action of near three hours." The Haitians, however, captured several of the ships in convoy and murdered the captain of one.

The Americans aboard the *Experiment* had one killed and one wounded. The ammunition was totally expended in the fight, but Toussaint replenished her magazines and also furnished one "long six-pounder to serve as a stern chase."

In the meantime, young Porter's exploits in the *Experiment* off Haiti on New Year's Day, 1800, had made him a marked young man. Captain Talbot, in the *Constitution*, asked for his services. The news occasioned Porter some dismay; not only had he acquired a taste for the excitement and freedom of small ship work, but there was a personal difficulty. The year previous, in the dispute between Talbot and Truxtun over their relative rank, Porter had exhibited rather violent partisanship for his old commander. He need not have been troubled. Silas Talbot was an honest man. When the new Lieutenant reported for duty, he was informed to his great delight that although borne on the frigate's muster roll, he was actually to command a Navy ship of his own.

She was a diminutive schooner with a crew of fifteen, bearing the odd name of *Amphitheater*; recently captured, she was now being fitted as a tender—a seagoing errand boy to *Constitution*. She mounted five little brass swivel guns from the latter's boat-gun stock. The date was March 1800. Porter and his fifteen men enjoyed two months of service in the craft doing all sorts of chasing before they found some real action.

The *Constitution* and her tiny consort were cruising the waters of the eastern end of Santo Domingo. Near Cape Samana there was a rather deep bay with a line of reefs at the entrance, then a frequent haunt of Picaroons. Talbot dispatched *Amphitheater* for a look. Sure enough, there were ships inside the reef; a brig which by her shape and rigging must have been American and alongside her a three-masted schooner and a lugger-rigged barge, one of the type that normally carried thirty to forty men. This seemed to Porter about the kind of odds that would provide good sport. He begged Talbot to let him go in, and the captain consented after putting half a dozen marines aboard and ordering a couple of the frigate's longboats to follow her. As Porter's schooner bore through the reef, both Picaroon ships came at him, armed not only with swivels, but with a long twelve-pounder and a pair of sixes. He held right on to close the action and defeated the enemy.

The newspapers had been so full of the exploits of the *Experiment* that scant attention was given to her sister schooner, the *Enterprise*. "Lucky little *Enterprise*," they called her in the Navy. Her greatest luck was in having Lieutenant John Shaw for a commander; a man out to make a name for himself. An Irish immigrant from a large family he had chosen to make his way in America. He was apprenticed as a sailor to pay for his passage and worked his way to the quarter deck, where Captain Alexander Murray found him and recommended him as a lieutenant.

Off Cuba on the way to battle position in April 1800 Shaw fell in with a heavy Spanish brig which attacked him during the night on the impression that he was an enemy. He gave the brig a hot battle but had to put in at St. Thomas for refitting. There was a large twelve-gunned three-masted French lugger in port, *La Diane*, carrying one hundred men more than the *Enterprise*. The French captain, seeing the battered American ship, concluded it was a good opportunity to assert French superiority. He sent Shaw a formal challenge for a battle outside the harbor. The American accepted eagerly and sailed outside the harbor waiting for the French lugger. But the latter refused to follow.

The *Enterprise*, finally tired of waiting, sailed away. A week or so later, when rounding the isle of Antigua, Shaw found himself face to face with *La Diane*, the challenging lugger from St. Thomas, which turned to run. The *Enterprise* caught up with her quickly and tacked to and fro across the Frenchman's stern, pouring in a broadside on each tack till she struck. The capture was important, for on board was Rigaud, the French partisan of Haiti. "This is the man, Sir," reported Shaw, "who has wrested from my countrymen, millions; the depredations, the piracies, plunder and murders he has committed on my fellow citizens are only too well known in the United States." Rigaud was imprisoned on St. Kitts but lived to return to Haiti with the French General LeClerc in 1801. Meanwhile, the news of his captivity brought better treatment to harshly handled American prisoners.

June and July 1800 were full of action for the *Enterprise*. On June 17, while becalmed, she was attacked by the French privateer, *Le Cygne*, four, with fifty-seven men, which had come out of Basseterre, Guadeloupe. Evidently, *Le Cygne* did not recognize the character of the *Enterprise* and engaged her for twenty minutes when she struck her colors. The privateer had five killed and fourteen wounded, while the American loss was one killed and two wounded. Shortly thereafter, the *Enterprise* took the privateer *Citoyenne*, six, after a hard fight.

On July 4, Shaw fell in with the French privateer *L'Aigle*, ten, with a crew of seventy-eight men. The *Enterprise* tacked across her enemy's wake and gave her a raking broadside; and then, running up on her weather quarter, boarded her. No further resistance was met, as all the French officers were badly wounded, leaving her leaderless.

A most important action was the battle of the *Enterprise* against the brig *Flambeau*, twelve, which carried half again the *Enterprise*'s weight of metal. She also had more men than the *Enterprise*, whose crew numbered eighty-three. The combatants sighted each other to leeward of Dominica toward night, and the next morning came together. The duel lasted about three-quarters of an hour, and most of the time the vessels were close-hauled in a light breeze, with the *Flambeau* at first leading off. As the *Enterprise* drew nearer the ships began with a brisk fire of small arms, then exchanged broadsides for twenty minutes. The fore-topmast of the *Flambeau* was struck, and in a sudden gust of wind toppled overboard, carrying six men with it. She lowered a boat to rescue the men and soon afterward struck her colors.

In October, Shaw's health broke down and he was relieved of his command by Lieutenant Andrew Sterett.

For their skill and gallant conduct the crew of the *Enterprise* was awarded by Secretary Stoddert the full value of their capture as prize money, instead of the usual half. At the end of the cruise Lieutenant Shaw's record amply justified that reward for he had "taken 18 vessels, captured 300 French prisoners, killed and wounded 61 men, and taken 42 guns."

In another act in the spring of 1800, the *Constitution,* whose Marine officer was that "man of spirit," Captain Daniel Carmick (who would later win fame in the Battle of New Orleans), took three prizes and cut out a captured British ship, *Sandwich*, held by the French in Puerto Plata, on the north coast of Santo Domingo. This affair, one of the most deft cutting-out expeditions of the early Navy, likewise involved the first landing on a foreign shore by marines of the new Corps.

The *Sandwich* lay in the harbor of Puerto Plata (where marines would again land 116 years later) under the guns of a Spanish fort and in water too shallow for the *Constitution*. To get the prize, Lieutenant Isaac Hull, the *Constitution*'s First Lieutenant, embarked eighty-nine marines and bluejackets aboard a commandeered American coaster, the sloop *Sally*, which could enter the harbor without suspicion. Captain Carmick and his junior officer, First Lieutenant William Amory, had the marines well hidden below, and, as Carmick related, "It put me in mind of the wooden horse at Troy."

Entering Puerto Plata in broad daylight on May 12, 1800, Hull put his schooner alongside the *Sandwich*, and, in Carmick's words, "The men went on board like devils." Then the marines landed, some in water up to their necks and stormed up to the fort where Carmick reported, "It was not half an hour after the ship *Sandwich* was taken that I had possession of the fort and all the cannon spiked." As soon as the prize could be gotten ready for sea, Hull reembarked the marines and took her out. Unfortunately, the raid, though widely acclaimed, turned out to be a breach of Spain's nominal neutrality and the *Sandwich* had to be returned.

Once again, on September 1, 1800, the *Experiment* was in the news. Though David Porter thought he might have been given command despite his youth, the skipper named was Lieutenant

Charles Stewart. After all, David Porter was still young for the rank he held.

Stewart and young Porter hit if off famously and had many adventures together, the most notable following the capture, after a ten-minute action, of the French schooner-privateer *Deux Amis*, eight. Porter with four men went to take possession, but before a single man of *Deux Amis* could be transferred to her captor, another sail came over the horizon. The *Experiment* ran off in chase and was soon out of contact. Now Porter was in as bad a situation as he had been aboard *L'Insurgente*, for the Frenchmen began to murmur and shuffle. This time Porter had no John Rodgers to follow, but he had his own high spirits and the precedent of the previous occasion. A pot of paint was produced. Porter drew a line across the deck just forward of the mainmast, cocked a pistol and announced he would blow the head off the first man who crossed. In the meanwhile his four seamen had dragged around one of the afterguns and loaded it with langrage—any sort of hard metal junk that came to hand—as a reinforcement for the pistol. There was no uprising, but no sleep either for Porter or his prize crew until they brought *Deux Amis* into St. Kitts three days later.

A short time later, on November 16, in the neighborhood of Antigua, *Experiment* successfully engaged and captured a schooner which turned out to be the *Louisa Bridger*, an English vessel. According to the ship's logbook, the *Experiment* "came alongside, fired a musket and ordered us to heave to or they would fire into us. Not minding this, she fired a gun at us. All hands being at quarters we engaged her for four hours, when we ceased firing as our hulls, sails, and rigging were very much injured." It would appear that after mutual apologies were rendered there was no further repercussion from this odd encounter.

The new frigate *Boston*, twenty-eight, Captain George Little, had distinguished herself when she destroyed a pirate force in the Bight of Léogane, not long after the *Experiment*'s clash with the Picaroons. Her next exploit was one of the most famous events of the war and the last major sea battle. The Massachusetts merchants in petitioning for an appointment in the Navy for George Little had said, "He will be the Nelson of our country!" While he couldn't be expected to live up to such expectations, he proved himself a solid captain. While cruising southward from Boston to Guadeloupe on October 12, 1800, the *Boston* encountered the French corvette *Berceau*, twenty-four, about six hundred miles northeast of the island. In a test of speed the *Boston*'s good lines enabled her to win. *Berceau*, seeing that she couldn't escape, shortened sail and fired a gun as an invitation to fight. About five in the evening *Boston* caught up. A battle of the long guns at broadside continued for an hour. The French, as was their custom, aimed for the masts and fired so accurately that it became almost impossible for the *Boston* to carry sail. Captain Little pulled away, however, made his repairs, and came back into range at nine o'clock. He began pounding the enemy masts and at ten o'clock the *Berceau*'s fore- and main-topmasts went by the board. Meanwhile there was a spirited musketry fight at close range. The damaged *Berceau*'s roll into the trough of a wave brought her mizzenmast down. With all power of movement gone, the only recourse was surrender. The *Berceau* had thirty-four killed and eighteen wounded out of a crew of two hundred; the *Boston,* seven killed and eight wounded out of 230.

In one of the last episodes of the war the Marines played a prominent part. The setting was the island of Curaçao into which, it will be remembered, the *Vengeance* had limped after her disastrous battle with the *Constellation*. It was a Dutch island and the governor had refused to assist in the repair of the French war vessel. The French then dispatched a large force from Guadeloupe to take the island. American citizens and their property suffered severely in that operation, which by September 1800 resulted in the French controlling all the island plus two of the forts at Willemstad. The Dutch withdrew into the other two forts. Some Americans voluntarily joined these garrisons. The U.S. frigates *Merrimack*, twenty-four, and *Patapsco*, twenty, in answer to a call for assistance, appeared off Curaçao on the twenty-second.

The Dutch had placed the island under British protection, but the French dominated affairs. Fifteen armed French vessels were lying close under the Dutch forts at Willemstad, threatening them.

In order to relieve the pressure, the *Patapsco,* Captain Geddes, reinforced with twenty marines of the *Merrimack*, stood into the harbor on the twenty-third, under small arms fire from the windows and roofs of houses. She ran up to within pistol shot of a French-held fort, and her cannon and musketry returned the fire. For more than two hours the fire was kept up, at half gunshot, until the French fire was practically silenced, although desultory cannonading continued that night and the following day. Two Americans were wounded.

The next day a *Patapsco* landing party, commanded by Second Lieutenant James Middleton, USMC, landed and assisted in the defense. They went to the aid of one of the town batteries and were stationed where they would have to bear the brunt of the expected assault. The French kept up a constant fire all the next day, but embarked on their ships precipitously during the night. The *Merrimack*, Captain Brown, entered the harbor the next morning, the twenty-fifth, and the British warship *Nereid* later took possession.

The actions above related were the more notable ones in the year 1800. There were many minor engagements, and many prizes were taken.

During more than two years of fighting the American Navy had captured 111 French privateers and sunk four. In addition, the Navy had recaptured seventy American merchantmen which had previously been taken by the French.

The actions by the small American naval force and the Marines brought France to the belief that it should sue for peace. At this time France was engaged in the Napoleonic struggle, with not only England, but with all of Europe.

Negotiations with France had been in progress throughout the latter period of the conflict, and finally resulted in a treaty signed at Paris on September 30, 1800. France agreed to recognize American neutrality and to refrain from seizing American vessels not carrying contraband. However, as the news of the convention was long in reaching the United States and there was much doubt as to its ratification, hostilities continued without interruption.

Then, as now, there was a great deal of controversy in the

United States not only in the halls of Congress, but also among private people regarding our quasi war. There were those who felt we should not be at war against France, but should be allied with France against England. The old fight between the Hamiltonians and the Jeffersonians was continued all through this period. On November 18 the Secretary of the Navy issued instructions that American vessels should be devoted especially to the protection of commerce, avoiding conflict with vessels belonging to the French Navy unless they were attacking our commerce. This policy remained unchanged, even while the treaty was before the Senate.

The treaty was finally ratified by the Senate on February 18, 1801, and proclaimed by President Adams. It should be noted that after France signed the treaty with the United States, it signed a secret treaty with Spain in which Louisiana was turned over to France. A few months later England and her allies made peace with France, though it was broken soon after when the Napoleonic Wars devastated Europe and again threatened the freedom of the seas.

Three years of warfare had proved to be an important period in the development of the American naval forces. A Navy Department had been established and had through vicissitude developed an efficient force. Officers, seamen, and marines had learned much of the business of fighting, and a training program was gradually developed in order to make the men more efficient in their duties. This early training in coordinated fighting and in shipboard organization was to prove of invaluable help when the United States went to war with Britain in 1812.

As always throughout the United States history, when peace came there was a scuttling of the military forces. The Army had never risen to the strength authorized, and demobilization made it an extremely small force. By an Act of March 3, 1801, the last day of President Adams' administration, the sale of many of the Navy vessels was authorized, except for thirteen frigates including the *United States*, *Constitution*, *President*, *Chesapeake*, *Philadelphia*, *Constellation*, *Congress*, *New York*, *Boston*, *Essex*, *Adams*, *John Adams*, *General Greene*, and the sloop *Enterprise*. However, only six of these vessels were to be kept in active commission, with two-thirds of the usual war crew. Twenty ships and nine galleys were sold. The other frigates were ordered laid up with a small naval complement and a marine guard of ten men each.

The Secretary of the Navy, Mr. Stoddert, had argued unavailingly with Congress in efforts to maintain the Marine Corps and Navy at what he considered defensive strengths. While the Act of March 3, 1801, did not expressly provide that the Marine Corps should be reduced, it did, as a matter of fact, bring about a material reduction, the extent of which was dependent upon the discretion of the President.

A new President—Thomas Jefferson, a scholar and a leader in American political life—now began an administration which started with a war against the Barbary pirates.

2

Wars with the Barbary Pirates, 1801-1816

It is always a temptation to a rich and lazy nation,
To puff and look important and to say:—
"Though we know we should defeat you, we have not the time to meet you.
We will therefore pay you cash to go away."
And that is called paying the Dane-geld;
But we've proved it again and again,
That if once you have paid him the Dane-geld
You never get rid of the Dane.
—From "Dane-geld" by Rudyard Kipling

Blackmail Unlimited

Blue water and hot sands, gleaming minarets and slavery; of such stuff was Mediterranean life to Yankee ships and sailormen from 1785 to 1802. For this was the lair of Blackmail Unlimited—Morocco, Algiers, Tunis, and Tripoli—the four Berber Muslim states bordering a two-thousand-mile stretch of the North African coast. Morocco was a flourishing monarchy, the other three were provinces of the Ottoman Empire, owing at least nominal allegiance to the Supreme Porte. Piracy was their trade, blackmail their price for immunity.

Here the Stars and Stripes meant nothing and the plight of the Boston brig *Polly* and her crew in 1793 was remarkable only because one of her forecastle hands was sufficiently articulate to put down on paper his grim story after they had been ransomed.[1]

The *Polly,* Cadiz-bound, was hailed and boarded by an Algerine brig off Cape St. Vincent.

> About one hundred of the Pirates jumped on board us, all armed, some with Scimetars and Pistols, others with pikes, spears, lances, knives, etc. As soon as they came on board they made signs for us all to go forward, assuring us in several languages that if we did not obey their commands they would immediately massacre us all. . . . They then went below into the cabin, steerage and every place where they could get below deck and broke open the Trunks and Chests there, and plundered all our bedding, cloathing, books, Charts, Quadrants and every moveable article. They then came on deck and stripped the cloathes off our backs, all except a shirt and a pair of drawers.
>
> When we had been taken into [Algiers] we were conducted to the Dey's palace by a guard. When we were brought before the Dey he said he was determined never to make a peace with the United States, adding, "Now I have got you, you Christian dogs, you shall eat stones." He then picked out four boys to wait upon himself and then ordered the rest of us to be conducted to the prison. . . .

Prison, wrote Foss, was a wretched place, crawling with vermin and filled with Turks, Moors, Arabs, Christians, and "a Jew or two." The Turks, he commented, were "drunken"; why, we do not know. Each prisoner was given a dirty blanket and a small loaf of black, sour bread; then he was loaded down hand and feet with chains weighing from twenty-five to forty pounds, all fastened to the waist.

The overseer's whip and goad, together with the bastinado for the more obdurate, spurred the half-starved captives in their incessant hard labor. Disrespect to the Muslim faith might bring roasting at the stake, or impalement. And the rebellious slave

[1]John Foss, *A Journal of the Captivity and Suffering of John Foss,* Newburyport, Mass., 1798.

who killed a Muhammadan was simply tossed off the city wall; were he lucky he would be dashed to immediate death below. But more probably he would lodge on one of the iron hooks studding it and hang there in agony for days before he died.[2]

Foss's story, supplementing the numberless other reports of atrocities to American sailormen and American pocketbooks, did much to harden the resolve of both Congress and administration for the excision of this ulcer, festering ever since the United States became a nation.

For centuries the Barbary corsairs had plied their trade, harrying Mediterranean traffic, despoiling the southern European coasts, and even moving north along the Atlantic. Despite their respectively great naval power in the seventeenth and eighteenth centuries, England, France, and Spain, immersed in successive wars with one another, had found it more to their advantage to pay tribute which—to a great extent—left their merchant trade unhampered. And, so far as the North American Colonies were concerned, their commerce, up to the time of the Revolution, was of course under England's protection. The smaller European maritime nations paid tribute also, in varying amounts.

American commerce in the Mediterranean had become very prosperous; the Mediterranean basin actually absorbing one-quarter of the colonial export of dried and pickled fish and one-sixth of its flour, wheat, and rice. Rum, lumber, beeswax, and onions were other fairly important American exports. The Revolution cut this traffic short. But it started again immediately upon the war's conclusion, and by 1790 nearly one hundred American merchantmen annually called at Mediterranean ports.

Unfortunately, being no longer under the wing of English treaties and the guns of the Royal Navy, this rich traffic was now fair game for the corsairs. The United States, a weak confederation, had no Navy and Congress had little desire to build one.

Appeasement, then, by palm-greasing, was the solution; ap-

[2]One of the authors once overheard a group of American tourists loudly debate the use for such hooks, as they craned their necks over the citadel wall of Rabat. Consensus was that the great ugly, rusted hooks were intended, like the little ones studding modern slate roofs, to support scaffolding for repairing the masonry.

peasement that grasped at straws insofar as results were concerned, for treaties unsupported by force meant nothing to the blackmailers.

There was one exception—Sidi Mohammed, Sultan of Morocco. With him it was possible to conclude a treaty in 1786 which was respected. It cost the United States some £5000, as well as a quantity of ordnance, but Mohammed—an enlightened and temperate ruler—freed all American prisoners and respected American ships. His successors, with some variations, followed his policy.

With the other members of Blackmail Unlimited, it was different. To Algeria, we gave $40,000 for relief of prisoners in 1793, nearly $1,000,000 for a treaty in 1796, and four ships in 1797, 1798, and 1799—the specially built frigate *Crescent*, thirty-six, the brig *Hassam Bashan*, and two schooners, *Hamdullah* and *Lalah Eisha*.

The United States paid $107,000 to Tunis in 1798, along with jewels, small arms, and other presents for the Dey in succeeding years. Tripoli demanded $100,000 yearly in tribute from 1787 forward, but it was never paid. However, we did pay over $80,000 in 1796 and 1799, and in 1802, the sum of $6500 to ransom the crew of the American brig *Franklin* who had been held in prison. All in all, the United States spent some $2,000,000 in tribute—sufficient to have built an imposing fleet. But we are getting ahead of our story.

It is interesting to note that Thomas Jefferson, who as President would win the reputation of being a pacifist, was one of the few American statesmen of the period who advocated taking a strong stand against the Barbary corsairs. As early as 1786, when Minister to France, he asserted that a fleet in being would arm the President "with the safest of all instruments of coercion."

For several years Portugal had provided some protection for American shipping, by patrolling the Straits of Gibraltar and keeping the pirates from entering the Atlantic. But in 1793 a treaty between Portugal and Algiers, oddly contrived by the British Consul at Algiers, unlocked the gate and Algerian corsairs surged out into the Atlantic. Eleven American merchantmen were captured. When the news reached the now constitutionally organized United States, public opinion forced congressional and administration hands, as maritime insurance rates jumped from ten per cent to a breathtaking thirty per cent. A Navy would be constructed. Six magnificant frigates, product of Joshua Humphreys' and Josiah Fox's drawing boards, were laid down in 1794. But the Congress, impecunious, in appropriating $668,-888 for the new ships, stipulated that construction should cease when and if a satisfactory treaty with Algiers be concluded.

Meantime diplomacy was at work. In 1795 Dey Hassan Pasha of Algiers after much dickering accepted an American offer to pay a lump sum of $642,500 for ransom of the prisoners and an additional annual tribute of naval stores equaling $21,600. In addition, presents were to be presented the Dey twice a year equaling similar blackmail imposed on Holland, Sweden, and Denmark. The shameful compact was signed in September and work on the new warships ceased [3]

For several years American merchantmen plied the Mediterranean in comparative peace under this thralldom, while our trade waxed. In 1799 an approximate $8,800,000 worth of goods moved in American bottoms to Spain and Italy, and by the next year it approximated some $11,000,000. This was too rich a morsel for the corsair states to ignore, so conditions worsened as Tunis and Tripoli screamed for bigger chunks of blackmail and Algiers, whose share of our tribute was the largest, became impatient for more. Meanwhile the quasi war with France in the Caribbean was in full flower, engaging the new United States Navy that had come into being in 1798.

So the United States continued to sign agreements and pay tribute. When tribute was sent in the fall of 1800, near the close of the quasi war with France, the Barbary buccaneers' bellicosity became even greater because of an unfortunate turn of events.

Captain William Bainbridge, in USS *George Washington*, twenty-four, arrived at Algiers in September 1800, carrying the annual tribute. Dey Bobba Mustapha—successor to Hassan—was having difficulties with the Sultan of Turkey, his overlord. So, when

[3]Fortunately for the United States three of the vessels were near completion at the time; see p. 29 supra.

Bainbridge, and our Consul, Richard O'Brien, paid their respects to the Dey, they received an amazing proposition.

Bobba Mustapha, whom William Eaton, our Consul at Tunis, later described as a "huge shaggy beast, sitting on his rump upon a low bench with his hind legs gathered up like a tailor or a bear, who extended his forepaw as to receive something to eat," informed Bainbridge that the *George Washington* would carry his presents and his Ambassador to the Sultan of Turkey at Constantinople. Bainbridge, hotly protesting, was answered, "You pay me tribute, by which you become my slaves. I have a right to order my slaves as I please." To a man of the American's temperament there could hardly have been anything more galling, but there was very little he could do about it. His ship lay under some two hundred guns of the Algerian fortifications; if he refused the insolent demand, not only would he lose his ship, but the corsairs would be loosed against American merchantmen.

So, after much haggling, the *George Washington*, Constantinople-bound, cleared Algiers harbor on October 19, loaded to the scuppers with the most heterogeneous cargo ever put aboard a United States warship. The frigate, we must remember, was a converted merchantman of 624 tons displacement and 108 feet long. Not only did she have on board her normal armament and stores and a crew of 130 souls, but packed in her steerage were the Algerian Ambassador and his suite—some hundred or more persons, including Negro slaves, half of them women. Stowed in her hold was *backsheesh* to the Sultan of Turkey—$800,000 in specie, plus an immense quantity of jewels and a menagerie of wild life for his zoo: lions, tigers, antelope, ostriches, and parrots. Two Arabian chargers for the Sultan topped the list. The Dey, it seems, was in the bad graces of the Sultan, hence his desire to make amends.

How they all existed in this modern Ark one cannot imagine. But Bainbridge ran a taut ship. His crew, put on a strict half-ration of rum, kept their tempers remarkably as they pushed their way through the crowded decks on their lawful occasions.

It was an extremely unpleasant trans-Mediterranean trip, against headwinds most of the way and in poor company. The

Americans derived what amusement they could from tacking the ship frequently while the Muslims were at prayer, so five times daily they had to flop back and forth on the deck like dying fish to keep their faces properly turned toward Mecca.

One can well imagine that Bainbridge, smarting under the humiliation imposed on his nation, his ship, and himself, was in no mood for trifling as the *George Washington*, with a brisk following wind, moved up into the Dardanelles at long last. Abreast of the guardian forts at the entrance to the Sea of Marmora—beyond which no foreign warship could move without personal permission of the Sultan—her eight-gun salute began to boom out as the ship slowed. The swirling cloud of white powder smoke surrounding her doubled in size as a shore battery promptly returned the courtesy. But no expected rattle of anchor chain through hawse-hole came to the ears of the garrison. Instead, *George Washington* emerged from the thinning smoke with topsails sheeted home again and before the Turks realized what was happening she was out of gunshot and bowling into the Sea of Marmora.

So it was that at dawn next day, November 9, 1800, a shocked captain of the harbor of Constantinople (Stamboul), came scurrying in his barge to hail this insolent armed stranger, anchored unbidden in the Golden Horn, and flying a flag whose like he had never seen before. He doubted the actual existence of the United States, until informed that the country was part of the new world discovered by Columbus. Rushing back to report, he later brought back word that the Sultan regarded it as a good omen that the Stars and Stripes, like the Turkish flag, bore a representation of heavenly bodies.

There was still some boggling by Turkish official underlings but, thanks to the good offices of Britain's Ambassador to the Sublime Porte, Thomas Bruce, Earl of Elgin, an *entente cordiale* was arranged with the High Admiral of Turkey, Capudan Pasha Hassan, who took Bainbridge under his personal wing. Hassan, brother-in-law to Sultan Selim III, shared his relative's dislike for the Dey of Algiers. He actually stamped on and spat upon the Dey's letter, while the unfortunate Ambassador was

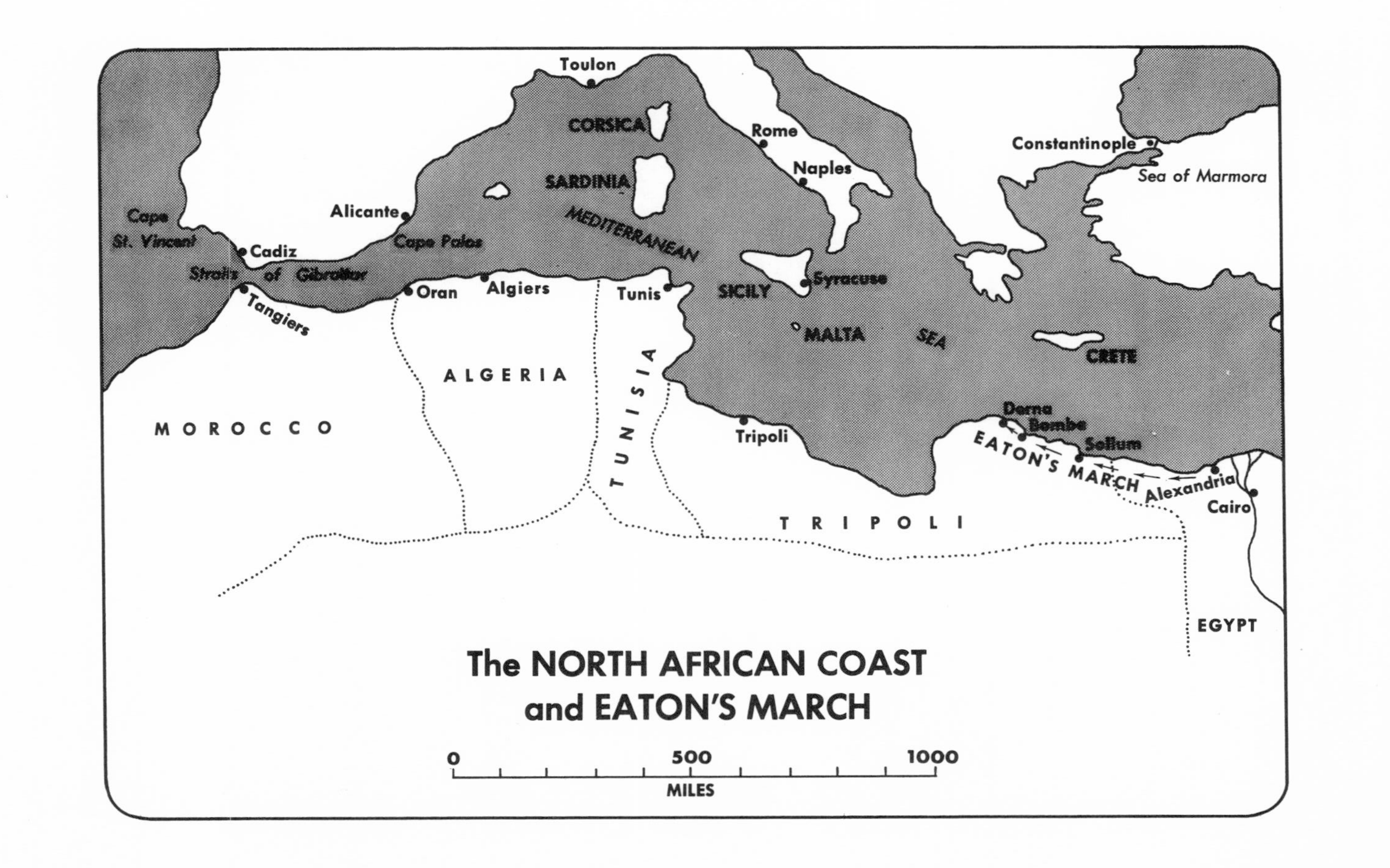

The NORTH AFRICAN COAST and EATON'S MARCH

refused acceptance, although his tribute, menagerie and all, was quickly grabbed.

Bainbridge's culture and natural charm stood him in good stead with the Capudan Pasha, who obtained a *firmin* (passport) which placed the American officer under the special protection of the Sultan. There was a series of friendly dinners; there was also some talk of a trade treaty with this nation discovered by Columbus. In such favorable circumstances Bainbridge may be said to have really laid the ground for the trade treaty which would later be negotiated with Turkey.

On December 30, 1800, the *George Washington* departed, honored by special salutes from the Dardanelles forts. This time a chastened Algerine delegation gloomed in her steerage. On January 21 Bainbridge brought her into Algiers, dumped his passengers, and presented the Dey with Sultan Selim's arbitrary demand for a hugh cash tribute, an immediate declaration of war against France, the liberation of all prisoners with English "recommendations," and an agreement to provision such British vessels as might ask for it.

Bobba Mustapha exploded, threatened Bainbridge. But when Bainbridge pulled the Sultan's *firmin* from his pocket and shoved it into the Algerine's face, Bobba, a deflated balloon, became fawningly agreeable. But there was more to come. The Dey, obeying the Sultan's orders, chopped down the French Consulate's flagpole as a declaration of war and ordered the immediate expulsion of the French delegation—some forty-odd men, women, and children. Disobedience would mean slavery; a foregone conclusion it would seem, for transportation was refused.

Once more the Sultan's *firmin* was waved. Bainbridge gathered the unfortunate French citizens on board the *George Washington*, cleared the port January 30, 1801, and deposited them at Alicante, Spain, on February 6. Then the *George Washington* pointed west for the United States, Bainbridge breathing his fervent prayer: "I hope I may never again be sent to Algiers with a tribute except it be from the mouth of a cannon." His prayer, as it turned out, would be answered shortly.

War and Tribute

The fact that Algiers had been able to commandeer an American ship of war was soon common talk along the Barbary Coast. American prestige sunk lower than ever, as did that of other Christian nations such as Denmark and Sweden, who had also been subject to depredations. Particularly obstreperous was the Bashaw of Tripoli, Yusuf Karamanli, a usurper, who for nearly two years had been haggling and bargling with our Consul James L. Cathcart, over his share of American largesse. He demanded ships, he demanded cash, he repudiated treaties. Finally, on May 10, 1801, despite the diplomatic efforts of Cathcart, he declared war on the United States. Following the symbolic cutting down of the flagpole at the consulate, his so-called "navy" —three small vessels under Murad Rais—put to sea to intercept American shipping at the Straits of Gibraltar.

The entire situation, in the opinion of United States Consul William Eaton in Tunis, was ridiculous. He constantly pointed out that the Barbary States were weak and so defenseless that any reasonable naval force could smash them. He could see no justification for permitting them to threaten nations possessing fleets of good ships and competent sailors. In a letter to the Secretary of State, Eaton, sarcastic, remarked: "What would the world say if Rhode Island should arm two old merchantmen, put an Irish renegade in one and a Methodist preacher in the other, and send them to demand a tribute of the Grand Signor?"[4]

What the Tripolitan despot didn't know was that already an American squadron was on its way to the Mediterranean. Thomas Jefferson, just become President, and enraged at the humiliating experience of the *George Washington,* and the demands of Tripoli, had dispatched Commodore Richard Dale with the frigates

[4]Eaton's "Methodist preacher" simile is obscure, but his "Irish renegade" refers to Tripoli's "High Admiral," a Scotch-Irishman named Peter Lisle. This individual, big, bluff, and blond, was a seaman in the Boston schooner *Betsy,* captured by the Tripolitans in 1796. He abjured Christianity, married the Bashaw's daughter, and under the name of Murad Rais cruised in his flagship *Meshouda,* actually the *Polly,* now carrying twenty-eight small guns and a crew of 246 men.

President, forty-four, Captain James Barron; *Philadelphia*, thirty-six, Captain Samuel Barron (James Barron's brother); and *Essex*, thirty-two, under Bainbridge; and the schooner *Enterprise*, twelve, Lieutenant Andrew Sterett. Dale, his flag in the *President*, had orders to visit the Barbary ports on a defensive mission but to open hostilities with any nation that declared war. In such case he was to "cruise off that port so as to effectually prevent anything from coming in or going out"; he was also to "sink, burn or destroy their ships wherever you find them." This latter injunction was Jefferson's own hair-splitting decision: he believed that without formal declaration of war by the Congress no prizes could legally be taken.

At Gibraltar, July 1, Dale learned of Tripoli's war declaration. Murad Rais, with his *Meshouda* and a sixteen-gun brig, was also nestling there, sheltered by English neutrality. Dale, leaving *Philadelphia* to watch the Tripolitans, dispatched *Essex* to collect American merchantmen in neutral ports and convoy them to the Atlantic. With *President* and *Enterprise*, he cruised the Barbary Coast and took up station off the harbor of Tripoli for eighteen days. The Bashaw, understandably disturbed, offered to treat for peace but before negotiations commenced Dale was forced to depart for Malta to get fresh water.

En route, Sterett's *Enterprise* fell in with the lateen-rigged polacca *Tripoli*, fourteen, manned by eighty men. The corsair moved in dangerously close to the *Enterprise* in preparation for boarding, a favorite tactic of the Barbary pirates. But Sterett, as good a seaman as the Navy had, maneuvered sharply, kept up a gunnery fight, and at the end of three hours had the satisfaction of seeing the enemy strike.

As soon as the *Enterprise* tried to take possession, however, the *Tripoli* broke out her colors again and came rushing in with the evident intention of boarding her stationary opponent. Evading her, Sterett's six-pounders were opened. Once more the Tripolitan hauled down his colors, only to resume action again. This time the *Enterprise* literally pounded the polacca into submission, raking her several times. The corsair captain, his ship dismasted, now personally threw his colors into the sea.

Sterett reported that action "commenced immediately at pistol shot which continued three hours with incessant firing. The *Tripoli* then struck her colors. The carnage on board was dreadful, she having twenty men killed and thirty wounded. . . ." Not a man was wounded on the *Enterprise* and she sustained no material damage to hull or rigging.

For his brilliant exploit the thanks of Congress and a sword were given to Sterett and an extra month's pay was awarded to the officers and men. The *Tripoli*, her guns and stores dumped overboard, was set free to make her way back to Tripoli as best she could. There the enraged Bashaw had her commander, Mohammed Sous, paraded through the streets mounted backward on a jackass, with the entrails of a sheep hung about his neck.

As for Sterett, his gunnery officer, the ever present David Porter, and the schooner *Enterprise*, they sailed for home in October 1801, since Commodore Dale did not believe it safe to cruise the Mediterranean in the winter.

Dale had ordered *Philadelphia* to base at Syracuse and cruise occasionally off Tripoli, and he assigned *Essex* to remain off Gibraltar and Algeciras to protect American merchantmen at the western end of the Mediterranean.

Before returning under orders to the United States, Dale in the *President* visited Algiers in the hope of persuading the Dey to agree to peace. He and Consul O'Brien made representations to the Dey but procured only airy promises.

On the way out of Algiers harbor on November 30, the *President* struck a rock and damaged her keel. Dale made for Toulon, France, the best place for repairs, but before he was allowed to dock he had to spend fifteen weary days in quarantine. The repair of the damaged keel forced him to stay at Toulon until early February 1802. He was visited there by the Admiral of the Swedish Navy with a proposal for joint operations against Tripoli which Dale's instructions did not permit. However, he did work out a joint plan of blockade and convoy.

Meanwhile the American squadron in the Mediterranean was temporarily reinforced in the early part of 1802 by the arrival at Toulon of the frigate *Boston*, twenty-eight, commanded by Captain Daniel McNeill. She had brought the new American Minister, Robert R. Livingston, to France. Dale decided to maintain *Boston* with the *Essex* on patrol in the Mediterranean; all other vessels of the squadron were ordered home because one-year enlistments of the seamen were about to expire.

For his part, William Eaton, our Consul at Tunis, was very distressed at the passive campaign forced upon the Americans by the inaction of Congress. As yet, war had not been declared against Tripoli, and Jefferson's administration still persisted in the illusion that we were at peace with the world. To his friend Congressman Samuel Lyman of Massachusetts, Eaton wrote describing the negligible effects of Dale's expedition and urging Congress to put more vigor into the campaign.

In the second year of the war against Tripoli, the United States Navy ordered a new squadron to the Mediterranean. Command was first offered to Commodore Thomas Truxtun, the hero of the quasi war with France. Because of a scarcity of captains, no one was appointed to command his flagship, *Constellation*, in which he had won two famous victories. Refusing to act as captain of his own flagship, the testy Truxtun declined the command and resigned from the Navy.

Captain Richard V. Morris succeeded Truxtun. As it turned out, no more unlikely naval commander could have been chosen. He took with him in his flagship *Chesapeake*, by special permission, his wife, baby son, and a Negro maid. He then permitted wives of other officers and men to make the cruise.[5]

Peppery William Eaton would later sum up Morris' Tripolitan saga with the acid remark in his letter-book: "The government might as well station a company of comedians and a seraglio before the enemy's nest."

Morris' instructions were explicit; he was to safeguard American shipping and maintain a strict blockade of Tripoli. Instead, he would scatter his ships throughout the Mediterranean while most of the time he kept far from the scene of action.

The new commodore got away in the *Chesapeake* in early April 1802 but the frigate sprung her mainmast four days out of Hampton Roads, so most of the ships in his squadron reached the Mediterranean before him.

[5]At least two babies were born on board the ship, and Mrs. Morris was delivered of her second child at Malta.

It was an imposing array. First to sail was the little *Enterprise*, still under Sterett's command. Then came *Constellation*, thirty-six, Captain Alexander Murray; *John Adams*, twenty-eight,[6] Captain John Rodgers; and *New York*, thirty-six, Captain James Barron. The *Adams*, twenty-eight,[6] Captain Hugh Campbell, was last to leave the United States.

Captain Murray, old, deaf, and headstrong, was senior officer in the Mediterranean until Morris arrived. Murray's first errand was to deliver a long-awaited present of jewelry to the Bey of Tunis. He was, understandably, received graciously. As a result, in his innocence of Barbary affairs, he reported to the Secretary of the Navy that Algiers and Tunis were now well disposed to the United States, and that Tripoli was ready to come to terms.

Actually, delivery of the jewels only brought a more exorbitant demand from the Bey of Tunis. In his boundless greed, he sent word that now he expected the gift of a brig of war.

Murray's education soon began. Tripolitan pirates had taken the Philadelphia brig *Franklin*, off Cape Palos, Spain; Murray just missed intercepting them as they raced for Tripoli, and had to content himself with a long-range bombardment of the port. One of the *Chesapeake*'s cannon balls crashed through the palace walls, to the terror of the Bey's seraglio, and his own rage. Then Murray sailed away.

In late May, Commodore Morris reached Gibraltar, where the *Chesapeake*'s mast was repaired. By the time she was again fit for duty, the Sultan of Morocco kicked over the traces, molesting United States merchantmen. This new complication kept Morris in the vicinity of Gibraltar for most of the summer, which delighted the seagoing Mrs. Morris, thus able to become a part of the social scene in the British colony.

Sultan Muley Soliman, son of the amiable Mohammed, came into the picture through one of the many fantastic incidents studding this Mediterranean campaign. In some fashion he had purchased from Tripoli the *Meshouda* (ex-*Polly*), Murad Rais's flagship, long bottled up in Gibraltar by American warships.

[6]This similarity of names is quite confusing. *John Adams* and *Adams* were sister ships, carrying identical armament; they were launched within three days of one another and rushed to completion in 1799.

Murad himself and his crew had long since returned to Tripoli by one means or another.

Muley Soliman wanted to send his new acquisition to Tripoli, loaded with grain and—possibly—contraband of war. When his demand for her free passage was turned down, he went into a tantrum, but actually had done nothing more warlike than make threats and take a few American vessels. Negotiations dragged on until August when our Consul at Tangier, James Simpson, announced that peace with Morocco had been restored. Simpson, as a mark of American good will, now gave the *Meshouda* a passport but with strict proviso that she was not to enter Tripoli.

During the fall of 1802 Sweden made peace with Tripoli, handing over a flat payment of $150,000 and promising an annual tribute of $8000. In addition, Napoleon sent the Bashaw a fine fourteen-gun sloop of war as a gift. These settlements left the United States not only with the problem of fighting the war alone, but also set a precedent as to the price of peace.

Morris' lackadaisical attitude made matters worse. From Gibraltar he went to Malta, where he found safe haven. Later, after Christmas 1802, he moved to a cozy anchorage at Syracuse in Sicily. So the great expectations in the United States for this naval expedition faded. Actually the nation lost ground, for the blockade of Tripoli was ineffectual, except as an irritant.

Also during the year, William Eaton, whose interest and operations along the Barbary Coast far exceeded his normal duties as United States Consul to Tunis, clashed with Commodore Morris. Morris gave a cold shoulder to Eaton's scheme to unseat the usurping Bashaw Yusuf Karamanli in Tripoli; as a result Eaton left for the United States to lay his scheme before President Jefferson, who approved. We shall hear more of the doings of this bustling American Machiavelli.

Not until the end of January 1803 did Morris make a real move. By that time *Constellation* had gone home. With *Chesapeake*, *New York*, and *John Adams* he put out for Tripoli, while *Enterprise* sailed for Tunis. But gale winds broke up the huffing, puffing commodore's plans. His provisions exhausted, he put back to Gribraltar, making brief visits to Tunis and Algiers, where he received cool receptions.

At Gibraltar, Morris shifted his flag to the *New York*, now under Captain Isaac Chauncey, with daring David Porter as first lieutenant. Isaac Hull took over the ubiquitous little *Enterprise*, Sterett going home in *Chesapeake*. Now Morris made another try for Tripoli, assembling *New York*, *John Adams*, and *Enterprise* at Malta, where the *Adams*, formerly blockading the *Meshouda*, also joined. But only *John Adams* was ready for a cruise and John Rodgers put out on May 3. Off the port he fell in with the *Meshouda* (ex-*Polly*), making for Tripoli under Moroccan colors, and picked her off.[7]

Morris at long last appeared off Tripoli, to establish the blockade. It was late May; he had been on the station for a year and now for the first time set eyes on his major blockading objective. A fleet of grain feluccas—lateen-rigged galleys—escorted by eleven gunboats, attempted to run into the port. Morris made chase but the gunboats huddled under the shore batteries, while the feluccas were beached beyond the old port. David Porter, reconnoitering, requested permission to make a night attack. Morris authorized a daylight assault. Porter with a detachment of some fifty marines and bluejackets made a landing under shore fire and the feluccas were set ablaze. After some heavy hand-to-hand fighting, in which Porter was wounded, the expedition disengaged, covered by the ships' guns, and under command of Lieutenant James Lawrence. American loss is uncertain; reports range from fifteen killed and wounded to just four men wounded beside Porter—one marine and three bluejackets. All casualties were retrieved. Approximately half the grain—some two hundred tons—was destroyed.

Under flag of truce, Morris now went ashore to dicker with Yusuf. But, like most of Morris' efforts, the gesture was abortive. Yusuf would talk only if money was forthcoming. He actually threatened to keep Morris as hostage, but was dissuaded. So Morris returned to his ship, and, amazingly enough, sailed

[7] Taken to Malta, the ill-starred little brig would be returned to Morocco in October 1803, when Preble brought the Sultan to terms. No one appears to have worried much over the fact that she was originally an American-owned ship whose owners had never been reimbursed for her capture by the pirates.

away June 10 in *New York*, leaving John Rodgers, senior captain, to command the squadron: *John Adams*, *Adams*, and *Enterprise*.

Forthright John Rodgers craved action, and he got it. The Bashaw, feeling his oats, on the night of June 21, sent his own squadron out—a twenty-two-gun polacca, escorted by nine gunboats. Rodgers, expecting some such move, had stationed *Adams* west of the harbor entrance, *Enterprise* to the east, and in *John Adams* lay in the center. Shortly after dawn *Enterprise* made signal that something was up. Rodgers, standing down, was informed that a large vessel had taken shelter in a cove some twenty miles to the east.

Both American vessels closed in, to find the corsair polacca moored in the bay, with springs on her cables, prepared to fire in any direction, while the gunboats crawling along the coast were assembling in the shoal waters around her. On the shore Rodgers also saw "a vast number" of cavalry and infantry. Rodgers worked his frigate in carefully, chose a good range, and opened fire. The Tripolitans could not match *John Adams'* long twelve-pounders, in range or accuracy. After forty minutes of it they abandoned ship, and Rodgers signaled *Enterprise* in "to amuse the enemy" while he skirted around some dangerous reefs and lowered his boats to take possession. Seeing that they had only the schooner to deal with, the Tripolitans began to come out and climb aboard their ship again, but *Enterprise* was now close in and firing fast the little guns of her broadside. By the time Rodgers retrieved his boats and brought the frigate into action again, smoke and flame were spurting from the polacca's portholes. A few minutes later she blew up.

Rodgers waxed almost poetic in his description of the explosion, which, he wrote, caused "a Huge Column of smoke, with a Pyramid of Fire darting vertically through its Centre interspersed with Masts, Yards, Sails, Rigging, different parts of the Hull &c and the vessel in an instant dashed to Attoms." Tripolitan losses in the explosion and from the naval cannonade of the shore must have been serious. Neither casualties nor damage were suffered on board the American vessels.

It was a nice little victory, badly needed to restore American morale. Unfortunately it was not followed up. By Morris' orders,

Rodgers was to raise the blockade five days after the commodore's departure, and the sea was again opened to Tripolitan corsairs.

However, the scenes were shifting. In July 1803 the smart topsail schooner *Nautilus*, twelve, Lieutenant Richard Somers, came winging into Malta with dispatches recalling Morris to the United States. He faded forever from the Mediterranean, September 25, 1803, in *Adams*[8] thirteen days after the arrival of his successor Commodore Edward Preble.

New Broom

Flint-faced Edward Preble, Captain, USN, his commodore's pennant flying in USS *Constitution*, forty-four, passed eastward through the Pillars of Hercules on September 12, 1803, bringing a breath of fresh air to all Americans in the Mediterranean. Both Jefferson and the Congress had decided in February 1803 that something had to be done.

Three small vessels, tailored to fit the needs of a Mediterranean coastal campaign, had been rushed to completion: the fine brigs *Siren* and *Argus*, both sixteen-gun sloops of war; and the schooner *Vixen*, fourteen. The schooner *Nautilus*, just completed, had been purchased and fitted to carry fourteen guns. These handy craft, together with the frigates *Constitution* and *Philadelphia*, made up a task force suited to the situation. The happy choice of Preble, tenth in rank on the captains' list, ensured real leadership.

Preble, as unyielding as the granite of his own Maine rock-bound coast, was forty-two years old—actually at least a decade older than any of the officers in his new command, whom he sarcastically lumped at first as "nothing but a pack of boys!" He was hot-tempered but not rash; dyspeptic (his constitution ruined by captivity in the notorious British prison ship *Jersey* during the Revolutionary War); the strictest of disciplinarians; a perfectionist. At the beginning of the campaign he was cordially

[8]In the spring of 1804 Commodore Morris was brought before a naval court of inquiry, which found him censurable for "inactive and dilatory conduct of the squadron." There was no court-martial. Irate President Jefferson summarily dismissed him from the service, May 14.

hated by most of his subordinates; by its end they adored him. Above all, as both friend and foe soon discovered, it could be said of him, as Lincoln would later say of Grant: ". . . He fights!"

He proved that at once to the satisfaction of his own officers and crew by threatening to fire on a British frigate off Gibraltar which had arrogantly refused his hail for identification. He proved it again when he learned on arrival that Sultan Muley Soliman of Morocco threatened war on the United States. Preble sailed into Tangier harbor October 5, with *Constitution* and *Nautilus*, followed by the home-going *New York* and *John Adams*, and the little *Enterprise*. The squadron, cleared for action, anchored off the fortress walls at point-blank range, presenting a combined broadside of more than sixty guns. Preble, leaving behind written instructions that should "the least injury" be offered him, bombardment must start "regardless of my personal safety," went ashore in style to beard the Sultan, with Tobias Lear, new Consul General to Algiers, beside him.

He was received courteously and escorted to the palace, where, stony-faced, he refused to surrender his sidearms, or to kneel to Muley Soliman.

"Are you not in fear of being detained?" asked Muley.

"No, sir. If you presume to do it my squadron in your full view will lay your batteries, your castle, and your city in ruins."[9]

This was language a North African despot could understand. The net result was that a placid Muley Soliman re-ratified his father's peace treaty of 1786. No more would tribute be paid; no more would American shipping be molested. Nor did Preble at the time even make a token gesture of *baksheesh*. The aroma of his saluting powder smoke was sufficient.

Preble moved to accomplish his principal mission; *Constitution* and smaller vessels cruising the Mediterranean, while *Philadelphia*, back again with Bainbridge in command, Porter her first lieutenant and Jacob Jones her second, sailed to Tripoli to establish the blockade. With her went newly arrived *Vixen*, Master Commandant John Smith. The commodore felt that this fast frigate-

[9] Glenn Tucker, *Dawn Like Thunder*, Bobbs-Merrill Co., Indianapolis, Ind., 1963, p. 206.

schooner combination could handle both offshore and close-in sweeps.

Bainbridge—unlucky Bainbridge—taking station, received information of two Tripolitan war vessels cruising the Mediterranean. In the belief they were probably going westward toward Gibraltar, he dispatched *Vixen* to look for them off Cape Bon. Toward the end of October *Philadelphia* was driven to sea by one of the storms common at that time, and as she was returning to her station on the morning of October 31, she sighted a Tripolitan vessel making for the harbor.

The *Philadelphia*, thirty-eight, gift of the city for which she was named, was a beautiful ship designed by Josiah Fox, Humphreys' assistant, as a somewhat lighter and less expensive version of one of the famous forty-fours. She carried twenty-eight eighteen-pounders along the gun deck, and sixteen thirty-two-pounder carronades topside. Underwater she had the famous Humphreys' lines, and aloft a quite unusual spread of sail which made her exceptionally fast.

The frigate now bore up in chase, with the lead line going constantly and getting seven to ten fathoms. It suddenly shoaled to a half six. Bainbridge had the helm put hard down and the yards braced sharp up, but the ship had so much way on that before she could lose it, misfortune once more struck at her captain. She went hard and fast on an uncharted reef. Bainbridge did everything a seaman's ingenuity could suggest, but to no effect. Canted over, unable to fire a gun at the numerous Tripolitan gunboats which presently came out, the frigate had to be surrendered, and for the second time in his career one of the best ship captains in the American Navy found himself a prisoner.

For Bainbridge and his men it was the beginning of an eighteen-month imprisonment. For Preble, who learned of the disaster when he spoke with a British frigate November 10, the news was shocking. He had lost one of his two frigates. Worse yet, it appeared that the Tripolitans had succeeded in floating the ship, repairing the Americans' hasty efforts to scuttle her, and that she was now resting in Tripoli harbor, her guns retrieved and remounted. This was a serious reversal of the balance of naval power, which could not be tolerated.

Establishing a base at Syracuse, Sicily, Preble kept up the blockade of Tripoli through the bitter winter months with his smaller ships. Transferring his flag from *Constitution*—far too valuable now to be risked except for a main effort—Preble cruised in *Enterprise* and *Vixen* when he was not busy working out plans for the *Philadelphia*'s destruction.

Meanwhile, the safety of the men and officers of the *Philadelphia* aroused international interest and brought offers of mediation from many sources. The United States diplomatic represenatives abroad were probably less than discreet in their appeals for help from the European powers. The American Ministers to Spain, France, and Russia all attempted to obtain the intercessions of those states. Sweden was asked for help, and Denmark was already assisting in the relief of the prisoners. President Jefferson was annoyed at the undignified tone of our many solicitations, saying, "I've never been so mortified as at the conduct of our foreign functionaries on the loss of the *Philadelphia*."

But Preble was not interested in ransom efforts; his method of bargaining would be by cutlass and fire. The Tripolitan ketch *Mastico*, lately captured by *Enterprise*, would be his vehicle, and twenty-five-year-old Lieutenant Stephen Decatur, Jr., skipper of *Enterprise*, the commander. Decatur had volunteered to take *Enterprise* herself in, daring the Tripolitan guns, but Preble would have none of that; the little schooner was needed with the squadron.

So on the night of February 16, 1804, under a full moon, lateen-rigged *Mastico*, rechristened USS *Intrepid*, slowly crept into Tripoli harbor, with English colors drooping from her masthead; to all outward appearance a slovenly Maltese trader. On her deck, in Moorish costumes, were Decatur, his pilot, a brave Sicilian shipmaster named Salvador Catalano who had volunteered for the job; and a couple of sailors.

Below decks, crouched and huddled amid barrels of gunpowder and pitch, were nine officers, fifty-odd bluejackets, and eight marines—volunteers all for one of the most extraordinary and daring raids ever attempted by the United States Navy. They were to board the *Philadelphia* as she lay under the Berber batteries, destroy her by burning and scuttling, and then—God willing—make their way out of the harbor and join USS *Siren* which was standing by outside the port to cover their retreat.

Among Decatur's nine young officers—nucleus of a United States Navy which would write its name large in the not too distant future—were Lieutenant James Lawrence—whose dying injunction of "Don't give up the ship!" would become a Navy slogan; Midshipman Charles Morris—known to a later generation as "Statesman of the United States Navy"; and another midshipman who one decade later would throttle a British invasion by his victory on Lake Champlain: Thomas Macdonough.

The *Philadelphia*, both broadsides double-shotted, lay under the guns of the Bashaw's castle, moored so as to sweep the harbor entrance. Her position and condition were known to Decatur, for not only had Bainbridge been in correspondence with Preble—using "sympathetic" ink—but Catalano himself had been in the harbor since her capture.

Intrepid got to within a hundred yards of *Philadelphia* when she was hailed and ordered to stand clear. Catalano, pouring out his troubles in lucid Mediterranean *lingua franca*, told of an anchor lost by storm; he begged permission to moor alongside until daybreak. Permission was granted, lines were passed. Then, as the ketch nosed up, someone on the frigate noted an anchor in plain sight on her bow.

A shriek of alarm was followed by an American cheer as willing hands tailing on the lines brought the vessels together. Then the boarders swarmed over to clear the frigate's deck with cutlass and boarding pike. Some twenty Tripolitans were cut down as they huddled on her forecastle; the remainder of her crew leaped overside into the harbor waters. Rehearsed in their duties, the boarding parties scattered their combustibles in cockpit, steerage, and storerooms, set the torch, then scampered for their ketch, even as flames were licking from *Philadelphia*'s gun ports.

The lines were cast off and *Intrepid*, propelled now by sixteen sweeps and towed by two small boats, moved out toward the mouth of the now illuminated harbor, target for every gun the excited Tripolitans could bring to bear. It was a thirty-minute job well done, with Decatur the last man to leave; he leaped for *Intrepid*'s rigging as she cast loose. Fortunately, the frantic gun crews on shore, strong in sound and fury, were short on expertise. One shot through the ketch's topsail was the net damage, although *Philadelphia*'s loaded broadside guns, discharged by the fire, also sent round shot splashing about in the channel as well as ashore.

Decatur and his little ship made the entrance, met *Siren*'s waiting boats sent by Lieutenant Charles Stewart to support his close friend and crony. Then the two vessels made off. Not a man had been scratched. Inside the harbor *Philadelphia*, her hawsers burned away, drifted crazily across the port, and blew up under the castle, to the shock and consternation of the entire city. There her timbers sizzled throughout the night.

Swift recognition of the amazing exploit followed. On Preble's immediate warm recommendation Decatur would soon be commissioned a full captain—the youngest man in the United States Navy to reach the grade. And from England's Lord Nelson came a terse sailor's acknowledgment of "the most bold and daring act of the age." In all probability Decatur would cherish that accolade even more than he did the sword that Congress presented him.

The question once was, and occasionally still is, debated as to why Decatur did not attempt to bring the frigate out instead of destroying her after he had gained possession. Those who argue that it could have been done seem to have forgotten one thing: Bainbridge had cut away her foremast before surrendering, and it had not been replaced. She, therefore, had no headsail and, as the breeze was onshore, could not have been worked out under canvas. It does not seem likely that seventy-four men in a sixteen-oared ketch could have towed her out by hand with everybody shooting at them and the Tripolitan gunboats certain to intervene.

The burning of the frigate completely restored the strategic situation. It was now no longer necessary to hold the *Constitution* in reserve; there was no longer any enemy heavy ship that could drive off our light cruisers. The big frigate could therefore be used in the direct attacks on the city which Preble had intended;

but it was late summer before the elimination of a threatened difficulty with Tunis and the end of the onshore gales gave opportunity.

During this time the Commodore maintained a blockade on Tripoli and kept two or three vessels of his squadron cruising the Mediterranean in search of any Tripolitan ship that might attempt escape from the port. He also arranged with the King of the Two Sicilies—Ferdinand IV—for the loan of six small flat-bottomed gunboats, each armed with one long twenty-four-pounder; and two bomb ketches, carrying each a thirteen-inch mortar. With the vessels came also the loan of ninety-six Neapolitan seamen. Junior officers from Preble's squadron commanded each of the vessels, with cadres of bluejackets to stiffen the crews. When these new additions had been shaken down Preble moved.

The walled city of Tripoli, with its castle and shore batteries, bristled with at least 115 heavy cannon. Tripolitan naval forces inside the harbor, which was protected by a screen of reefs, were a ten-gun brig, two armed schooners, two large galleys each mounting several guns, and nineteen gunboats; each of these last carried either an eighteen- or a twenty-four-pounder and two small howitzers. The corsair navy was commanded by our old acquaintance Murad Rais, the renegade. On shore the Bashaw mustered some twenty-five thousand troops.

On July 25, when Preble commenced his bombardment, the American squadron consisted of the *Constitution*, four brigs—*Argus*, *Siren*, *Vixen*, and *Scourge*; two schooners, *Nautilus* and *Enterprise*; the six Neapolitan gunboats and two mortar ketches. Its fire power totaled 156 cannon of all calibers.

After several days of boisterous weather, during which the little gunboats and mortar ketches were only saved from foundering by excellent seamanship, the weather cleared. On the morning of August 3 the squadron stood in. *Constitution*, followed by the brigs and schooners, engaged the shore batteries, while the mortar ketches hurled their big projectiles into the town. The gunboats made for the enemy's defensive line of gunboats spread in front of the two gaps in the reefs.

Decatur, commanding the flotilla, led one division of three

gunboats against five Tripolitan vessels clustered in front of the eastern pass; Somers led the other three against the hostile boats screening the western pass.

As the shooting against the castle began, the Tripolitan gunboats came straight on toward contact, banging through the powder smoke, for they prided themselves greatly at hand-to-hand fighting, and their equals in their game had not been found in the Mediterranean during three hundred years. They got their bellyful from Decatur, who slammed his bow against one of their boats, boarded against odds of two to one, and in ten minutes had the adversaries all down or overboard except five who hid in the hold.

Lieutenant John Trippe carried another after a desperate battle in which he drove a boarding pike through the Tripolitan skipper after taking eleven scimitar wounds. Joseph Bainbridge's boat of Decatur's division had her lateen yard shot away and could not close; neither could two of Somers' craft, which were unable to beat against a contrary wind fast enough to reach hand-to-hand action. Somers finally found himself alone against five enemy gunboats, "advancing and firing," as he later reported. But with round shot and grape from his one twenty-four-pounder, Somers halted them. They wove ship to escape under the protection of the shore batteries, and the amazing Somers actually chased all five of them back behind the reefline. Meanwhile Lieutenant James Decatur of Somers' division came down to join his brother's battle and delivered into one of the Tripolitans a fire so fierce that she hauled down her flag. He swept alongside to take possession; just as he mounted the rail, the Tripolitan captain produced a pistol and shot him through the head.

The news came to Stephen Decatur as he was towing out his own prize. He shouted to the eleven men who remained unhurt in his own boat and, casting loose his prize, turned back toward the treacherous Moor in a frenzy of rage, slamming into her side and leaping aboard almost in unison. The Tripolitan captain was a giant of a man; Decatur's cutlass snapped off against his boarding pike, and the American took a thrust that tore his arm and chest, but he grappled with the big man, and the two went to the deck, Decatur on top. Another Moor was swinging a deadly blow at Decatur's head when an incredibly courageous seaman named Daniel Frazier, already wounded in both arms, pushed in to take the blow on his own skull.[10] The struggling pair rolled, the Tripolitan captain working one arm free to yank out a dagger; but Decatur managed to hold his wrist with one hand while with the other he fired a pistol through his pocket, bringing down his huge enemy like the carcass of a bear.

That finished it; the rest of the Tripolitans on the gunboat gave up; the other vessels had fled. The wind changing, Preble broke off action and the squadron hauled offshore. The captain's barge was sent for James Decatur, who would die before sunset, and there was a sad, proud evening in the squadron as it prepared for another bout. Another there would be—and more than one—but the Tripolitans would try handgrips no more.

Lieutenant Stephen Decatur boarded the *Constitution* to make his report to Commodore Preble. As young Decatur stepped on the quarterdeck, his uniform torn and bloody, face pale and eyes sad at the loss of his dearly loved brother, he saluted and said, "I have brought you three of the enemy's gunboats, sir."

Preble seized the lieutenant, shaking him, and shouted, "And why did you not bring me more?" Then swinging on his heel he strode into his cabin. Decatur and his fellow officers were dumbfounded. A few minutes later, an orderly came with the message that the commodore wished to see "Captain" Decatur in his cabin.

No sound came from the cabin for a long time while the officers listened. At last, some of them, fearing the worst, rapped on the door and opened it. Preble and Decatur were seated side by side on the narrow bench, and both men were in tears.

Four days later the squadron again bombarded Tripoli, but on this occasion none of the enemy vessels closed in for an attack. During this attack one of the gunboats of the United States force blew up, killing and wounding eighteen of her crew.

That same day the frigate *John Adams*, bringing dispatches and

[10] Frazier survived.

news—both good and bad—from home, joined the squadron. Promotions and encomiums for Decatur and the others engaged in the *Philadelphia* raid were accompanied by the bitter news that Preble would be superseded.

Aroused by the *Philadelphia* disaster, the administration had decided to increase the naval effort. One million dollars had been appropriated. Four fine frigates were on their way to the Mediterranean—*President*, Captain George Cox; *Congress*, Captain John Rodgers; *Essex*, Captain James Barron; and *Constellation*, Captain Hugh A. Campbell. Commanding, with his broad pennant in *President*, would be Commodore Samuel Barron, senior captain in the Navy. So, because of seniority and despite his age, stodginess, and ill health, Barron would displace Preble and the fine edge of leadership be blunted. Navy Secretary Robert Smith wrote Preble his regret that the Department had been "unavoidably constrained" in the matter; "as the Frigates cannot be commanded but by Captains, we of necessity have been obliged to send out two Gentlemen senior to yourself in Commission." [11]

Preble, not unnaturally chafing under the situation, nevertheless pressed his efforts against Tripoli. The *John Adams* was no reinforcement—her gun carriages had been removed so that she could carry supplies to the squadron. So the force in hand must do. On August 24 the squadron anchored off the harbor in the dusk and all through the night pounded the place. Another night attack, August 28-29, showered the town, the Bashaw's castle, and all the shore batteries. At dawn the little gunboats, which had pushed close in, withdrew, having exhausted their ammunition, and *Constitution* stood boldly in to batter the castle and nearby batteries. Tripoli had become an unhealthy place in which to live.

Preble stressed this by bombarding again in broad daylight, September 3. Murad Rais brought this action on by moving his gunboats and galleys out east of the inner harbor. The commo-

[11] As quoted by Tucker, *op. cit.*, 336. Tucker also points out that the Secretary apparently overlooked the fact that *John Adams*—also a frigate—was then commanded by Master Commandant Isaac Chauncey, who would not be promoted until 1806. It should be noted, too, that Barron was given Captain Cox to command his flagship.

dore sent his own gunboats after the enemy, supported by his brigs, while the mortar ketches once more pounded the town. *Constitution* capped the climax by moving so close in shore that she was able to put no less than eleven broadsides into the Bashaw's castle. Then the squadron hauled off once more.

At eight o'clock that night the little *Intrepid*—the ketch in which Decatur and his band had bearded the Bashaw and burned the *Philadelphia*—moved toward Tripoli's harbor mouth. In her hold she carried one hundred barrels of gunpowder, over which were laid 150 fused shells. The entire combustible mass was linked by a powder train calculated to burn not more than fifteen minutes.

Preble's plan was that *Intrepid*, transformed into what in naval parlance of those days was termed an "infernal," should be brought into the harbor, and under the castle walls, where the Tripolitan light craft nestled at night. There the match was to be ignited. If all went well, Richard Somers—it was Captain Somers now—and his twelve volunteer companions, Lieutenants Henry Wadsworth and Joseph Israel and ten bluejackets, would jump into the two lightest and fastest pulling boats in the squadron and make their getaway before *Intrepid* blew up and devastated castle and shipping. Off the harbor mouth the escorting *Argus, Vixen,* and *Nautilus* waited in the night.

They waited for more than one hour. Then the black of the harbor mouth was split wide in a blinding flash, and the roar of a great explosion rumbled out. What had happened? No one to this day knows. Perhaps the premature explosion was an accident. More probable—and this was the opinion of Preble—*Intrepid* was assailed by Tripolitan guardboats and Somers, as he had declared he would do, simply hurled a lighted lantern into his magazine and blew his ship up.[12]

On September 10, word came of the *President*'s arrival at Malta with Barron. Preble, hauling down his pennant, sailed for Malta in *Constitution*, whose command he had given to Decatur. He took care that the gunboats and personnel loaned

[12] Fourteen mangled bodies were hauled out of the harbor waters and buried by the *Philadelphia* prisoners next day. No identification was possible. Timbers of the *Intrepid* were also washed ashore.

by the King of the Two Sicilies be returned to him. On January 10, 1805, in *John Adams*, Preble put the Straits of Gibraltar hull down behind him. He carried with him many comments, and letters of commendation, from old friends and acquaintances on the station—from the governor of Malta to the Pope of Rome. Pius VII had taken care to write to President Jefferson that "The American Commander, with a small force and in a short space of time, has done more for the cause of Christianity than the most powerful nations of Christendom have done for ages."[13]

But greatest treasure of them all to Preble was a document presented by young Captain Decatur just before his departure, in a little scene on quarter deck.

Fifty-three men had signed that scroll, with Stephen Decatur's name leading; fifty-three of that galaxy of Navy folk who would forever be known as "Preble's Boys." They were the youngsters whom he had molded and trained, bullied and praised to become iron men in wooden ships. They had hated him in the beginning. Now they would proudly announce: "We, the undersigned officers of the squadron under your command, cannot in justice suffer you to depart without giving you some small testimony of the very high concern in which we hold you as an officer and a commander."

The stormy Mediterranean winter had set in even before Barron's arrival, causing cessation of naval operations. The new commodore, returning to Malta and then to Syracuse, took with him most of his squadron, and the war against Tripoli drifted to a stalemate, with another token blockade.

But over to the east, a backfire was about to be ignited, far beyond the sands of the Libyan Desert.

General William Eaton

Restless William Eaton had never ceased seeking opportunities to permanently solve the problem of Tripoli. He believed that the

[13] As quoted in Tucker, *op. cit.*, 399.

only way to deal with the Bashaw was to dethrone him. Now he was back from the United States—a passenger in the *President*—with the nebulous title of Naval Agent, and Jefferson's blessings to prosecute his scheme to restore the rightful Bashaw of Tripoli —Hamet Karamanli—to the throne from which his half brother Yusef had ousted him.

Hamet, whom Eaton always referred to as the "rightful Pasha of Tripoli," was somewhere in the interior of Egypt, where, after escaping from Yusuf's clutches, he had thrown in his lot with a group of rebellious Mamaluke beys warring with the Turkish viceroy. Eaton's problem was to find his candidate, rally around him an army of dissident Arabs and Tripolitans, and launch him on the path of conquest.

This man Eaton was a fighter. He was also a leader, who had been weaned on the discipline and daring of Anthony Wayne at Fallen Timbers. His pugnaciousness and rigid sense of honor had plunged him into several scrapes with higher authority, so in 1797 he had resigned his captaincy in the 4th Infantry to take up the post of Consul at Tunis.

Eaton had authority to draw upon Commodore Barron for money, men, and munitions. However, Navy Secretary Smith's weasel-worded orders to Barron, combined with the Commodore's own indifference and the diplomatic dabblings of Tobias Lear, choked the supply line. The net result was that Eaton's fantastic scheme became one of the most bizarre adventures in the history of American military action.

Eaton sailed to Cairo in the smart little *Argus*, now commanded by Lieutenant Isaac Hull. While Hull waited, Eaton ferreted out Hamet, far inland, and persuaded him to make the move. Back in Cairo and Alexandria, Eaton, with Hull and First Lieutenant Presley N. O'Bannon, USMC, Hull's marine officer, set about gathering a rare assortment of adventurers, Christian and Muslim. As finally assembled at a rendezvous some thirty miles west of Alexandria, the "army's" backbone consisted of ten Americans—Eaton, O'Bannon with a sergeant and six marine privates, and Midshipman Pascal P. Peck, all of the *Argus*. A shady Levantine who called himself "Colonel" Eugene Leitensdorfer served—when he did serve—as interpreter and "engineer adjutant general." There was also a young Englishman from Malta—George Farquharson. Then there were twenty-five cannoneers, scraped from the streets of Cairo, and thirty-eight Greek Christians who turned out to be stout soldiers indeed. Hamet had arrived with ninety followers and an additional Arab force of cavalry headed by two sheiks lured in with their men on promise of money.

On March 6, 1805, this heterogeneous mob moved out, led by Eaton, now clad in a general's uniform as Hamet's commander in chief. Counting camp followers there were some four hundred people in the mass, with two-hundred odd camels and donkeys. Ahead of them were a good thousand miles of desert. Behind them the *Argus* was on the way back to Malta, with Eaton's report and the not unreasonable request that foodstuffs, two fieldpieces, one hundred additional stands of arms, ammunition, $10,000 in specie, and one hundred marines meet him at Derna, 550 miles away along the coast, and halfway to Tripoli.

On April 15 Eaton and his horde arrived on the shores of Bomba Bay, within two days' march of Derna. For forty days the indomitable Eaton had kept his unruly flock—half-starved, thirsty, and mutinous—together by sheer will power and his own two fists, ably aided by O'Bannon and his tough marines. Even Hamet—reluctant dragon—once refused to go on and had to be coerced. The Arabs mutinied at least five times as they clamored incessantly for money. Desertions there had been; they was unavoidable; but not a single casualty. In fact the strength had been increased to twelve hundred souls, of whom 650 were fighting men, by the addition of a forty-seven-tent nomad Bedouin tribe—150 fighting men and their families.

They were out of the sandstorm and drought of the desert now into fertile country, but anxious eyes could find no sail on the horizon. Not until next day did the *Argus* heave in sight. Hull had kept his rendezvous. He brought words of encouragement from Barron; supplies were coming. And come they did shortly in the sloop *Hornet*, ten, Lieutenant Samuel Evans, a converted merchantman purchased at Malta, and *Nautilus*, now under Master Commandant John H. Dent. The *Hornet* brought welcome beef, pork, bread, and other foodstuffs, also a quantity of water. She also brought a welcome $7000 (Spanish). But of the ammunition, cannon, muskets, and marines Eaton craved, there were none.

In front of him Eaton had a fortified walled town, garrisoned by eight hundred troops. Somewhere to the west, he knew from the Arab grapevine, another field force from Tripoli was moving to attack him. Hamet and his Arabs were once more in a ferment of indecision. To Eaton there was but one solution: attack!

On April 26, Eaton sent a formal demand for surrender to Mustafa Bey, governor of Derna, saying that he wanted no territory, but that he wanted passage through the city and he wanted the supplies which would be needed. Mustafa bluntly replied, "My head or yours!"

The *Nautilus*, *Argus*, and *Hornet* stood in the harbor. The time for action had come. *Nautilus* and *Hornet* took up positions opposite a battery on the water's edge, and Hull sent a boat from *Argus* with two fieldpieces to the foot of the precipice which had been occupied by Eaton's cannoneers. The cliff was so steep that but one gun could be hoisted up.

Hull, maneuvering the *Argus* into range, poured twenty-four-pound shot carronade shells into the loophole houses, while the other ships engaged the water battery. Eaton divided his forces and attacked from three sides. With him were Midshipman George Mann from the *Argus*—replacing Peck, who had been retained on board—and Farquharson. He led a group on the right flank nearest the sea, while Lieutenant O'Bannon, with his handful of marines, twenty-four cannoneers, twenty-six Greeks, a few Arabs on foot, came in from the southeast and attacked the breastwork from the center. Hamet's own forces swept around the head of a deep ravine and attacked from the southwest where friendly sheiks had promised they could expect the most help from the populace.

The ships silenced the battery on the sea side by 2 P.M., but the enemy did not abandon that position. O'Bannon was stalled in the center, and Hamet's men were useless as shock troops. Eaton found the pressure on his flank increasing. The battle was hanging in the balance when he decided upon a desperate charge.

"We rushed forward against a host of savages more than ten to our one," he reported later to Commodore Barron. "They fled from their coverts irregularly, firing in retreat from every palm tree and partition wall in their way. At this moment I received a ball through my left wrist which deprived me of the use of the hand, and, of course, of my rifle." Eaton, wounded, seized his sword and continued the advance, while O'Bannon, his marines, and Midshipman Mann led the charge of the rest of the Christians and the Arab infantry.

The Americans reached the water battery, drove out its remaining defenders, and planted the American flag on the walls. Tripolitan guns still serviceable were turned against the fleeing enemy. All the while the ships poured a destructive fire into houses which harbored snipers. By four o'clock the city had surrendered.

The capture of the city was fortunate, for Yusuf's forces were only two days' march away. The American losses were relatively heavy. Eaton reported that he lost fourteen killed and wounded, three of whom were Marines—one dead and another dying; the rest being chiefly Greeks. Eaton was full of commendation for his subordinates, praising without stint O'Bannon, Midshipman Mann, and the young Englishman George Farquharson, for whom he recommended a United States Marine commission.

When Eaton sent his report to Commodore Barron on April 29, Derna was firmly in American hands. With the support of the Navy, the conquest of the rest of Tripoli seemed assured. Eaton was in high spirits. For a brief moment he experienced the exultation of a conquering hero. As for Derna, the old town would not see such carnage again for 136 years to come, when Rommel's armor boxed in and captured a brigade of British tankers within its walls.

The force from Tripoli was reported to be but a short distance away, so Eaton worked feverishly to restore the defenses of Derna. True enough on the morning of May 1, this force, some three thousand strong, part foot, part horse, hove in sight, under command of one Hassen Bey. Hassen, it seemed, was in no hurry to attack. Not until May 13 did he move. Eaton kept his small force of "regulars"—the marines, the Greeks, and the Levantine gunners—in the waterfront castle, left it up to Hamet to run his own show. Astoundingly enough, Hamet developed not only ability but fortitude. Most of the operations were cavalry skirmishes, with the town's artillery and Hull's little ships occasionally taking a hand at long bowls. The townspeople, too, were now all for Hamet. After a final fight on June 11, when Hamet's troops—covered by artillery fire from the ships—brilliantly repulsed the best that Hassen could produce, the attackers withdrew, this time for good. Hassen's retreat was doubtless expedited by the sight of a large frigate entering the harbor, flying the Stars and Stripes.

But Captain Hugh G. Campbell, commanding *Constellation*, brought neither reinforcement nor comfort. Instead, he informed Eaton that Tobias Lear had negotiated a treaty with Yusuf, handing him $60,000 cash ransom for the *Philadelphia* prisoners. Commodore Barron washed his hands of Hamet and ordered Eaton to evacuate Derna immediately.

Such was the heartbreaking conclusion to an amazingly successful campaign; such the shameful abandonment of an ally. Eaton and his troops were evacuated by the *Constellation*'s boats that night. With them went Hamet and his suite. Behind were left Hamet's sympathizers, cursing the infidels who had betrayed their trust.

The fact that money had been paid in blackmail at the very time that a powerful squadron lay off the Port of Tripoli, and Eaton's expedition was threatening the Bashaw from the east, seemed inexcusable to many people. Preble summed it up for these dissenters as "a sacrifice of national honor" caused by "an ignominious negotiation." But the war with Tripoli was over and no more tribute was to be paid. Algiers and Tunis still remained as potential further blackmailers. Bey Hamouda Pacha of Tunis, emboldened by the Tripolitan outcome, now demanded the return of one of his vessels, which Captain John Rodgers had captured when she with two Neapolitan prizes attempted to run the blockade into Tripoli.

Rodgers, commodore now, for Barron had returned to the United States sick, paraded five frigates and several brigs under the Bey's nose in Tunis harbor on August 1, 1805, and queried whether Hamouda desired peace or war. When the Bey quibbled and frothed Rodgers demanded—and got—immediate agreement that the United States would be placed on a "most-favored-nation" basis. And that was that; a welcome breath of fresh salt air after the Lear-Barron devious hocus-pocus.

Meanwhile Eaton went home to wrestle unsuccessfully with Congress for the private money he had spent in government service. Hamet became an exile, finally to be reunited with the wife and children Yusuf had held in prison. O'Bannon received a sword from the State of Virginia, but was refused promotion in the Marine Corps. So he resigned to take an Army commission which was never approved by Congress. Bainbridge, back in the Navy, would redeem himself during the War of 1812 by his victory in the *Constitution* over HMS *Java*. However, most of "Preble's Boys" distinguished themselves in that war so some good came of it all.

Poetry of Justice

While the treaty with Yusuf ended for a time the depredation of the Tripolitan pirates, the situation with the other Barbary rulers had not been completely resolved. There was chronic displeasure by the current Dey of Algiers—Achmet—over the delays in the receipt of the tribute and naval stores which were to come to him from the United States. The Algerians captured three merchantmen, but one later escaped. Consul General Lear managed to patch up a temporary peace and secured the release of the vessels and prisoners. But this did not deter the Dey, who kept on demanding indemnity for Algerians carried off in the escaping vessels.

As the danger of war with England increased, the American warships had to be withdrawn from regular patrol in the Mediterranean. As could be expected, the Barbary rulers immediately became more arrogant. The Bey of Tunis threatened war in 1810 when the United States tried to recover a merchantman captured by French privateers and sold to the Bey's chief minister. Unable to enforce its demands, the United States had to permit the Tunisian to keep the prize.

A new Dey—Hadji Ali—was on the throne of Algiers when the War of 1812 became fact. He was old but ambitious, and his naval commander, Rais Hammida, was daring. Hadji threw in his lot with England. When the merchantman *Alleghany* arrived on June 18, 1812, with tribute of American naval stores, Hadji quibbled over the quality and amount of the blackmail and threatened to lock up Tobias Lear, who bought himself and the United States—he thought—out of bondage by obtaining a cash loan from the Levantine banking firm of Barci. As soon as Hadji received the cash he broke diplomatic relations, ejected Lear bodily, on board *Alleghany*, and loosed Rais Hammida on all American shipping.[14]

Fortunately, or unfortunately, the war and the British blockade choked all American commerce to a trickle, so Rais Hammida made only one prize and that not until 1815, when the little Salem brig *Edwin* was captured and her skipper and crew of ten men robbed and put to hard labor. Meanwhile Hadji Ali had been assassinated and a Turk from Lesbos—Omar Aga—assumed the throne. Omar was in for an education, for the Treaty of Ghent had been signed and President James Madison had both the will and the means to make the Mediterranean safe for democracy.

Madison asked for a declaration of war against Algiers. Congress gave it to him March 3 and by early May two powerful squadrons were readying for the Mediterranean. Heading them were two men who each had a score to settle with the Barbary pirates—Stephen Decatur and William Bainbridge.

Decatur sailed first, from New York, his commodore's pennant in a spanking new forty-four, USS *Guerriere*, named after the Britisher sunk by Isaac Hull in *Constitution* in 1812. The *Macedonian*, thirty-eight (captured by Decatur in the *United States*), *Constellation*, thirty-six, *Epervier*, eighteen (another ex-Britisher, captured by *Peacock*), and *Ontario*, sixteen, followed. Then came

[14]Wheeling-dealing Tobias Lear, off on his "slow boat to America," would undergo one more humiliation. A British frigate bagged *Alleghany* as a prize and Tobias didn't reach home until April 1813.

three fourteen-gun brigs, *Firefly*, *Spark*, and *Flambeau*, and the schooners *Torch* and *Spitfire*, both twelves.

In Boston, Bainbridge was preparing to follow close on Decatur's heels, with the great new ship of the line *Independence*, seventy-four, *United States*, forty-four, *Congress*, thirty-six, and eight smaller vessels. The new USS *Java*, forty-four (named after the Britisher sunk by Bainbridge), would soon follow.

The Marine Corps was hard put to supply contingents for such a congregation of warships. So, as it turned out, the United States Army would have a hand in this, the final act of the Barbary Wars. Brevet Major Samuel B. Archer's Company H, Corps of Artillerists, was hurriedly mustered into Decatur's squadron in lieu of marines. Archer and Brevet Captain Luther Scott, with forty-odd men were in *Macedonian*; Second Lieutenant Francis O. Byrd and Third Lieutenant James Monroe (nephew of ex-President Monroe), with approximately fifty men in *Guerriere*.

Decatur, in a hurry, entered the Mediterranean, touching briefly at Gibraltar where he learned that Rais Hammida, with a heavy frigate and another vessel, was in fact loose in the Mediterranean, and probably off the southern Spanish coast. Decatur departed at once, lest the news of his arrival should reach his enemy, his ships scattered wide, in a great eastern sweep.

Constellation, nearest the coast, on June 17 sighted a large frigate, topsails backed, twenty miles southeast of Cape de Gata and made for her, signaling the flagship. It was Rais Hammida, in his flagship *Mashuda*,[15] a well-found forty-six-gun frigate.

Either by accident or overenthusiasm, *Constellation*'s battle flag was broken out when she was still a mile from *Mashuda*, and the shocked Algerine, who had taken the squadron for British vessels, at once made all sail. By this time Decatur in *Guerriere* was on *Constellation*'s right hand, with little *Epervier* trailing, and *Ontario* making up fast. *Constellation* opened with her bow guns at long range, and a lucky shot wounded Rais Hammida, who would not, however, quit his quarter deck. The Algerine now wore ship, making for the Spanish coast and neutral waters. But

[15] Not to be confused with our old friend, the little *Meshouda* (ex-*Polly*).

Guerriere, a handy sailer, crept up and finally overhauled her. Decatur nosed in, paying no attention to *Mashuda*'s broadsides and small arms fire, and then let her have the full weight of his metal—seventeen long twenty-four-pounders and five forty-two-pounder carronades—these latter served by the seagoing artillerymen of Company H. The broadside swept *Mashuda*'s decks, one of the many casualties being wounded Rais Hammida himself, cut in two by a carronade ball as he sat in a chair directing the action.

Guerriere swept past the staggering *Mashuda* and little *Epervier* closed in, under Lieutenant John Downes, to give the *coup de grâce* in a twenty-five-minute-long pounding. When she struck, the Algerine had twenty dead and a great number of men wounded. *Guerriere* lost four killed and ten wounded, the majority of the casualties being caused by the explosion of a gun. But Lieutenant Monroe was wounded and one of his artillerymen killed by small arms fire.

A prize crew—including six artillerymen—was hurriedly put on board the captured ship and Decatur went charging across the Mediterranean for Algiers, after hunting down and capturing *Mashuda*'s consort—the twenty-two-gun brig *Estido*.

On June 29, 1815, Decatur's squadron sailed in Algiers harbor to give Omar from Lesbos the shock of his life. For the first time he learned that his one powerful frigate was captured, his vaunted maritime piracy spoiled, five hundred of his subjects held as hostages. He learned something more; Decatur's cannon-mouth ultimatum that tribute had ceased, as must the capture of American ships or enslavement of American citizens; the United States must enjoy a most-favored-nation status. All Americans now in slavery must be released and the owners of the brig *Edwin*—Algiers' sole prize in this fracas—recompensed by $10,000 in cash. Not only that, but these things must be agreed upon immediately and on board the *Guerriere*.

A truce of three hours was asked, to which Decatur bluntly refused. As the *Guerriere*, cleared for action, moved to attack the few remaining Algerine ships, now seen approaching the harbor, the Dey's barge came skipping alongside, carrying the ten prisoners and flying the signal of assent, a white flag.

And that was that. Almost anticlimactic were the visits of the squadron to Tunis and Tripoli. At Tunis the Bey surrendered on demand $46,000 cash recompense for two American ships captured and turned over to a British warship. At Tripoli, ten Christian slaves were surrendered, a cash fine of $25,000 exacted, and a salute of thirty-one guns demanded and received.

Meanwhile the one sad note in the affair was taking place. The *Epervier*, Lieutenant John T. Shubrick, cleared Algiers July 12, 1815, carrying a copy of the Algerine treaty and the ten rescued American seamen. She was never heard of again.

On Bainbridge's arrival, the combined squadrons then paraded the Mediterranean in strength which would not be surpassed for 127 years to come. The Barbary Wars were over. The United States Navy had presented the nation with its first taste of sea power.

3

The Philippines, 1899-1916

Take up the White Man's burden,
And reap his old reward:
The blame of those ye better,
The hate of those ye guard—
The cry of hosts ye humor
(Ah, slowly!) towards the light:—
"Why brought ye us from bondage,
"Our loved Egyptian night!"
—From "The White Man's Burden" by Rudyard Kipling

On February 4, 1899, two oddly contrasting military forces glowered at one another around the land perimeter of Manila on Luzon, capital city of Spain's Philippine archipelago. Behind a rudely constructed trench contravallation some twenty thousand or more poorly armed and untrained Filipinos in an extemporized military formation confronted approximately eleven thousand American soldiers—adequately armed but mainly inexperienced volunteers with a small leaven of regulars. Even their leaders were in violent contrast. Major General Ewell S. Otis, USA, sixty-one-year-old Civil War veteran, Regular Army Medal of Honor man now mummified into a prototype of "Colonel Blimp," was opposed by thirty-year-old Emilio Aguinaldo, fiery patriot and vigorous political leader of Filipino nationalism.

At 8:30 P.M. that night a three-man patrol of the 1st Nebraska Volunteer Infantry, probing the front area of the regimental sector, ran into a group of intruding Filipinos. Following close on an unanswered challenge, Private Willie Grayson's itchy trigger finger loosed off a round and the Philippine Insurrection was on. Let's establish now just why Willie and the rest of his blue-shirted, slouch-hatted comrades were over there at all.

The history of American military operations in the Philippines during the years 1898 to 1916 comprises three successive wars. The first, the Pacific segment of the Spanish-American War, was quickly and conclusively over in seven months. It commenced with Commodore George Dewey's spectacular naval victory over Spain's Pacific fleet in Manila Bay on May 1, 1898, and ended with the signing of the Treaty of Paris on December 10, 1898.

The second war was against the Philippine insurrectionists, during the period February 4, 1899, to July 4, 1902, when President Theodore Roosevelt proclaimed the establishment of peace throughout the Christian-inhabited portion of the Philippine archipelago and the establishment of a civil government. Concurrently he offered amnesty to all rebels who would take an oath of allegiance to the United States.

The third conflict was with the insurgent Muslim Moros inhabiting the southern islands—principally Mindanao and Jolo. This struggle continued until 1916.

Our particular concern is with the Philippine Insurrection and the later long drawn-out Moro pacification period; the birth pangs of a proud Malay nation, ushered in by Willie Grayson's hard-kicking Springfield.

Dewey's victory in Manila Bay had demolished Spanish sea power in the Pacific. But the Spanish Army still held Manila itself and Dewey could not put ashore a landing force capable of investing and assaulting the city. It was essential, then, that troops be rushed overseas to complete the job, a development entirely unexpected. It took a fumbling Administration, an unrealistic Congress, and a doddering War Department exactly two months to place the first contingent of less than 2500 men overseas.

Meanwhile, assisted in the first place by Dewey's speedy ferrying of Aguinaldo back from exile in Hong Kong, the still-glowing embers of past Filipino rebellion against Spanish rule had flared like a prairie fire. Aguinaldo, setting himself up as a dictator on June 23, 1898, established a revolutionary government and declared Philippine independence.

A rag, tag, and bobtail Philippine Army—more of a mob than a military force—gathered about Manila's walls, while Spanish rule in the remainder of Luzon and most of the other islands in the archipelago collapsed. Only through some tactful juggling by American commanders were the United States troops landing on Luzon able to move through the Filipino lines to take up positions for the attack which ended with Manila's surrender on August 14. The Filipino forces participated in the short final assault (met only by token defense) but were more of a hindrance than a help.

Major General Wesley Merritt, go-getting Regular Army leader, was snatched from his Philippine command a few days after the surrender to attend the peace conference in Paris, and General Otis replaced him. Throughout the dreary four-month period until the Treaty of Paris was signed, relations between Americans and Filipinos worsened, since despite the strenuous efforts of Filipino leaders the United States military authorities refused to recognize Aguinaldo's claim that the islands were now independent.

Publication of the treaty terms, which included cession of the Philippines to the United States for a payment of twenty million dollars, confirmed the worst fears of the Filipinos. It seemed that they had but changed masters. So while in the United States itself angry argument broke out between so-called "imperialists," who favored the treaty, and die-hard isolationists, affairs around Manila were nearing the breaking point. Otis was able to persuade Aguinaldo to withdraw his troops from the city itself, where they had penetrated in the final assault. But the Filipino leader either would or could not move his forces from the trenches surrounding Manila.

Arms, Men, and Terrain

Otis' immediate problem was threefold: to clean up the city, establish a stable government, and protect its population and the surrendered Spanish troops from threatened Filipino ravages. An administrative and sanitary program had gone into effect at once. In the city three infantry regiments, less than three thousand men, provided for internal security. The remainder of his forces, some eleven thousand men, were bivouacked outside the walls, confronting the Filipino Army encirclement.

Manila, fronting on the eastern side of Manila Bay, lay astride the Pasig River, winding in from the east. This unfordable stream split the land perimeter into almost equal segments. Outside the city itself and running through the edges of suburban villages, the Filipino trench line and blockhouses made an irregular loop some sixteen miles long, with its extremities resting on the bay north and south of the city and five miles apart.

Otis' plan was a defense in depth, mobile, elastic, and well suited not only to the terrain but also to the instructions from Washington which bound him to remain strictly on the defensive. Of necessity, the unfordable Pasig River split the defense, but Otis rested content in the fact that he held interior lines and the only three bridges lay deep in his own lines, facilitating mobility of support. Furthermore, he had an ace up his sleeve; the shallow-draft steamboat *Laguna de Bay*, protected by bulletproof sheet metal and armed with two three-inch guns, two 1.65-inch Hotchkiss revolving guns, and four Gatling guns. The *Laguna de Bay*, only armed craft on the Pasig, manned by infantrymen and commanded by a veteran Western steamboat man, Captain Frank A. Grant, Utah Volunteer Artillery, as it turned out would furnish invaluable mobile firepower deep within enemy lines. Conversely, the river blocked any quick shifting of enemy forces.

An adequate wire network linked headquarters and all units, while arrangements had been made with Dewey (now a full admiral), for long-range naval artillery support.

One important ingredient lacked—troops to man this defensive position should hostilities flare. The majority of Otis' troops were volunteers, enlisted "for the duration" of the Spanish-American War. And by December 10, when the treaty was signed ending that war, their contract was ended, and the enlisted men made no bones of expressing themselves. The debilitating humid environment was no place in which to soldier. They were hot; they were bored; many of them were sick. They were tired of tamely taking a succession of insults from the Filipinos surrounding them. "We wanna go home!" was more than a wish—it was pithily and loudly expressed in solder doggerel:

For it's home, boys, home, boys,
Home we ought to be;
Home, boys, in the
Land beyond the sea!

Otis' dilemma was crucial. By law and Army Regulations he must take immediate steps to ship home a full three-quarters of his available troops, the time-expired men. This would leave him less than five thousand fighting men. Yet he was also charged with maintaining American sovereignty in the Philippines. The situation was no secret, either to officers or men. And the volunteers, together with such Regulars whose enlistments were expiring, in an almost spontaneous action, did what no American troops before or since have willingly done—they announced they would stay until the replacements that Otis was clamoring for arrived![1]

Otis' northern sector, under Major General Arthur MacArthur (father of Douglas), was manned from left to right by the 1st Montana, 10th Pennsylvania, 1st South Dakota, 1st Colorado, and 1st Nebraska Volunteer Infantry regiments. In this sector also, deep in the Tondo area where they could be utilized as needed on either side of the river, were the 20th Kansas and 3rd U.S. Artillery (acting as infantry). Two batteries of the Utah Light Artillery furnished sector support.

The southern sector, commanded by Brigadier General Thomas N. Anderson, from left to right consisted of the 1st Washington, 1st Idaho, 1st California, 14th U.S., and 1st North Dakota

[1] In 1906 Congress belatedly awarded this sincere patriotic stand by establishing the Philippine Congressional Medal for all members of the Army who had volunteered to remain in the Island beyond their discharge date. Inscribed "Philippine Islands, 1899, For Patriotism, Fidelity, Loyalty," this proud symbol of the real Volunteer spirit was criticized at the time, by many unthinking persons, as an alleged debasement of the Congressional Medal of Honor itself. See Dupuy, R. Ernest, *The Reserve Story,* unpublished ms., Washington, D.C., 1967; also Ganoe, William A., *The History of the United States Army,* rev. ed., D. Appleton-Century Co., New York, 1942, p. 398.

Infantry regiments, supported by two batteries of the 6th U.S. Field Artillery.

Each regiment on the perimeter had an outpost in contact with the Filipino trench line, while the respective main bodies lay in support well in rear. The volunteers were armed with the single-shot, black-powder, breech-loading Springfield rifle, caliber .45, while the Regulars had the Krag-Jorgensen .30-caliber repeater, using smokeless powder.

American field artillery pieces were 3.2-inch quick-firing breech-loaders. Lighter artillery available included a few three-inch mountain guns—pack artillery. A few hand-operated Gatling and Hotchkiss machine guns also were in the infantry regiments.

Filipino armament, as it turned out, was a miscellaneous assortment of handguns, varying from a comparatively few Mauser repeaters captured from Spanish troops, to antique muzzle-loaders. Ammunition was in short supply, and although several small ammunition plants were later erected by the Filipinos they were of necessity inadequate in machinery and personnel. Used cartridge cases would be assidiously gathered by Aguinaldo's forces, but the reloading was poor and the results deplorable—from the Filipino viewpoint. Additional handicap would be the poor marksmanship displayed by the average Filipino soldier.[2]

The supply of firearms was far below Filipino needs. Probably not more than fifty per cent of any unit had firearms of any sort. Unarmed men in combat picked up the weapons of killed or wounded comrades. Aside from a very few Krupp fieldpieces captured from Spanish garrisons, the artillery consisted of ancient muzzle-loaders. In some cases Filipino ingenuity later actually reamed out hollow logs, bound in wire, to use as cannon.

One weapon, however, the Filipinos had in plenty. This was the bolo, a heavy-bladed jungle knife about twenty inches long. One old-time campaigner in the Philippines called it "a cross between a carving knife and a hatchet,"[3] a very neat description. The Filipino peasant used the bolo—always kept at razor

[2] Due only to lack of training. Later, the Philippine scouts of the United States Army speedily became crack marksmen. A scout infantry company which did not qualify one hundred per cent of its personnel in marksmanship annually was rare, indeed.

[3] Rear Admiral Bradley A. Fiske, USN, *War Time in Manila,* The Gorham Press, Boston, 1913.

edge—for everything from cutting grass to building a hut. It was also convenient in slicing off an enemy's head.

On every count except numbers, American forces were seemingly superior to their opponents. However, two factors—climate and sanitation—leveled the balance to some extent. The Filipinos were primitive people and their Spanish overlords were almost as primitive in sanitation. Even in Manila, sewage disposal was practically nil. Smallpox, bubonic plague, beriberi, malaria, yellow fever, and all the kindred tropical diseases thrived.

This aura of malaise permeated a climate, where the temperature—except in the mountainous regions of Luzon—never fell below eighty degrees Farenheit; where there were but three seasons: the so-called "cool" season, from October to March; the hot, dry season, from March to June, with all the tropical sun's deadly intensity; and the rainy season—June to October—when rainfall was constant, leather rotted, roads became quagmires, and rivers flooded.

And now the Americans were suddenly plunged into combat.

Battle of Manila

Fortunately for the inexperienced American troops, the Filipino assaults that night of February 4 were entirely uncoordinated. As result a succession of little firefights dotted the perimeter. Two assaults, in the northern sector, made some preliminary penetration but as soon as MacArthur's men rallied from their initial stage fright the lines were reestablished.

At dawn MacArthur received permission from Otis to take the offensive and by afternoon the Filipinos had been pushed well back beyond their original positions. The supporting fire of the field artillery was augmented on the far left by USS *Charleston*'s long-range support. All of this was too much for the inexperienced Filipinos.

Anderson's sector on the American right, quiet during the night, now flared as he, too, received permission to advance. On his left the Idaho and Washington infantry, long infuriated by the taunts of the insurgents on their front, charged them. These

Filipinos were a so-called brigade of seven hundred men, commanded by a former bandit named Pio del Pilar. In the valor of their ignorance they had filled a bend on the west bank of the Pasig. Now they were rushed off their feet, driven against the river and most of them killed, captured, or drowned.

On Anderson's right the going was heavy despite artillery support and the thunderous explosions of the heavy guns of USS *Monadnock*. The old-fashioned light-draft monitor waddled to within a thousand yards of the shore, but it seems that noise, rather than armor-piercing projectiles that simply dug themselves harmlessly in the ground, was her most effective effort.

It was during this conflict that First Lieutenant Charles K. Kilbourne, Signal Corps, climbed a telegraph pole within 250 yards of the enemy and under heavy small arms fire coolly repaired a break in telegraphic communication. Kilbourne won the Congressional Medal of Honor for his deed.

On February 6 a task force of MacArthur's command struck out across country and captured the waterworks pumping station supplying Manila with water. By the end of that day insurgent forces had been driven well beyond the city. There was now no doubt as to the outcome.

Of overwhelming assistance to the American forces was their artillery. Against its fire, the insurgents had no defense and no counter. The battle ended when the insurgents retreated and dispersed into the surrounding countryside. The two American divisions lost fifty-nine killed and 278 wounded. It was impossible to assess the insurgent casualties, but American troops buried 612 insurgents, and General Otis estimated their total loss at about three thousand.

A week later a Navy force landed and took an insurgent fort on the island of Ilo-Ilo. Almost simultaneously, American seamen and soldiers also captured the city of Cebu on the island of that name, and went ashore on the island of Panay.

Early Operations in Luzon

During the latter part of February and the month of March 1899 more American troops arrived in the Philippines, including

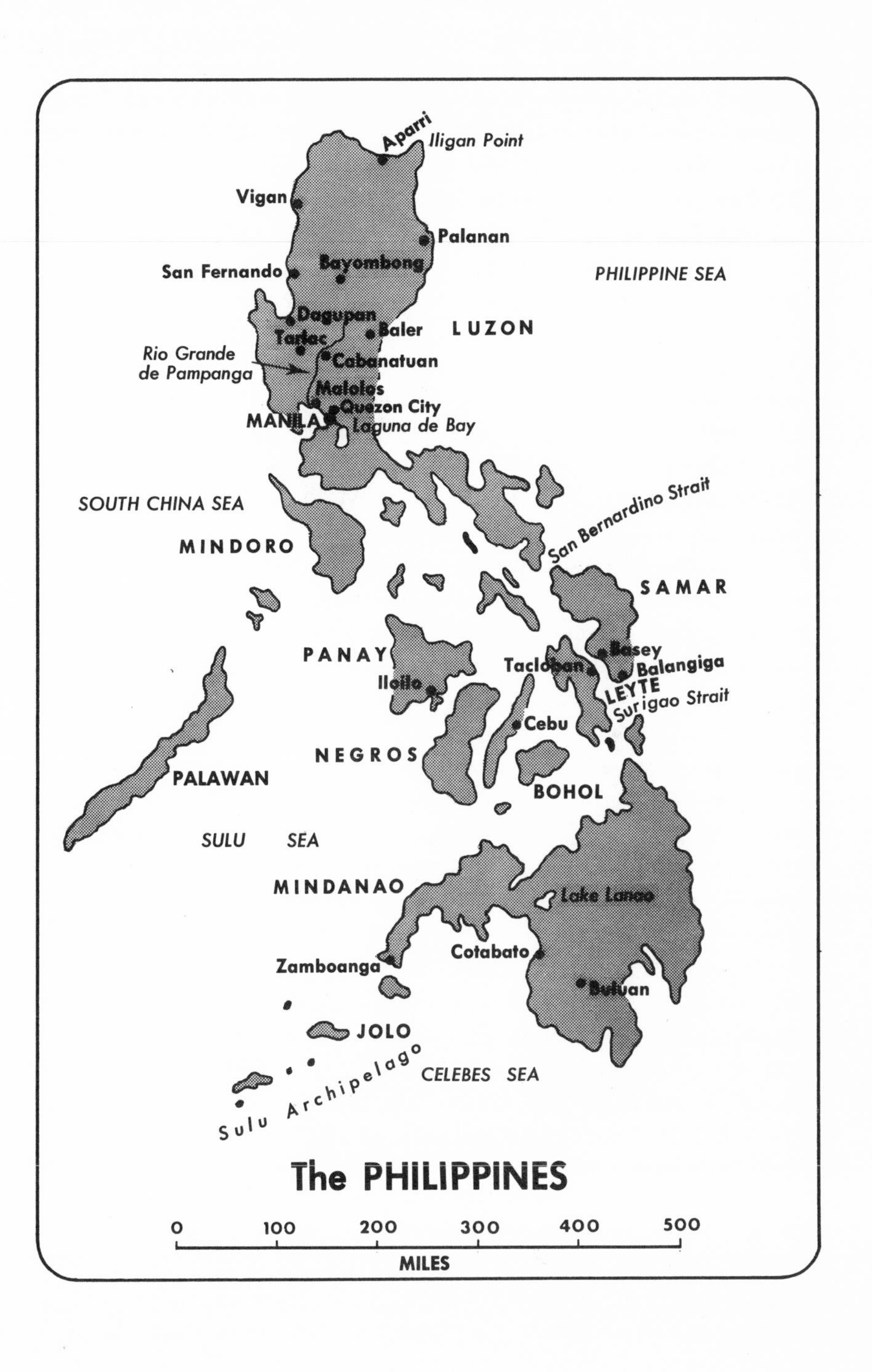
Aparri
Iligan Point
Vigan
Palanan
San Fernando
Bayombong
PHILIPPINE SEA
Dagupan
Baler
LUZON
Tarlac
Rio Grande de Pampanga
Cabanatuan
Malolos
Quezon City
MANILA
Laguna de Bay
SOUTH CHINA SEA
San Bernardino Strait
MINDORO
SAMAR
Basey
PANAY
Tacloban
Balangiga
Iloilo
LEYTE
Surigao Strait
Cebu
NEGROS
PALAWAN
BOHOL
SULU SEA
MINDANAO
Lake Lanao
Cotabato
Zamboanga
Buluan
JOLO
CELEBES SEA
Sulu Archipelago
The PHILIPPINES
0
100
200
300
400
500
MILES

Regular Army units freed by the ending of the Spanish-American War.

Since the cool season was nearing its end, it was imperative that American occupation forces make as many strikes as possible.

A flying column under Brigadier General Lloyd V. Wheaton, with river gunboats cooperating, moved out of Manila along the Pasig River to the Laguna de Bay and pushed the insurgents eighteen miles from the city. This operation opened the Pasig River to traffic from its sources to Manila Bay, while to all intents and purposes it split the insurgent territory in two.

The other major operation occurred in the last week of March 1899 when MacArthur's troops moved northwest from Manila and captured the insurgent capital at Malolos, some twenty miles away.

MacArthur's reinforced division reached out along a number of small streams, using river transportation where available but reduced to the pace of the caribou-drawn supply carts. Expecting considerable insurgent resistance at Malolos, MacArthur on March 31 prescribed an artillery preparation of twenty-five minutes to be followed by an envelopment of the insurgent left flank.

Colonel Frederick C. Funston, a soldier of fortune who was to make his name in the Philippine Insurrection, led the 20th Kansas on the left. An extensive trench near the railroad, less than a quarter of a mile from the suburbs of Malolos, was found deserted, and here the Kansas regiment halted. The commander sent a small reconnoitering party into the town and two squads cautiously moved up the principal street. A convent which had been occupied by Aguinaldo as a residence was in flames. The Americans were fired upon by a dozen men behind a stone street barricade. The detachment returned the fire and charged, putting the enemy to flight, and seized the town. Aguinaldo's "government" had fled to the north.

Following the capture of Malolos, General Otis had a golden opportunity to settle the insurrection in short order. With the season of unbearable tropic heat coming on shortly, he had perhaps a month in which he could have extended and consolidated American authority. Instead of sending small mobile columns in all directions to occupy insurgent territory, he sent comparatively large forces in two or three directions. This idea of thrusting large forces did not envision retaining occupied territory under American control. As soon as a key point was gained, Otis required the expedition to return bag and baggage to Manila. The scattered, disorganized insurgent forces then moved into the vacuum and reoccupied the territory. The kindest thing that might be said is that Otis was cautious, but the fact is that because of his dilatory action it took three years to do a job which many subordinates thought could have been accomplished in a matter of months.

During the late spring of 1899, MacArthur continued making thrusts north of Malolos to seek out and to defeat insurgent groups. One operation brought his troops into contact with some six-thousand insurgent forces entrenched on the north bank of the Rio Grande de Pampanga at the town of Calumpit. The Rio Grande, unfordable, was about eighty yards wide and with a five-mile-an-hour current. The insurgent troops, commanded by General Antonio Luna,[4] had removed all boats from the river. The occupation troops had no pontoon bridges, so their only possible means of crossing the river was by a partially dismantled railroad bridge. On the north bank of the river on both sides of the bridge were six thousand insurgents securely protected in thickly embrasured entrenchments.

In General MacArthur's words, the crossing was a remarkable military achievement. Funston, commanding the Kansas Volunteers, conceived and carried through the plan. On May 26, he took with him Corporal A. M. Ferguson and Captain Charles S. Flanders and made a reconnaissance of the bridge. Ferguson took off his shoes and, armed with only a revolver, crawled through the network of iron braces underneath where the floor had been and worked his way hand over hand until he was underneath the insurgent outpost stationed on the other end of the bridge. He returned with a complete description of the insurgent position, reporting that all of the ties, rails, and planks were gone in the bridge and at its farther end all but one of

[4] Luna, educated in Europe, was a strong-willed student of military strategy who had been appointed Minister of War and also combat commander of the insurgent forces. He was actually a rival of Aguinaldo, and plotted to make himself dictator.

its steel girders.

The next day Colonel Funston determined to force a passage across the river about six hundred yards below the railroad bridge. Covered by one hundred riflemen, Privates Edward White and W. B. Trembly, naked and unarmed, swam the river with the end of the rope which was to be attached on the farther shore and used as a trolley for rafts. Although fired upon repeatedly, they landed within twenty feet of a small enemy earthwork, fastened the rope to one of the uprights in the trench, and then fought off several insurgent soldiers. Funston and eight men boarded a raft and pulled themselves across hand by hand. After the raft had returned several times, he had three officers and forty-one enlisted men on the opposite bank. This force made a flank attack on the enemy's entrenchments at the end of the bridge and, after a sharp fight, routed them.

For this action, White, Trembly, and Colonel Funston received the Congressional Medal of Honor, and Funston was promoted to the grade of Brigadier General of Volunteers.

From an Army standpoint Funston was a paradox. An adventurous youth of twenty-six, he had engaged in a botanical expedition in California's Death Valley. Two years later in Alaska he floated alone down the Yukon River in a canoe. In 1896 he accompanied an insurgent expedition to Cuba as a a soldier of fortune and fought against Spain. Wounded and a victim of malaria, he returned to the United States in 1898, just at the time the 20th Kansas Volunteers were being organized for war. The governor of Kansas appointed this comparatively youthful man of thirty-three to command the regiment. Only five feet, five inches in height, he was, however, absolutely fearless in regard to his personal safety. Because of his youth he looked to the soldiers like a boy among the sixty-year-old officers of his rank in the American army.

Two days after the capture of Calumpit the insurgent government, now at San Isidro, sued for an armistice of fifteen days in order to discuss putting an end to the war. General Otis agreed to permit an insurgent delegation to go to Manila and appear before the Philippine Commission, but he refused an armistice. The delegation—actually a "rump" party, appointed by Luna—was received by Otis who informed them that the cessation of hostilities depended entirely upon the surrender of arms and the disbanding of their military organization. The insurgent party then appeared before the American-appointed Schurman Commission and after discussing the situation promised to return within three weeks. It never returned. Luna's attempt to gain control of the insurgents was to result some three weeks later in his assassination.

One other expedition in the spring of 1899 deserves mention because of its commander, Major General Henry W. Lawton, a soldier's soldier. He was instructed to march in April against the insurgents in the Province of Laguna, southeast of Manila. With a fifteen-hundred-man force, primarily dismounted cavalry, Idaho and North Dakota Volunteers, and two battalions of the 14th Infantry with two mountain guns, he captured the city of Santa Cruz on Laguna de Bay.

Lawton, Civil War veteran, Medal of Honor man, and well known as Indian fighter and hell-for-leather cavalryman, then swung northward up the valley of the Rio Grande de Pampanga to capture San Isidro, from which Aguinaldo and his government had fled but minutes previously.

Between them, now, MacArthur and Lawton had swept the terrain immediately north of Manila of all insurgent activity. Their troops, however, exhausted by the climate and by continuous marching and fighting, also were hard hit by heat and amoebic dysentery. In MacArthur's command alone, of a strength of 3700 men, 1003 were sick and wounded. Otis stopped all offensive movement to reorganize his forces, which were still further depleted by the necessity of sending sizable detachments to the islands of Negros and Jolo.

Since the beginning of the year combat casualties had amounted to 107 officers and 1667 enlisted men—more than the losses in the entire Spanish-American War. Intermittent guerrilla operations continued all through the hot summer, and it became more and more obvious that the American occupation force was not strong enough to put down the insurrection. By June 1899 there were approximately 35,000 troops in the Philippines, over half of whom were volunteers with their departure imminent.

Between June and October all the State Volunteer regiments returned home to their points of origin, primarily the West and Midwest. The volunteers had done their work well, but now were to be replaced by Regular Army units, some organized from volunteers from the regiments being sent home.

In October 1899 new Volunteer regiments—federal troops, raised for the duration of the war only—numbering about twenty thousand men, began arriving in the Philippine Islands. General Otis decided that he was sufficiently strong to deliver the *coup de grace* to the insurgent army. A Fabian policy, which the insurgents had adopted after the first few fights with the Americans, made decisive action extremely difficult. The farther the Americans advanced into insurgent territory, the greater became the supply problem, and the number of troops required to protect the line of communications. Between February and October of 1899, a period of eight months, no American soldiers ventured more than sixty miles from Manila. Now came action again.

Hunting Aguinaldo

The bulk of the insurgent army was north of Manila, being pushed by MacArthur's division toward Angeles. As the American forces thrust northward, a logical line of withdrawal for the insurgents was along the railroad, which had its terminus on Lingayen Gulf, 150 miles north of Manila.

Otis' plan was to have MacArthur's division—now on the railroad at San Fernando—pin Aguinaldo and his troops down somewhere in this area, until encircling forces could get around his rear and gain access to the mountains in the north. Thus there would be no further retreat for Aguinaldo. The geography of central Luzon suited this plan. In the center was a broad, flat plain extending from Manila to the mountains in the north, and flanked both east and west by mountain ranges.

On the east, Lawton, whose mobile force included cavalry, would move north from San Isidro to block off the passes into the mountains fringing the east coast of Luzon. Wheaton, now a major general, Civil War veteran, and Medal of Honor man, would command the other arm of the pincers. Moving by water from Manila to the San Fabian-Dagupan area on the Lingayen Gulf[5] he would seal Aguinaldo's escape routes to the west and north.

The theory was fine, but Otis did not specify where the encircling forces should meet, and he kept—or tried hard to keep—rigid control over all elements of his field forces.

MacArthur's steady advance, after several sharp encounters, brushed all opposition ahead of it. By November 12, Aguinaldo and his few remaining loyal commanders held a council of war at a town on the railroad about twenty-six miles north of Tarlac in the wilds of Luzon. They decided that united insurgent resistance was useless, and that the only alternative was to break up into small groups and engage in guerrilla warfare. Generals Concepción and Alexandrino, who had been opposing MacArthur's advance, marched into the Zambales Mountains to the west; Aguinaldo with a small group of followers and the troops of Generals Pio del Pilar and Manuel Tinio moved toward the mountains to the north. From this time on MacArthur encountered no insurgent resistance, but suffered much from disease and weather.

Wheaton, with two thousand men—the 13th and 33rd Infantry regiments, a platoon of artillery and engineers and signal detachments—left Manila by transport November 6, with naval escort. He landed at San Fabian next day with but little interference. Had he pushed out in accordance with his orders "to prevent the retreat of the insurgent army to the north," the trap would have been closed and MacArthur's legitimately slow but steady movement north would have crushed the insurgents. As it was, he stayed put in the landing area and left the northern gateway open wide.

Our interest lies with the amazing campaigns of Lawton, and his cavalry leader, Brigadier General Samuel B. M. Young, a six-foot-four Civil War veteran of true United States Cavalry heritage and aggressiveness.

Lawton had moved out first from San Fernando and Calumpit

[5]Where the principal Japanese invasion occurred forty-two years later.

—railhead—with an all-Regular command: the 24th (Negro), 16th and 34th Infantry regiments, and one battalion of the 22nd, a provisional cavalry brigade—eight troops of the 3rd and nine troops of the 4th Cavalry—a provisional artillery detachment whose unorthodox composition belied its accomplishments, and three companies of the newly organized Philippine Scouts. In all, he had some 3700 men. Young, the cavalry commander, although obedient to orders, took little stock in Otis' dilatory policies. The artillery consisted of four horse-drawn Hotchkiss twelve-pounders, manned by two companies of the 37th Infantry—one being the gunners, the other furnishing infantry protection. Captain Ernest D. Scott, later to become in World War I an artilleryman of renown, commanded this scratch unit.

By October 19 the command had crossed the Rio Grande at Arayat and pushed north up the valley to San Isidro, where some nine hundred insurgents under Pio del Pilar were routed. Supply had already become a problem, for water transport only could be used between Calumpit and San Isidro and it was subject to harassing enemy fire. Here weather and floods on the river complicated matters, but by great exertion a base was established, and mule teams and ox carts assembled for forward movement.

Young's cavalry brigade now plodded through mud to Cabanatuan, while the rest of the command toiled at assembling supply. Floods washed away bridges, barges grounded on sandbars, while both Lawton and Young fretted. On November 5 an insurgent proclamation was captured, announcing the coming move of Aguinaldo's "capital" from Tarlac to Bayombong, well north in the mountains. Lawton at once unleashed Young—much to the latter's glee—on a stripped-saddle, live-off-the-country march to block the passes. The remainder of Lawton's force followed.

Marching and occasionally fighting under almost indescribable conditions of weather, Young's command actually overran Aguinaldo's rear guard, capturing his supply train. One detachment almost nabbed the insurgent chieftain himself, but through the negligence of its commander the enemy party slipped away. That same day another detachment rode into San Fabian to contact General Wheaton, whose command had been dilly-dallying for a week in the San Fabian-Dagupan area since their debarkation. Young, arriving at San Fabian in person, pushed north in pursuit of Aguinaldo, borrowing from a reluctant Wheaton some of his troops to reinforce his own cavalry, now scattered in small packets over the countryside.

Enlisting the aid of naval units lying in the Gulf, the port of Vigan was captured; the thirteen-inch guns of USS *Oregon* sent the insurgent garrison fleeing in terror. A detachment of bluejackets and marines marched in, directed by a staff officer of General Young, while the townsfolk cheered. A battalion of the 34th Infantry then pushed north through Tila Pass, scattering Aguinaldo's bodyguard, whose commander, the twenty-eight-year-old del Pilar, was killed. Aguinaldo himself fled northeast with a small party.

One organized body of insurgents still remained, under Tinio. This outfit was chased north, putting up a bitter resistance. The pursuit ended up in the northwest tip of Luzon, where the insurgent force disintegrated. Some eight hundred Spanish prisoners were liberated. Finally, sixteen Americans—sailors and soldiers—were released and Young's detachment, seventeen officers and 133 men, in rags and practically barefoot, staggered into Aparri, where naval units were waiting to help them.

Otis could thank Lawton and Young for spearheading a pursuit through the jungle which ended—seemingly—all organized resistance. True, Aguinaldo himself was still at large, but only as a harried fugitive. His army and his government no longer existed; his family had been captured. But Otis thanked neither man. Lawton he had relieved shortly before the end of the campaign; to put him in charge of a relatively minor expedition in the south. Young, instead of being promoted to Lawton's place, was also relieved. Into Lawton's shoes stepped a relatively junior officer, Brigadier General R. H. Hall; a man who could see eye to eye with a commander who had proved his kinship with Kipling's "elderly, heavy-sterned old men who 'amper and 'inder and scold men."

Young would go on; ending his career as Chief of Staff of the United States Army. Lawton, in the forefront of a minor engagement against guerrillas in southern Luzon, would fall to a sharpshooter's Mauser at San Mateo, December 19, 1900. But we cannot leave their northern campaign•without mentioning one of the most remarkable sideshows of this fantastic jungle-mountain expedition.

In late November Captain Joseph B. Batchelor, 24th Infantry, with his battalion of fine Regular Negro infantrymen and three companies of Philippine Scouts was detached from Lawton's command to strike over the mountains for Bayombong, where Aguinaldo had planned to establish himself. Young's sweeping end run had killed the Filipino leader's hope, but Batchelor, with orders to live off the country, had kept on. At Bayombong—where a detachment of the 4th Cavalry had already been established—Batchelor, entirely on his own, struck northward for the fertile but unexplored valley of the Cagayan River, which empties into the sea at the northern end of Luzon.

He and his footsloggers crossed over eighty miles of mountainous jungle in five days, lived for three weeks on what food they could find—and it wasn't much. They forced the surrender of all local Filipino forces in the area of three provinces, captured a seagoing steamship, a river steamer, more than a hundred barges. They liberated more than four hundred prisoners, bagged a quantity of cannon, small arms, and eleven hundred Filipino soldiers. Best of all, they left the people of the valley enthusiastic supporters of American soldiers and American ways.[6]

Batchelor and his command reached Aparri and naval support in triumph. But an infuriated Otis "abused him like a pickpocket," when he returned to Manila.

So much for Batchelor. But we must also mention an amazing instance of Spanish bravery, which caused the capture of the Americans whom Young liberated.

On the northeastern coast of Luzon the little town of Baler sits below the Sierra Madre mountain range, which blocks communication with Manila. In 1898 the townsfolk rose against the small Spanish garrison, commanded by Second Lieutenant

[6] The Cayagan Valley people have long memories. In 1942 they welcomed and sheltered another American officer and his troop of Philippine Scouts who established an astounding guerrilla resistance against Japanese occupation. See R. Ernest Dupuy, *Men of West Point,* William Sloane Assoc., New York, 1951, pp. 203-207 incl.

Don Saturnio Martín Cerezo. The Spaniards took refuge in the local church, where they withstood determined assaults for 337 days. They refused to believe insurgent claims that the Spanish-American War was over, and rejected as spurious all efforts to convince them they could surrender and go home with the Spanish troops. Even an assault by General Tinio, with support of a modern field gun, was unsuccessful.

Word of the amazing defense of Baler church reached the American authorities. The USS *Yorktown* in April 1899 dropped anchor offshore and a boat party under Lieutenant J. C. Gillmore, USN, attempted to move upriver to contact the Spaniards. But an insurgent ambush wrecked the boat, killed nine men, and the eight survivors, including Gillmore, were made prisoner. *Yorktown* steamed away.

Actually, when the last scrap of food was gone, Cerezo and thirty-two Spanish soldiers surrendered to the insurgents on June 6, 1899. They had been promised their liberty and the promise was kept. They reached Manila after a terrible journey over the mountains, were warmly received, and finally got back to Spain to be showered with honors.

By the end of 1899 Otis, down in Manila, and even MacArthur, reorganizing his troops after their grueling campaign, felt that the insurrection was over. Brigadier General William A. Kobbé, Jr., with the 43rd and 47th Infantry regiments and a battery of field artillery had been lifted south to Sumar, Leyte, and Catanduanes, in conjunction with a naval force—the gunboats *Nashville*, *Helena*, and *Marivales*—opening up the hemp ports to commerce. Except for the Benguet Mountain range in the north, where Aguinaldo hid, Luzon appeared to be pacified. The principal ports of the other major islands were in the hands of US troops.

Actually, the occupation forces were sitting on a volcano.

Guerrilla Warfare

Aguinaldo's decision of November to conduct guerrilla warfare was flaring throughout the islands. The Katipunan, as it was called—"Worshipful Association of the Sons of the People"—a bastard freemasonry of sorts, originally Tagalog but later spreading through all but the Moro provinces in the south, furnished the mechanism. At its height it boasted of at least a hundred thousand members who with terroristic ritual set up a very effective secret government network. Its devotees and the peasants whom they enlisted by terror or persuasion, were peaceful farmers by day who stalked outposts by night and laid lethal traps for small bodies of American soldiers.

Whereas during the last four months of 1899 American casualties in 229 engagements amounted to sixty-nine killed and 302 wounded, in the first four months of 1900, 442 guerrilla clashes cost the Americans 130 killed and 322 wounded.

General Otis was relieved in May, at his own request (he felt that his task had been accomplished), and General MacArthur took his place. Before leaving, Otis had regrouped his forces into occupation status on a geographical basis. The Army, scattered in small garrisons—there were 413 of them by September 1900—was attempting to supervise civil government but the Katipunan actually maintained undercover control of most of the *barrios*. The very individuals designated by the military as local officials were either members of the dreaded secret society or came completely under its sway.

The guerrilla movement came to its peak in August. As in all such widespread operations, the American forces controlled only the ground upon which they stood. Guerrillas fought from ambush with firing at close range or by sudden attacks on small parties of American soldiers in brutal type of combat. Soldiers were hacked to death by bolos instead of being wounded or killed by Mauser bullets. As General MacArthur put it at the time: "Each little command had to provide its own security and information gathering by never-ceasing patrols, explorations, outposts, escorts and regular guards."

Pro-American Filipinos—and by this time there were many—were completely terrorized, their lips sealed. Informants, men, women, and children, were beaten to death with clubs or stones. Some were simply chopped down by bolos. But where inspiration of terror was desired, the unfortunates were buried alive—sometimes in the *barrio* street.

In the meanwhile the insurgents had been receiving a certain amount of moral support direct from the United States, where the "Philippine Question" had become a political football in the coming Presidential election. Early in 1899 isolationist elements —among them reputable citizens like Senator George F. Hoare (R. Mass.), Samuel Gompers, Andrew Carnegie, David Starr Jordan, and Charles F. Adams—organized an Anti-Imperialistic League in Boston early in 1899 to protest the annexation, and urge granting of independence. The isolationist movement quite naturally snowballed into a Democratic Party Presidential platform plank. President McKinley's reelection in November 1900 plainly showed the American people's temper, but much harm had been done, for the insurgents' hopes had been raised and the *ignis fatuus* that a tired United States would elect an anti-imperialist—William Jennings Bryan—and bring about immediate independence, kept up the hopes of the guerrillas.

So serious became the situation that MacArthur, who as military governor had endeavored to give the Filipinos free rein in governing themselves, on December 20, 1900, proclaimed martial law throughout the islands. Some seventy-nine guerrillas were tried for murder and hanged; and thirty-two other prominent irreconcilables, including the civilian leader Apolinario Mabini, were deported to the island of Guam.

McKinley's inauguration, March 4, 1901, was followed on the twenty-second by the capture of the fugitive Aguinaldo under most dramatic circumstances. From his mountain hide-out in the little town of Palanan, near the northeastern coast of Luzon, due east of Illagan, Aguinaldo sent a coded message to a cousin, a guerrilla leader, directing him to send four hundred armed insurgents to him. They were to be guided by the courier himself. The courier was captured, and the code broken by General Funston, his aide, and a Spanish interpreter after several hours of effort.

Since the one trail to Palanan from the coast was under constant guard, a surprise American raid was impracticable. Daredevil Funston proposed to General MacArthur that with eighty Macabebe Philippine Scouts and a few Tagalogs posing as insurgent officers, he and four other American officers—ostensibly their prisoners—march to Aguinaldo's headquarters and capture him. The party, guided by the original courier, who had entered into the scheme, would supposedly be the vanguard of the four hundred men the Filipino leader had asked for.

MacArthur agreed. The expedition, lifted from Manila in United States gunboat *Vicksburg* March 6, landed in great secrecy on the east coast more than a hundred miles south of Palanan. The Scouts were clad in nondescript insurgent uniforms and armed with Mauser and Remington rifles. The American officers marched as prisoners and as they passed through native *barrios* the Macabebes made great play of herding along their dejected "captives." Messages were sent on to Aguinaldo reporting their advance, using stationery captured from the insurgent General Lacuna, and bearing his forged signatures. Aguinaldo later admitted it was these forgeries which completely allayed his suspicions.

For ten days the expedition followed the irregular coastline. The rain never ceased. Drenched to the skin, they waded streams and fought their way through the dense grass. Their food was soaked into a soggy mess and after a time the force was on half rations. There was little opportunity for sleep because the ground was so wet, and the men were able to stave off their hunger only by gathering a few fish, snails, and limpets.

By March 22 the little band had reached a town ten miles from Palanan. There it was met by a messenger from Aguinaldo who directed that the American prisoners be left on the coast and not brought to his hide-out. In his fear that the American officers' absence might make the whole plan go awry when they reached Palanan, Funston decided to disregard Aguinaldo's instruction about leaving the American prisoners behind. En route to Palanan the Americans had to dive into the brush and hide when the insurgent patrol sent from Palanan to guide them in to the hide-out met the expedition.

The twenty-second of March was Aguinaldo's birthday, and the town was bedecked in festive colors. As the disguised Macabebes marched into the town plaza, Aguinaldo's bodyguard of about fifty men lined up to present arms as a band played. The Macabebes swung into line opposite Aguinaldo's troops. The

Americans momentarily waited in the brush outside the *barrio*.

In the second story of the municipal building overlooking the plaza stood Aguinaldo with several aides. Segovia, Funston's Spanish interpreter, and one of the Tagalogs walked upstairs to report to Aguinaldo. After a few congratulatory words from the President about their difficult march, Segovia walked to a window and gave the signal to the Macabebes below. At once they opened fire on the insurgents lined up a few yards away, sending them scattering to the nearby woods. In the municipal hall Segovia drew his pistol and fired at Aguinaldo's aides, who escaped by jumping out the window. The Tagalog assistant to Segovia, Tel Pacido, tackled Aguinaldo and threw him under the table, shouting, "You are a prisoner of the Americans!" When Funston and the other Americans entered the town a few minutes later, the situation was well in hand.

Aguinaldo, well and very tactfully treated by General MacArthur, recognized the situation and on April 19 issued a proclamation acknowledging the sovereignty of the United States "without any reservation whatsoever." A true patriot, he devoted himself thereafter to the interests of his people. The backbone of the insurrection was broken. However, two subordinate leaders, more bandit than patriot, invoking the terrorism of the Katipunan, tried to keep the fires of rebellion aflame. On the island of Samar, Vincente Lucban, and in the province of Batangas on Luzon, Miguel Malvar, instituted reigns of terror in mid-1901. On July 4, 1901, William Howard Taft, chairman of McKinley's civilian Philippine Commission, became civil governor, and General MacArthur returned to the United States. He was replaced by Major General Adna R. Chaffee, who had been in command of American troops during the so-called Boxer Rebellion in China.[7]

Malvar's conspiracy, practically at Manila's back door, was ingenious and insidious. It embraced both political and military factors, for the man—with the Katipunan's terror trail interwoven—established an almost complete *insurrecto* government, in parallel with the American provisional civil government. Public

[7] This expedition is the subject of Chapter IV.

officials, rendering lip service to the *Americano*, were in fact Malvar's men. Meanwhile his guerrillas nibbled at American outposts and small detachments of troops.

When the scandal broke into the open General Chaffee placed matters in the hands of Brigadier General Bell, who took the field with task forces totaling four thousand men at all times, and swept the province clean. "Protective zones" were established about all sizable towns, where peaceable Filipinos—this included the majority of the population—could be sheltered from the inroads of their brethren. Outside these zones, *barrios* were burned, stores destroyed, and life made unbearable for the guerrilla. By April 1902 most of the outlaws were starving. Many captives had to be immediately hospitalized. Malvar, after several sharp clashes, surrendered April 16. Somewhere between eight thousand and ten thousand Filipinos, engaged in one way or another, had been captured.

Balangiga

A different situation existed in semi-wild Samar, where Lucban's guerrillas spread fire and sword. The coastal towns of Samar had been occupied, but the interior was left to Lucban's tender mercies. There he chivvied the *barrios* at will. At Balangiga on the southwest coast, Company C, 9th U.S. Infantry, Captain Thomas W. O'Connell, with two other officers and seventy-one men, was bivouacked in a public building. Relations with the townspeople were good; so good, that when the *presidente* of the town suggested to O'Connell that a number of natives from the vicinity be brought in to assist in the major cleanup the officer had initiated, he gained ready assent. Some eighty men came in, and were housed in conical tents across the plaza from the barracks.

The company was at breakfast at six-thirty on the morning of September 28, 1901. In the plaza the workmen were lining up, under the eyes of the three sentinels in front of the barracks. The village *presidente*, strolling up to one of them, suddenly snatched his rifle, and the "workmen"—actually picked bolomen of Lucban's guerrillas—swarmed over the other two and rushed the mess hall. The church bell began clanging and all the men of the *barrio* followed to make the butchery complete. Most of the soldiers died at the mess tables, chopped and dismembered in shocking fashion. So, too, died the three officers. The company cook, hurling a pot of boiling water at his assailants, grabbed a meat cleaver and with a scant dozen other men, most of them wounded, reached the arms racks. This little group fought its way to the beach and in *barotas*—native outrigger canoes—clawed their way along the coast to the neighboring town of Basey and the safety of another American garrison.

Company G, 9th Infantry, Captain Edwin V. Bookmiller, at Basey, was rushed to Balangiga, drove out the insurgents and buried the dead; the soldiers lashed to frenzy by the sights they found. Not one American body was unmutilated.

C Company's score:

Killed during the massacre	—36
Wounded, died later	— 8
Wounded	—22
Missing	— 4
Uninjured	— 4
Total	74

The men of C Company, veteran Regulars just returned from the China campaign, had sold their lives dearly, although surprised. Bookmiller's company, before withdrawing to Basey, found 250 dead Filipinos.

Brigadier General Jacob H. (Hell-Roaring Jake) Smith, commanding the Department of the Visayas—a Civil War veteran, brevetted for gallantry in the 2nd Kentucky Infantry at Shiloh in 1862—had not won his Army nickname for nothing.

In a general order to his entire command Smith now enunciated his intention in retaliation and pacification ". . . to wage war in the sharpest and most decisive manner possible . . . every native whether in arms or living in the *pueblos* (towns) will be regarded and treated as an enemy until he has conclusively shown he is a friend. . . . Neutrality will not be tolerated . . . if not an active friend, he is an open enemy. . . ."

He had available at Tacloban, his headquarters, a battalion of marines, under Major Littleton W. T. Waller. Smith sent him into the Balangiga area, admonishing him: "I want no prisoners. I wish you to burn and kill; the more you burn and kill the better it will please me."

Waller on October 24 landed his four-company battalion, 315 strong, at Basey and Balangiga and began a hunt for Lucban and his followers. Between November 7 and 10, 1901, Waller's patrols burned 255 houses, killed thirty-nine *insurrectos*, captured eighteen more, destroyed a ton of hemp and a half ton of rice, and captured fifty native boats.

Lucban pulled his men, who at one time numbered three thousand, back into a deep jungle stronghold on the bluffs of the Sojoton (Basey) River. Here in caves and terraces overlooking each other across the two-hundred-foot river gorge, the natives, using captive labor, had spent years fashioning a defensive labyrinth. Hidden trails, camouflaged pits and traps, bamboo cannon, poisoned stakes, vine nets slung full of boulders—"everything that savage, treacherous minds could conceive"—encircled the tortuous approaches of the fortress. Although its existence was well known to the Spaniards, the place had never been explored. Until the Sojoton fastness was penetrated and reduced, there would be no peace on Samar, and Major Waller knew it.

On November 15, 1901, Waller's battalion set out in three columns, commanded respectively by Captain Hiram I. Bearss and David D. Porter and himself. Next night, all three parties bivouacked within striking distance of the objective. Before daylight Porter and Bearss joined, while Waller moved upriver behind them.

Surprising an outpost, the marines jumped two enemy camps, cleared them out and then, crossing the river, stormed the fastness above them. Lucban's men fled. Both Porter and Bearss won the Congressional Medal of Honor for their gallantry in leading the assault.

By this time other punitive expeditions began slashing into the interior of Samar from all coastal points. Lucban's forces, driven from spot to spot, disintegrated and by February the chief himself was captured and Smith in April began relaxing his restrictive policy.

"Hell-Roaring Jake" had pacified Samar. Unfortunately he had also created a "do-gooder" backfire in the United States. Stories of his coercive measures, some of them distorted, had come across the sea, where many hearts were bleeding, it seemed, for the Filipinos, but few for the dead of C Company, 9th U.S. Infantry. A Congressional investigation was followed by a general court-martial for Smith. Found guilty of "conduct to the prejudice of good order and military discipline," the general was sentenced to be admonished. Shortly afterwards, he retired.

Meanwhile, General Smith had ordered Waller to reconnoiter a telegraph route fifty-two miles across the unmapped island, from Lanang on the east to Basey on the west coast. Setting out from Lanang three days after Christmas 1901, the expedition —six officers and fifty men—was dogged by disaster. Boats foundered in swollen rivers; provisions, even matches, were lost; bearers mutinied; and marines dropped dead of fever and exhaustion, while one man went mad. To save the strongest, Waller divided the force and pushed ahead to Basey for help, leaving Porter to make the best of it with the weak. Search parties from Basey then combed the jungle. Not until January 15, 1902, were all survivors out of the bush. Ten marines had perished.

Enraged by the repeated treachery of the Filipino guides and bearers, who had plotted to massacre the whole party, Waller now convened a drumhead court at Basey on January 20, 1902. In his own words, "When I learned of the plots and heard everything, I sent them out and had them shot."

All told, Waller conducted eleven summary executions in the town plaza of Basey, not only for the guides' gross betrayal of his marines, but in reprisal for the Balangiga massacre. As might be imagined, political pressure from the United States caused him to be charged with murder before an Army court-martial. Once all the facts were known, the court gave him a full acquittal.

All this leads up to an assessment of the behavior of the American soldier in the islands. He was no angel, for, as Kipling has well put it, "single men in barracks don't grow into plaster saints." But it must be remembered that most of the alleged brutality charged against our troops by "do-gooders" at home during this period—and the charges were many and vociferous—was the result of "third degree" methods of obtaining military information. It was essential that the whereabouts of the *insurrectos* and their munitions stores be disclosed. When prisoners or suspected *insurrectos* found in the *barrios* wouldn't talk, steps were taken to loose their tongues. These steps were not always legal, and at times the soldiers were excessive in their brutality, as were the Filipinos. But guerrilla war is always brutal. And the military authorities were quick to punish definite abuses, as the court-martial records show.

Aside from the cases of General Smith and Major Waller, cited above, one more is remarkable for its aftermath. Lieutenant Preston Brown, 2nd Infantry, charged with "the murder of an unarmed, unresisting prisoner of war," was found guilty by a general court of manslaughter, and sentenced to dismissal and five years' penal servitude. President Theodore Roosevelt, however, commuted the sentence to reduction of thirty files on the promotion list and loss of half-pay for nine months. Brown would command a regiment, a brigade, and then a division in combat during World War I, and would retire in 1940 as a major general famed throughout the Army as a martinet. And that, as soldiers say, is the way the ball bounces—sometimes.

By July 1902 civil government had been established throughout the Christian portion of the island. A well-disciplined Philippine constabulary kept the peace from the northern tip of Luzon south to the Sulu Sea and the Surigo Strait. Occupation troop strength had been reduced from a peak of 70,000 to 34,000, and the military posts from 552 to 195. On July 4 President Roosevelt proclaimed the end of hostilities, with complete pardon and amnesty to all former *insurrectos*, except in the Moro Province of the southern islands.

The bill to Uncle Sam was some eight million dollars. More than a hundred thousand American troops had been employed, who had fought in 2811 separate engagements, lost 4243 of their number killed in action, and 2818 more wounded. Approximately sixteen thousand Filipinos had been killed in combat and approximately a hundred thousand more had died of famine and pestilence.

But south of that Sulu Sea-Surigo Strait line, another and even more savage conflict was breaking out.

Kris and Krag

The Moro Province of the Philippines embraces the island of Mindanao—second largest in the group—and a cluster of smaller islands known as the Sulu peninsula, lying just off the southwestern tip of fantastically shaped Mindanao. The Army's Department of Mindanao and Jolo embraced the area.

The Moros—there were 300,000 of them, as compared to the seven million Christian Filipinos—were Muslims; a warrior Malay tribe living in a feudal slaveholding environment. They practiced polygamy, they fought one another. They were an uninhibited piratical congeries of warriors living in fortified settlements, whose local leaders—*datos*—claimed full authority over their respective groups. They detested Christians, they despised other Filipinos. They gave lip service—of a tenuous sort—to the Sultan of Sulu, who lived on the island of Jolo. They had never accepted the Spaniard, whose garrisons were few and who after several centuries of futile effort had given up any pretense of occupying other than a few coastal ports. To these coastal settlements, too, had come, on sufferance only, some northern Filipino traders and, of course, the ubiquitous Chinese merchant.

The Moro was proud, vain, and fearless. He dressed in gaudy turban, embroidered jacket, tight-fitting trousers, and bright colored sash into which was stuck his personal weapon—the razor-edged *kris* or *barong*; a far more terrible weapon than the bolo of the northerner. He liked his way of life and his objection to any change or limitation was immediate and drastic.

"We could not help but admire the Moro," wrote an American officer who had fought him frequently. ". . . You meet a Moro on the trail and he looks you straight in the eye. There is nothing menial or subservient in his make-up."[8]

[8] Colonel Horace P. Hobbs, *Kris and Krag,* privately printed, Washington, D.C., 1962, p. 50.

There was the key to the Moro troubles. The Moro *dato* respected force but cared not one whit whether Spain or the United States claimed dominion over the islands. All he wanted was to be left alone to rob, plunder, take slaves or women, as he saw fit. So in 1899 the Sultan of Sulu and other prominent *datos* graciously received Brigadier General John C. Bates, USA, and the few existing coastal towns were garrisoned without incident, American soldiers walked their streets and the countryside unarmed.

For a while local commanders hoped that a "laissez faire" policy would maintain peace. However, they were continually being drawn into Moro vs. Moro conflicts, and when, in obedience to public clamor in the United States, slavery was abolished in October 1903, the lid came off the Moro caldron.

Here the American soldier for the first time met the *juramentado* (the Spanish word means one who has made a vow), a Moro who has worked himself up to a religious frenzy and, kris in hand, runs *amok*, as the Malays have it. He charges blindly, seeking to kill and keep on killing, until he himself is disposed of. *Juramentados* were known to keep on coming despite several mortal wounds. A number of Americans were mowed down before two drastic steps were taken: the first, to bury the dead assassin publicly with the carcass of a pig beside him—thereby shutting Heaven's gates to a devout Muslim; the second, which came later, was to replace the .38-caliber service revolver by the .45-caliber automatic pistol, whose slug would stop a galloping horse in his tracks.

The first major expedition against Moro recalcitrants on Mindanao had come in April 1902, when Colonel Frank D. Baldwin with a fifteen-hundred-man force, cavalry and infantry, thrust against the Sultan of Bayan into the Lake Lanao country, and captured two Moro *cottas*, villages protected by substantial fortifications in which brass muzzle-loading *lantakas*—a species of small cannon—were mounted.

The anti-slavery proclamation brought flaring outbreaks on both Mindanao and Jolo. The Sultan of Bacolod, in the Lake Lanao area, having made slave raids, Captain John J. Pershing led a punitive column into the area and stormed Moro *cottas* on Mt. Taraka. At the same time, on Jolo, a mapping expedition—two companies of infantry, two troops of the 14th Cavalry, and a mountain-gun platoon—were attacked on Suleiman Mountain by Moros led by two local *datos*—Panglima Hassan and Andung. The attackers were driven off and Major General Leonard Wood, the department commander, then organized and accompanied an expedition to quell Hassan's outlaws. The 28th Infantry, a battalion of the 23rd, two troops of the 14th Cavalry, and a battery of mountain guns, accompanied by a pack train, engaged in a whirlwind campaign from November 12 to 21, 1903. It included a nasty assault on a *cotta* in a swamp, which was stormed by Major Robert L. Bullard's battalion; a madman charge of forty-odd *juramentados* upon a cavalry detachment—repelled with the loss of twenty-seven of the assailants; and a final full-dress assault on a chain of eight *cottas* on Suleiman Mountain.

Some five-hundred Moros had been killed, wounded, or captured; the forts and neighboring villages destroyed. The island was temporarily at peace, but Hassan was still at large. Not until March 1904 was Hassan brought to bay and killed by a column led by Major Hugh L. Scott, in a crater on Mt. Bacsak.

In 1904 the principal offender on Mindanao was one Datu Ali, who with several other local chieftains dominated the Cotabato Valley and the Rio Grande, in the south-central area of the island. Acting on intelligence reports that Datu Ali was preparing for a full-scale anti-American sweep down the Rio Grande valley, General Wood on March 5 arrived at Cotabato from his headquarters at Zamboanga with an assortment of river boats carrying two companies of the 23rd Infantry, one dismounted troop of the 14th Cavalry, one field gun, and a detachment of marines and sailors. A company of the 17th Infantry was added, from the Cotabato garrison.

The expedition arrived in the vicinity of Ali's stronghold at Serenaya, some forty miles from the coast, on March 7, after a brush with Moro outposts. Ali's position was actually a masonry fort, one thousand yards long; more than a score of *cottas* linked together, and bristling with *lantakas* and some old Spanish cannon.

Reconnaissance showed that the position was surrounded by

marshy ground except for one spot. An artillery bombardment—Wood's own fieldpieces had been augmented by some 3.2-inch rifles dismounted from the river gunboats—swept the position all day long. The fire was answered by the Moro cannon. The gunfire ceased at nightfall. An assault was prepared for daybreak, but the opening light revealed a white flag flying from the fort walls. Since no Moros came out to surrender, a cautious reconnaissance revealed that the place was empty save for one wounded warrior. Ali and his forces—estimated at some five thousand men, women, and children—had fled in the night!

Wood now turned his attention to the Lake Lanao region, where Pershing and his squadron of the 15th Cavalry had been keeping a partial peace by a mixture of ruthless activity and friendly gestures which delighted most of his Moro charges. Bullets and banquets were intermingled successfully in the majority of the native settlements. However, the Taraca River mountain Moros kept up an incessant guerrilla warfare.

When a reconnaissance patrol was ambushed with the loss of two officers and thirteen men, Wood acted. An expeditionary force of eighteen infantry companies, four troops of dismounted cavalry, and a battery of field artillery, gathered from the garrisons of Jolo and Mindanao, moving in two columns, by forced march, converged on the upper Taraka River, swept its valley to the lake and destroyed all hostile *cottas* on the way. An armed post—Camp Vicars—was established and peace descended on the Lanao region.

But the elusive Datu Ali was still loose in the Rio Grande valley. An expeditionary force, moving by river boat and on foot, combed the upper reaches of the river and Lakes Liguasan and Buluan without success during November 1904. Then General Wood went on leave to the United States. His aide, Captain Frank R. McCoy, Cavalry, proposed a quick drive into the *bontocs*, which was approved by the acting department commander, Brigadier General James A. Buchanan.

McCoy took with him Lieutenant Philip Remington, the provisional company of the 22nd Infantry, ten Moro soldiers of the Philippine Scouts, and a Moro guide, one Datu Enok—seventy-seven men in all. Landing at Digos on the east coast, they struck through the jungles on a five-day march, carrying nothing but one day's cooked rations and ammunition.

On October 22, 1905, Ali's hide-out, a house in a clearing beside the Malalag River, some six miles south of Simpetan, was discovered. McCoy, Remington, and the advance guard, a handful of men, rushed the house, exchanging shots with ten of Ali's retainers, and the two officers crashed through the door and shot Ali dead. Mindanao was at peace—for the time being.[9]

Meanwhile, back on Jolo in 1905, before Wood's departure on leave, the hill Moros had again risen. Their leader was one Datu Pala, who on Hassan's death had fled to British North Borneo with his band. He was driven out of there by the British and returned to Jolo with additional recruits. Quick dashes and *juramentado* outrages, almost to the gates of Jolo city's walls, now demoralized those coastal Moros who had settled down to peace.

Scott, commander on Jolo, was unable to control the situation with his now reduced force. So General Wood in April brought reinforcements of about a thousand men and initiated the so-called Third Sulu Expedition. Provisional companies of the 17th and 22nd Infantry, a squadron of the 14th Cavalry, and detachments of Moro Scouts and Philippine constabulary, pushed out from Jolo. Several skirmishes brought the column under the shelter of Mt. Talepao, a bare volcanic mass where Pala's *cotta* was found and destroyed. The outlaws fled east, to be cornered on a rocky ridge. An assault was met by a *juramentado* rush of three Moros, one of them Pala himself. All three were killed, and the position was overrun.

The column then moved east to a large blasted crater on the very edge of the coast, where, on May 9, to the Americans' amazement a large force of Moros surrendered without a shot having been fired. It appeared that the previous night two United States destroyers and a gunboat, lying offshore, had sent their searchlights flashing into a gash in the crater's side. At daylight the superstitious Moros were willing to surrender to the

[9] Accounts differ as to who actually tackled and shot the Moro chieftain. One of the authors has the distinct impression that General McCoy, years later, said he had done it. Other accounts give Remington credit for firing the fatal shot. It makes little difference. The plan and its execution were McCoy's; a very daring operation.

enemy they knew, rather than face again what they believed to be the devil's eyes.

This, however, was far from the end of the Moro question. The hill Moros in the Bud Dajo-Bud Bacsak hill-mass of Jolo—where the Suleiman Mountain fight had taken place in 1903—became so unruly that their *juramentado* raids threatened Jolo city again. Colonel James W. Duncan, with a task force of the 6th Infantry, and a platoon of mountain artillery, was sent by General Wood to attack their stronghold, a fortified crater on Bud Dajo itself. Initially impregnable, the fortress was bombarded by the artillery and Lieutenant Gordon Johnson with a handful of men penetrated the place. The two-day combat, March 6-8, 1906, ended when the Moros—men, women, and children—were cut down by the artillery and final infantry assault; all of them perishing.

Once again came cries from the United States when the details of the fight became known; the home folk could not understand that the Moros kept their families with them, that they refused to surrender, and that the women and children fought beside the warriors.

Sporadic fighting and small outbreaks kept American garrisons on the alert for four more years. In 1911 a flare-up in the Serenaya valley in central Mindanao necessitated another punitive column and by executive order all Moros were to be disarmed. This was easier said than done, but General Pershing, commanding the Mindanao-Jolo Department, kept at the job with dogged persistence. The final major clash came on Jolo, where the Dajo-Bacsak hills erupted again.

Pershing summed it up in a letter to the governor general on February 28, 1913. He said, in part: "The . . . Joloano Moro . . . is not at all overawed or impressed by an overwhelming force. If he takes a notion to fight, it is regardless of the number of men he thinks are to be brought against him. You cannot bluff him. There are already enough troops on the island of Jolo to smother the defiant element but . . . if we attempt a thing the loss of life among the innocent women and children would be very great. . . . I am not prepared to rush in and attack them while they are surrounded by their women and children. . . .''

Nevertheless, all efforts to induce the women and children to leave their crater on Bud Dajo failed. On June 15, 1913, after a three-day fight in which it was necessary to use artillery, the position was assaulted. Nearly all the three-hundred-odd warriors and as many women and children died. This marked the end of Moro resistance to law and order.

The entire Philippines was now in full peaceful development; a development which would result by 1934 in the granting of Commonwealth status within the United States, with the promise of complete independence in 1946. In 1942 that development would be halted by the inroads of war, but in 1946 the promise did become fact. Meanwhile the people of the Philippine Islands had proven their loyalty to the Stars and Stripes in blood and tears, the only Asian people of any Western colonial empire who had stood faithful to their salt when the chips were down.

4

The China Relief Expedition, 1900

Which I wish to remark,
And my language is plain,
That for ways that are dark
And for tricks that are vain,
The heathen Chinee is peculiar.
—From "Plain Language from Truthful James" by Bret Harte

The Dragon's Teeth

During the spring of 1900 China went momentarily beserk. The result was the Boxer Rebellion, so-called; no rebellion at all, but a fanatical anti-foreign crusade aided and abetted by the Chinese government, and aimed at extirpation of all foreigners and foreign influence throughout the confines of the Empire.

The blood bath, in which some two hundred missionaries, men, women, and children, and probably fifty thousand Chinese Christians died, brought the troops of seven European nations and the United States onto Chinese soil in a fantastic campaign ending with the occupation of Peking, and the flight of the Chinese government. It paved the way for the fall, a decade later, of the Manchu Dynasty. The China Relief Expedition, although miniscule in light of later overseas military clashes, is of particular importance to Americans because, for the first time in our history, United States troops were participating in a joint interallied military operation.

The objective of the expedition was the relief of the foreign legations in Peking, where the international diplomatic corps, and a handful of soldiers, sailors, and marines, also including Americans, plus some civilians and a horde of Chinese refugees, were defending themselves against raging mobs of Boxers and Chinese regular troops. The ferocity of the conflict may be judged by the fact that sixty Congressional Medals of Honor were awarded for deeds of American gallantry performed during both the campaign proper and the siege of the legations.

All these events took place within a comparatively narrow theater: from the coast of the Gulf of Chihli at the mouth of the Pei-Ho (North) River, and including Peking, some seventy-five miles northwest as the crow flies. Thirty-five miles upriver from the Taku Bar, off which allied warships at this time were gathering, was the throbbing commercial city of Tientsin, with a large foreign settlement outside its walls. Fifty miles beyond lay Peking, where the foreign diplomatic corps would be besieged for fifty-five days. A single-track railway line and the telegraph linked Taku, Tientsin, and Peking. One so-called highway—actually a rutted trail—paralleled the river and the Grand Canal from Tientsin to Peking.

The terrain, from the coast inland, was the broad, arid, almost treeless loess plain of northeast China, pitilessly hot in summer, and covered by millet fields intolerably dusty.

The Chinese explosion had been long in the making. For a half century the major European nations had been systematically nibbling at China's vast periphery; a nibbling accelerated in pace after Japan's smashing victory of 1894-1895. Russia, France, Germany, and Great Britain moved in to deny Japan full fruits of victory. By 1900 Russia was crawling through Manchuria and had seized the Laiotang peninsula, establishing bases at Dalny and Port Arthur; Germany had grabbed the treaty port of Kiaochow (Tsingtao); Great Britain had wrested a concession at Weihaiwei in the north, and on the mainland opposite Hong Kong in the south. France, adding to her initial grab of Indo-china, had exacted spheres of influence in the three southernmost Chinese provinces. Even Italy was nibbling, in a typically Italian effort to keep up with the European "Joneses," at San Men

Bay in Chekiang.

The one holdout against this quite ruthless dismemberment was the United States. Its "Open Door" policy—aimed at preserving the integrity of China—demanded equal opportunity for trade in all the "spheres of influence" staked out by Europe—in thirteen of China's eighteen provinces and in the three additional provinces of Manchuria. The policy, enunciated in September 1899 by Secretary of State John Hay, received lip service from Europe, but didn't in fact make much change. China was herself helpless, and American interest certainly didn't go so far as threatening use of force. Added to China's travail was reaction against the extraterritorial rights of foreign missionaries, demanded and exacted by the respective powers, sometimes in direct violation of Chinese ethics, customs, and superstitions.

To the sixty-four-year-old enamel-faced, tyrannical Tzu-Hsi, Dowager Empress of China, commonly known to the diplomatic corps in Peking as "the old Buddha," this situation had become intolerable at the close of the nineteenth century. It was threatening the very roots of her regime. So she listened with interest to a certain clique of her Manchu favorites when they suggested that she had in her hands a force which would wipe out forever the "foreign devils" and all their works. This was the *I Ho Chuan*—"Fists of Righteous Harmony"—a secret society dedicated to the overthrow of all foreign influence, and which played upon the emotions of an ignorant population vastly susceptible to all the mumbo-jumbo of superstitition and sorcery. This society apparently started in the northeastern provinces of Shangtung and Chihli. The depredations in those provinces in 1899, violent but momentarily minor in scope, attracted foreign attention to the Boxers, who were also known as the *Chuen-fei*—"Bandits of the Fists." Hence the colloquial and later popular name of "Boxers."

The Boxers claimed to enjoy the special protection of China's gods and to be invulnerable to bullets. Their desire was to rid the country of the "foreign devils," who were accused of forcing the Chinese government (a) to give away territories and ports, (b) to offend the spirits of wind and water by allowing the buildings of railways and the exploitation of mines, and (c) to grant the foreign missionaries immunity from Chinese law.

In general, the rank and file of Boxers were recruited from the poorer classes, extremely ignorant, and lashed to fury by the appeals of their leaders to religious fanaticism. In this society, recruited from a countryside torn by famine and disrupted by floods, some of the Manchu leaders saw the answer to their prayer. In January 1900 the "old Buddha" indicated her pleasure with the Boxers in an Imperial edict which gave them full rein. In April a wave of murder and arson gave rise to another edict favorable to the Boxers. Some foreign missionaries and thousands of their converts—"devil's disciples," the Boxers called them—were murdered. It should be remembered, however, that a number of prominent Chinese officials protested against the Boxer inroads.

The Boxer menace crept closer to Peking during May 1900. Prince Tuan, a violently anti-foreign Manchu, was appointed to head the Tsungli Yamen (Foreign Office) and, although the Dowager Empress issued a proclamation denouncing the Boxers, it became evident to Bishop Alphonse Favier, Catholic Vicar-Apostolic of Peking, that, as he told the French Ambassador, Stephen J. M. Pichon, "This religious persecution is only a façade; the ultimate aim is the extermination of all Europeans."

But the Bishop was a prophet without honor in the legations, where the foreign diplomats, while loudly protesting to the Tsungli Yamen the atrocities being perpetrated on their nationals elsewhere, refused to believe that they themselves might be in danger. But on May 28, when a Boxer mob attacked and burned a railway station on the Tientsin line just sixteen miles from Peking, the diplomatic corps requested armed guards from an assortment of foreign warships now gathering off Taku Bar. Among these ships were USS *Newark*, a protected cruiser, and *Monocacy*, an ancient paddle-wheel gunboat. The American vessels were under Rear Admiral Louis Kempff, second in command of the Asiatic squadron.

The request was promptly filled. On May 31 the guard detachments came up the railway line to Peking—337 officers and men, American, British, French, Italian, Japanese, and Russian bluejackets, and marines. The United States contingent numbered fifty marines, three bluejackets, and two officers, Captains John T. Myers and Newt Hall, USMC. Myers commanded.

On June 3 additional detachments of German and Austrian sailors, eighty-nine men all told, also arrived. About this time thirty French sailors and sixteen Italians were detached from the legation guard proper to protect the Pei-Tang compound, Bishop Favier's French Cathedral and mission in the west-central area of the Imperial City.

Matters now worsened rapidly. So threatening was the Boxer horde ringing the Legation Quarter that on June 9 Sir Claude MacDonald, British Minister, wired his Consul in Tientsin an urgent call for help. Then the curtain dropped as the telegraph went dead and the railroad service ceased.

The Siege of the Legations

For fifty-five days the representatives of the United States, the British Empire, Germany, France, Austria, Italy, Japan, Russia, Spain, Belgium, and Austro-Hungary, their families, and their retinues, together with refugee missionaries and others of the Chinese capital's small foreign colony, were besieged in the Legation Quarter, an area roughly three-quarters of a mile square. To their number had been added an indeterminate group of Chinese Christians. The defense of this enclave rested primarily upon detachments of soldiers and sailors of eight nations—fifty-five Americans, eight-one Russians, eight-two Britons, fifty-two Germans, forty-seven French, twenty-seven Austrians, twenty-nine Italians, and twenty-five Japanese; a total of twenty officers and 389 men. Aside from their small arms, these troops possessed four light guns; an Italian one-pounder, an American Colt heavy machine gun, an Austrian Maxim, and a British rickety, jamming-prone, five-barreled Nordenfelt. Later an extemporized nine-pounder was built up by the United States marines from an old gun barrel found in the compound. Ammunition for all arms was, of course, limited.

Supplementing this force were some 125 volunteers from the

civilian males present—armed with everything from sporting rifles to carving knives lashed on poles.

Food and water was more than adequate to support a total beleaguered population of some three thousand men, women, and children. Foodstuffs came from shops in the Legation Quarter, from a neighborhood granary, and from the Peking Hotel, while the 150 or more polo and racing ponies in legation stables provided fresh meat. The British compound contained five wells of water. In addition, well-stocked wineshops in the Quarter furnished great quantities of champagne!

Isolated since first the Tientsin wire and then the Russian line that linked up with Kiachta in Siberia were cut, these folk lived and fought off incessant attacks of howling Boxers and equally vociferous regular Chinese troops who surged against their makeshift barricades and loopholed compound walls. The first Boxer assault came on June 13. It was followed by a "come into my parlor" coaxing ultimatum from the Tsungli Yamen. Unless the foreigners evacuated Peking in twenty-four hours and trusted themselves to the tender mercies of a Chinese military escort down to Tientsin, the Chinese government regretted that it could not guarantee their safety.

Wisely, the proposition was rejected. The German Ambassador, choleric Baron Wilhelm E. von Ketteler, called for a sedan chair and hustled off unescorted to the Yamen to make his own official protest. He never made it; a mob murdered him on the way—indicative of what would have happened had the legations trusted themselves to Chinese mercy.

From that time on the Legation Quarter was the target for continued attacks. Artillery fire was poured into it, fanatic charges stormed at its barricades. Sir Claude MacDonald, the British Minister, was elected to command the defense. He appears to have played the part of administrator, interfering little with the professional military men of the guard. On the other hand, Pichon, the French Minister, and some other civilians were later accused of playing busy-body roles.

Meanwhile the legation area was ringed by enemies, alive and dead; the almost intolerable stench from the unburied bodies of Chinese attackers was added to the torments of heat, continuous conflict, and anxiety. In the very beginning the United States marine guard established a strongpoint on top of the Tartar City wall to prevent harassing Chinese fire on the garrison below. In this they were joined by German marines in a sort of back-to-back defense barring attacks along the ramparts from both east and west. When the Germans were driven out by a particularly severe Chinese assault the American marines took over the entire wall defense, assisted by volunteers.

From time to time Chinese attempts to tunnel and undermine the defenses were discovered and eradicated. The greatest anguish was caused by the pall or uncertainty hanging over the terrorizing situation. People had only to look over the walls to witness the horrible atrocities the Boxers were committing on their fellow

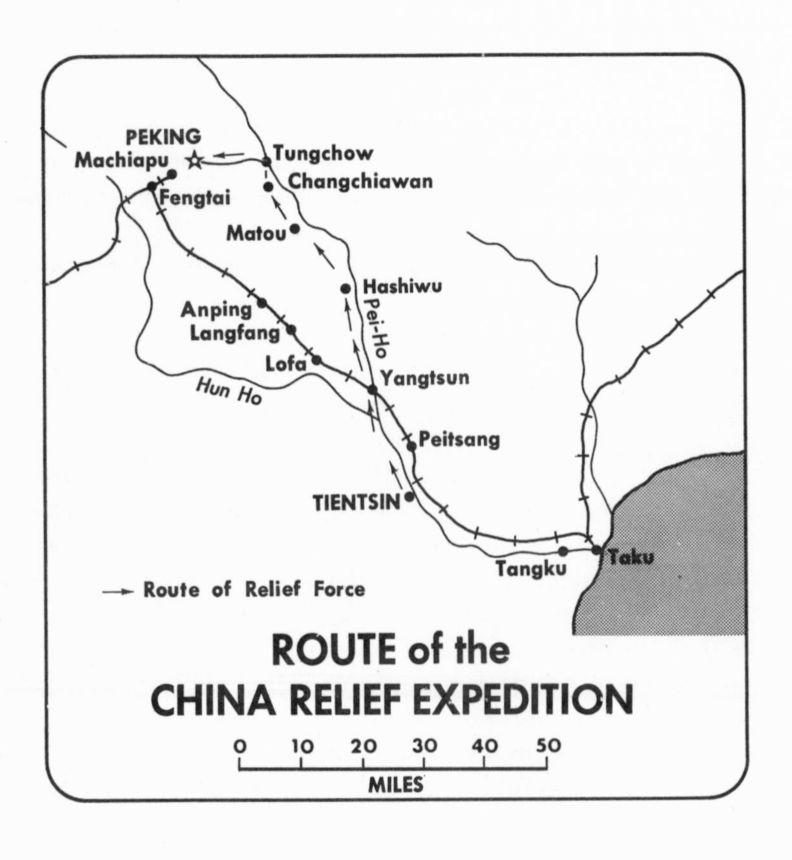

Chinese, while refugees had told grim stories of foreign missionaries immolated. Would the legations be rescued? From time to time rumor and—oddly enough—several palpably false messages alleged that relief was on the way. But not until August 10—when the situation was one of touch and go—did messages come in from British General Gaselee to Sir Claude MacDonald and from Japanese General Fukushima to Colonel Shiba, Japanese military attaché, bluntly stating that the relief expedition was on the way and would probably arrive on the thirteenth. The welcome outbreak of firing along the west walls during the night of the twelfth to thirteenth was followed by a savage assault of several hours' duration, covered by renewed artillery fire. Then it faded as suddenly as it had begun, but the sound of combat to the west grew louder. Watchers on the Tartar City wall about the Legation Quarter put up three flags—American, British, and Russian—as evidence they still lived, and a signalman, seeing troops moving in the Chinese city beyond, wigwagged directions to an unguarded sluice gate below him, where a canal was channeled through the wall. Moments later British Indian infantry surged inside the embattled compound, to be welcomed with champagne.

The road of the rescuers from Taku Bar to Peking had been long and tough.

The Thrust That Failed

By early June, as international concern turned to events in China, European and American warships were gathering in the open roadstead of the Chihli Gulf off the Taku Bar, where a dozen miles of shoal water separated them from the mouth of the Pei-Ho River, watergate to Peking. Already foreign detachments were landing, moving by lighter and by shallow-draft gunboat to Taku, where the estuary was guarded by four well-armed Chinese forts.

From Taku these troops were moved by rail to the foreign settlements area outside the frowning walls of the Chinese city of Tientsin, itself now seething with rioting Boxers. Naval commanders on the spot had been ordered to take what steps they could were a call for help to come from Peking and the diplomatic colony, and to protect defenseless missionaries; not forgetting, also, the commercial interests involved.

Among the detachments moving into the Tientsin area was a landing party from USS *Newark*; 112 men, led by *Newark*'s skipper, Captain Bowman H. McCalla, USN. They arrived June 6. Rear Admiral George C. Remey, commanding the U.S. Asiatic Squadron, had passed on instructions from Washington to protect American interests and McCalla felt that his primary responsibility was to Edwin Conger, United States Minister to China, in Peking.

The improvised chain of command-communication, which, like Topsy, "just growed," was from the legations—with Sir Claude MacDonald at its head—by wire to the international consular corps at Tientsin, thence to the naval commanders, who themselves had established an *ad hoc* command, headed by Admiral Sir Edward H. Seymour, RN, who flew his flag in HMS *Centurion*, but who had proceeded to Tientsin.

One June 9 Sir Claude MacDonald's urgent call for help from Peking brought a hurried conference between the naval commanders and the consular corps at Tientsin. The meeting bogged down when the consuls, emphasizing the seriousness of Boxer threats to the settlements, urged that their need for military protection take precedence over any help to the legations.

McCalla, impatient, broke the impasse by stating categorically that he and his American contingent would march next morning for Peking.

Seymour picked up the ball. As a result, on the morning of June 10 some 2100-odd men, American, British, German, Russian, French, Japanese, Italian, and Austrian bluejackets, marines, and soldiers (Russian, these), left Tientsin, Peking-bound, on five railway trains. With them they carried seven field guns, ten machine guns, and a gang of coolies for rail line repairs. The leading train, in which was Seymour, held half of the British 915-man contingent and all McCalla's bluejackets.

It is interesting to note that Seymour's Chief of Staff was Captain John Jellicoe, RN, of later Jutland fame. Also aboard was Commander David Beatty, who would lead Jellicoe's battle cruisers at Jutland. Both men would be wounded during the present operation, Jellicoe most severely.

What started out as a journey of a few hours turned into a seventeen-day nightmare. By the night of June 11, the expedition had reached Langfang, halfway to Peking, to be stalled there by damage to the rail line. They got but four miles farther by the fourteenth, when the trains were attacked by a flood of fanatic Boxers. Convinced of their invulnerability, the poor wretches came on in berserk fury, brandishing knives and spears, to die in windrows under machine gun and small arms fire.

Next day the rail line behind—on which the last troop train had been shuttling back and from from Tientsin—was cut and the telegraph went out. Seymour was on his own, with water and food lacking, and ammunition limited.

Between him and Peking lay masses of Boxers, in roadless country. Nor did he have field transport. He decided to fall back to Yangtsun, where the railway crossed the Pei-Ho River, and then move on Peking by water. Four junks were obtained. But in addition to the constant Boxer sniping and skirmishing now came a more serious blow. Regular Chinese troops attacked his last train on the return trip to Yangtsun, and were only beaten off after a sharp action. That settled it. Seymour started to fall back down river on Tientsin, only twenty miles away. But he was falling back on foot, his wounded and his artillery on the four junks he was dragging with him. Boxers contested the way at each village, Imperial Chinese cavalry was threatening his flank, the heat was appalling, and food, water, and ammunition were running low.

It was nightfall on June 21 when the stumbling column, which had just fought its way through a village, found itself confronted by a great walled enclosure from which came small arms fire. The junks in the river piled up in the shallows. British bluejackets and marines stormed the enclosure walls with the bayonet, while McCalla's American contingent held the Boxer packs outside at bay. The Chinese garrison was swept out, the wounded in the junks rescued, and the expedition coiled itself inside this shelter.

They were in luck. They had captured the Hsiku Arsenal, not only a defensible stronghold, but a storehouse of field guns, machine guns, and small arms, with ample supply of ammunition. Fifteen tons of rice assured food of a sort, while a stock of medical supplies brought relief to the wounded. And, of course, there was water.

The arsenal was but six miles from the foreign settlements, but was surrounded by a sea of enemies. Several attempts were made to gain contact with the settlement; one messenger, a Chinese servant, did get through, as it turned out, but Seymour's command, fighting off incessant attacks, had no means of knowing this.

On June 24, Chinese fire outside the arsenal slackened; troop movement became apparent through the tall millet fields—infantry and some mounted men. Moments later the first wave of sweating foot soldiers came tumbling through the opened arsenal gates. They were American marines, commanded by Major Littleton W. T. Waller. How they got there will be told later.

Two days later Admiral Seymour and his force were safely back in the foreign settlements perimeter, itself now under siege. They had lost 62 killed and brought back 232 wounded men. Of these, four of McCalla's American bluejackets had been killed and twenty-eight more wounded, in addition to the captain himself.

So much for Seymour's futile effort to reach Peking. What had been happening in the Tientsin area is another fantastic story.

Prying the Gateway Open

Seymour's departure had left the Tientsin settlements very short of defensive manpower, but on June 12 a Russian transport from Port Arthur disembarked at Taku sixteen hundred Russian troops (the Russians had one hundred thousand men in Manchuria), who marched without opposition into the settlements next day, bringing the garrison strength to 2400 men. An improvised defensive barricade of the five-mile perimeter was erected under the supervision of a young American mining engineer named Herbert Hoover. On the seventeenth, Chinese thrusts from the native city pounded it and communication with Taku and the warships was cut.

During this while, the major powers were hurrying troop reinforcements toward the Chihli Gulf and Taku roadstead. They came from European colonial posts and from the Philippines. But the Boxers were all over the countryside. Communication between the coast and Tientsin was essential. Worst of all, the Taku forts guarding the Pei-Ho estuary were being reinforced. Should these forts turn definitely hostile there could be no landings. Such was the situation confronting the allied naval commanders in the international fleet off the Taku Bar.

A hasty meeting on June 15 brought resolve to take the forts at once. Rear Admiral Louis Kempff, USN, senior American officer present, alone dissented. The United States did not yet consider the Chinese government to be involved.

On the face of it the proposition was madcap. Nine small unarmored vessels—seven of them antiquated gunboats—would engage the heavy modern armament of four large forts, which lay two on each side of the two-hundred-yard-wide channel. Landing parties from these vessels, totaling nine-hundred officers and men, would tumble ashore in the mud flats, assemble under command of Commander Christopher G. F. M. Cradock, RN, and storm each fort in succession. It was madcap, but it worked.

The gunboats, one British, one German, three Russian, one French, and one Japanese, filed into position at nightfall, June 16. With them went two modern destroyers, HMS *Fame* and *Whiting*. Ahead, her tired old paddle wheels churning the muddy current, USS *Monocacy* moved upriver to lay off the railroad station pier and take aboard any foreigners seeking shelter. All this was accomplished without any hostile reaction from the forts.

But at two-fifteen next morning the forts opened heavy but happily ill-directed fire on the flotilla. *Fame* and *Whiting*, knifing out of the line, steamed into the little navy yard lying under the guns, and cut out four modern Chinese destroyers, which could, between them, have wiped out the entire assaulting force.

The allied gunboats answered the forts and the landing party splashed ashore on the north bank. Led by Cradock[1] they carried Fort No. 1 with the bayonet. Naval gunfire blew up magazines in the two south bank forts—Nos. 3 and 4—and resistance in Fort No. 2 on the north bank faded.

The *Monocacy*, with thirty-seven foreign women and children rescued from the Taku mission, came sedately down river. Her skipper, Commander F. M. Wise, USN, reporting the event and his part in it, added wistfully: "I feel a natural regret, shared no doubt by the officers, that duty and orders prevented the old *Monocacy* from giving her ancient smooth-bores a last chance."

The gateway to Tientsin had been opened, but the path was not yet cleared.

Tientsin

In from Cavite to Taku on the day the forts fell came Major Waller and his battalion of marines, 137 strong. Ferried ashore, they moved by rail on June 20 from Taku for Tientsin but bivouacked for the night still twelve miles short of their destination. Waller sent the train back. Next day strong forces of Boxers and regular Chinese troops barred the road. Waller was joined by an advancing group of 450 Russian troops, but the combined force was forced to retire to their bivouack. Three marines were killed and seven more wounded in this clash.

But more transports were arriving off Taku by this time—from Hong Kong, from Port Arthur, from Weihaiwei; from Kaiochow, Yokohama, and from the Philippines. Up the line came a battalion of the Royal Welch Fusiliers, 250 British bluejackets from HMS *Terrible* and a handful of Italians, all under command of Commander Cradock. Up, too, came a second train, carrying one thousand Russians and 250 Germans. Waller joined Cradock's command and the combined force battled its

[1] Eighteen years later Admiral Cradock, RN, leading another and larger forlorn hope, would go down with his flagship under German fire at the battle of Coronel.

way into the beleaguered settlements on June 23.

Next day Waller and his marines, with a detachment of Cossacks, pushed on to the relief of the Seymour force, already described. On their return they assisted Russians and British in clearing the Tientsin-Taku line. Waller put in in his report: "Our men have marched 97 miles in the five days, fighting all the way. They have lived on about one meal a day for about six days. . . . They are like Falstaff's army in appearance, but with brave hearts and bright weapons."

In the settlements the allied forces repelled several sharp attacks, but the enemy strength in and around the native walled city was growing, and harassing artillery fire from its walls pounded the settlements. The Taku line was kept open, and up it in driblets came more allied troops. Nevertheless, the fact was that the settlements were under siege and no attempt could be made to relieve the legations at Peking until the Chinese stronghold of Tientsin had itself been taken.

No word was received from Peking until June 29 when a native Chinese messenger brought an extraordinary communication addressed "To the officer commanding any European troops: Besieged in British Legation. Situation desperate. Make haste." The message, written four days earlier, was the first to be received since June 9.

By this time allied strength outside Tientsin was approximately fourteen thousand men. Among the new arrivals were the 9th U.S. Infantry and another battalion of marines from the Philippines. Tientsin city was a walled affair, with four gates—one in the center of each side. An outer mud wall ringed the city. Chinese forces were estimated at some twelve thousand Imperial troops and about as many Boxer auxiliaries, superposed on a population of about one million. Each gate could be approached only over a causeway across marshes, canals, and irrigation ditches. The walls were impervious to the fifty-six pieces of light artillery in allied hands.

Tientsin was attacked July 13; Japanese General Yasumasa Fukushima commanded the principal assault. A Japanese column charged up the causeway to the south gate, taking heavy losses, while American and British forces under English Brigadier General A. R. F. Dorward supported it. Commanded by Colonel R. L. Meade, American marines had the left flank; on their right were the Royal Welch Fusiliers; still farther to the right were the British Naval Brigade, and the 9th Infantry, Colonel Emerson H. Liscum. Herbert Hoover, as he later related, accompanied the Marines "as a sort of guide in their part of the attack on the Chinese City." The heat was suffocating (temperatures of 140° Fahrenheit were recorded within the next fortnight), and the terrain between the two walls consisted of rice paddies, huge salt mounds, Chinese graves, and muck from sewage canals. While this was going on Russian and German jabs were being made at the north side of the city.

The south gate assaulters were met by artillery and small arms fire from the walls and from across the Pei-Ho River. The 9th Infantry, which had reached Tientsin only three days previously, had particularly heavy going.

Dorward's disposition and the orders he gave have been criticized as having forced the 9th into a situation where it suffered both from the walled city fire and from the flanking Chinese troops across the river on its right. Dorward later blamed himself for the 9th's predicament. In any event, by 8 P.M., when the attack was called off, the 9th had lost ninety-five men out of seven hundred engaged, including Colonel Liscum, shot as he attempted to pick up the regimental colors when the color-bearer fell. Liscum's last words were: "Keep up the fire!"[2]

Before dawn the Japanese broke the stalemate. In a skillful night attack, they blew up the south gate of the Chinese city and swarmed through. All allied forces followed and the place was systematically looted, many of the Chinese civilian population cheerfully joining.

The American marines on the left had lost thirty-odd men. Total allied casualties were more than eight hundred killed and wounded, the Japanese, naturally, taking the greatest loss. Chinese casualties have never been totaled.

[2]Now the motto of the 9th, whose most treasured trophy is a huge punch bowl—the Liscum Bowl—melted from Chinese solid silver *lycees* (shoe-shaped bullion ingots) captured later in the city.

On to Peking

The better part of a month now was lost while the allied commanders argued among one another on the feasibility of a thrust to Peking, and the rest of the civilized world tensed with rumor—there was no definite word—as to the fate of the foreigners besieged in the legations. Fantastic reports that they had all been murdered floated unconfirmed. Kaiser Wilhelm II of Germany, enraged by the news—verified—that his Ambassador had been murdered in Peking, foamed and thundered, prepared a grandiose expeditionary force, naming Field Marshal Count Alfred von Waldersee as its commander, and through diplomatic discussions wangled a somewhat reluctant assent from the other powers to Waldersee's assuming supreme command in China. (As it turned out Waldersee and a sizable German force would not arrive until long after the legations had been relieved.)

Meanwhile among additional troops gathered at Tientsin were the 6th U.S. Cavalry, 14th U.S. Infantry, Light Battery F of the 5th U.S. Artillery, and a service detachment whose big mules and roomy Studebaker wagons were the envy of all the other contingents. These troops had come direct from the United States. Best of all, perhaps, was the fact that Major General Adna R. Chaffee, strait-laced cavalryman, veteran of Civil War, Indian fighting, and Cuba, had also come over, to command the American force, now over two thousand strong, including the 1st Marine Regiment.

Galvanized into action by frantic messages received July 20 from Sir Claude MacDonald and Mr. Edwin Conger, the American Minister, the relief expedition took the field August 4. The word from Peking, dated July 4, stated that the legations were still holding out, but that their provisions would not last much more than a week.

The most fantastic thing about this expeditionary force was that its campaign would be fought on the basis of cooperation only; there was no appointed supreme commander present. Naturally, national rivalries made themselves felt from the very beginning. It is in fact remarkable that this balky team pulled together at all.

Taciturn Chaffee was well able to hold his own with the other principal commanders at Tientsin. These were Major General Sir Alfred Gaselee, whose effective British force was now three thousand strong; Russian General Nicolai P. Linievitch, with approximately four thousand; Japanese General Baron Yasumasa Fukushima with a well-balanced force ten thousand strong; and French General H. Frey, who had but two thin battalions of Annamite Marine Infantry, five hundred men. All in all, the expeditionary force numbered about sixteen thousand strong (some four thousand men were left in the Tientsin garrison), including one hundred Germans and two hundred Italians and Austrians. Its artillery appears to have been adequate, but it was short of cavalry; the Japanese had but one mounted regiment, the Russians a *sotnia* (squadron) of Cossacks, the British a battalion of the 1st Bengal Lancers. The United States Cavalry contribution consisted of one troop, M of the 6th, the horses of the remainder of the regiment having not yet recovered from the effects of the long sea voyage from the United States.[3]

The Americans, British, and Japanese first marched on the west bank of the river, the Russians, French, and smaller contingents on the east. Initial opposition occurred next morning at Peitsang, some ten miles beyond Tientsin. There Chinese forces, strongly entrenched, for a short time halted the advance, but were decisively defeated and thrown out by a systematic Japanese attack, supported by the British. American troops took no part in this fight.

Lack of sufficient cavalry prohibited immediate pursuit, but the expedition pushed on next day, in an attempt to keep the enemy off balance. At Yangtsun—another ten-mile hike under appalling conditions of heat and thirst—once more the way was barred. An elaborate trench system with plentiful artillery

[3] The above figures are approximations only. In all probability the effective field strength of the expeditionary force, after the Tientsin garrison is subtracted, was never more than sixteen thousand. Some sources trim this down to fourteen thousand.

necessitated a formal assault, which—remarkably enough under the circumstances—appears to have been coordinated at least in principle. That a European battery dropped several salvos in the ranks of E Company, 14th U.S. Infantry, killing four men and severely wounding eleven others, was pure accident.

The United States 9th and 14th Infantry, and 1st Marine Regiment, made a frontal attack, with the Russians and part of the British on their left. On the right the British 1st Bengal Lancers and M troop, 6th U.S. Cavalry probed the Chinese left, covering the advance of a brigade of Japanese infantry in an enveloping movement. The American guns, posted between the American infantry and the cavalry, furnished supporting fire. The Chinese position was taken after a four-hour fight.

Completely exhausted by the heat, the force rested here for a day before taking up the march again. Regroupment was necessary. The German, Austrian, and Italian contingents, lacking any supply transport, had returned to Tientsin without firing a shot. The French force, also hampered by lack of transport, halted at Peitsang, to the chagrin of its commander, General Frey, who could only volunteer to maintain the line of communications.

By August 11 the force had pushed up to the walled city of Tungchow, only fourteen miles from Peking, against Chinese resistance that was weakening by the hour. Early next morning Japanese engineers blew in the south Tungchow gate, and the invaders surged in.

A commanders' conference later that morning brought mutual agreement that the assault on Peking would be in two stages—this to compose, if possible, national rivalries. The entire command would move west at once, in parallel national columns. Bivouacking for the night, they would assault simultaneously early next morning, each contingent taking one of the four gates studding the eastern face of the complex. The Russians were on the right. Next were the Japanese, then the Americans, and finally the British. A scanty French force scraped up by the diligent General Frey would follow between the Japanese and the Americans.

The Storming of Peking

This attempt at coordination faded into a free-for-all during an unexpected pounding rainstorm. During the night a Russian reconnaissance in force suddenly slid southward across the front of both Japanese and Americans, to attack and hold the outer portion of the Tung Pien gate, at the junction of the Tartar and Chinese cities, the allotted American objective.

Let's pause to look at Peking, that puzzling conglomeration of four walled cities. The four-square Tartar City with sides three and a half miles long, enclosed the Imperial City, an oblong roughly one and a half miles deep by one mile wide, with its southern face contiguous with that of the Tartar City. Inside these walls again, lay the Forbidden City—holy of holies of the Manchu Dynasty. it was a scant mile wide, and one and a half miles deep. Against the south face of the Tartar City wall rested the Chinese city, an oblong four miles wide by two miles deep. Inside the southwest corner of the Tartar City, its west limit nestling into the walls of the Imperial City, was the Legation Quarter.

The walls enclosing these teeming population centers were approximately forty feet high, and wider, as one historian has it, than New York's Fifth Avenue. Each gate consisted of a high tower, through which a passage channeled, guarded by outer and inner gates. The Russians in this case had merely pierced the outer gate of the Tung Pien, and had been caught in the inner confines under the tower. There they clung, under heavy fire.

Aroused by the cannonading, the other allied forces stood to arms, then commenced uncoordinated dashes for the walls. The Japanese moved steadily for their objective, the Chih Hua gate, thus neatly cutting off and long delaying any attempt by the Russian main body to reinforce its embattled reconnaissance group. The Americans, forced slightly south of their objective where the Russians were now battling, ended up in mud under the walls just south of the Tung Pien gate. The British closed in on their allotted target, the Hsia Kuo gate of the Chinese city. The bewildered General Frey, just arrived with his little scratch French-German-Italian force, later in the day became sucked up in the long-delayed advance of the Russian main body, after barging through the American columns, much to Chaffee's wrath.

The 14th Infantry, heading the American advance, reached the area of the Tung Pien just south of the gateway itself. The leading elements, clustering at the wall, thought the jagged, roughened stones might give slim handhold and young trumpeter Calvin P. Titus, of E Company, dared it. Amazingly, he made it to the top. Others followed. Before the startled Chinese defenders knew what was happening, the Stars and Stripes went up, and two companies of the 14th had gained toehold on the ramparts. With Reilly's battery in close support at the gate itself, a combined Russo-American drive cleared the gateway and surrounding area, while the troops on the wall cleared the ramparts, enabling the British column to close on the Hsia Kuo gate of the Chinese city without loss.

That gate was blown in by artillery fire and the British advanced west through deserted streets. As they passed the Ha-Ta gate they received desultory fire. Then on the wall above they sighted first three flags—American, British, and Russian—mute evidence that the legations were still holding on.

It was then they found that unguarded sluice gate through the Tartar City wall and burst through into the Legation Quarter, with General Gaselee himself in the van. Not long afterwards American infantry and marines came sweeping along the top of the broad walls from the direction of the Tung Pien and Ha-Ta gates, whence they had cleared all Chinese operation.

Mission accomplished!

Losses among the defenders of the legation—military and civilian—had been serious. Sixty-six had been killed, more than 150 wounded. Eight noncombatant civilians, six of them babies, had died. Two enlisted men of the American marine guard were among the killed, and their leader, Captain Myers, severely wounded. No records were kept of the Chinese refugees within the compound, and the loss to the attacking Chinese will never be known.

The End at Peking

In a somewhat amazingly lackadaisical fashion, it was not until the next day that the legation people broke the news to their rescuers that there might still be another siege going on in Peking.

This was at the Pei-Tang compound, housing the Catholic Cathedral and French missionary complex—Bishop Favier's fold and flock. Here the Bishop, his priests and nuns and several thousands of their Chinese Christian converts had undergone a tragic experience compared to which the siege of the legations was a Sunday School picnic.

At the Pei-Tang there was no stock of food. There was no stable of polo and racing ponies to furnish fresh meat. Its sole military protectors were thirty French and sixteen Italian bluejackets, detached from the guard force which had arrived in Peking in late May. Commanding that little group was twenty-three-year-old Ensign Paul Henry, French Navy, who in some miraculous manner managed to fashion a fighting force out of the Chinese refugees crowding the compound. Paul Henry was killed on July 30, but it wasn't until August 15 that two companies of Japanese infantry bucked their way through the Tartar and Imperial cities to relieve the Pei-Tang and its starving inhabitants; this to the red-faced embarrassment of the legation people, who had seemingly forgotten the very existence of the Pei-Tang.

Other things happened on August 15. The Russians and the Japanese completed their conquest of the Tartar City, the British dominated the Chinese city, and General Chaffee's American force undertook the reduction of the Forbidden City. Chaffee's first task was to smash in the south gates of the Imperial City, behind which the Forbidden City and its cowering Imperial court were hidden.

Chaffee began his attack in the morning. Captain Henry J. Reilly drove his Battery F, 5th Artillery, in section column up the ramp and onto the south Tartar City wall, went into battery at the Chien gate tower, exactly opposite to the outer gateway of the Imperial City and began a methodical bombardment of the area beyond. Below, in the broad courtyard, the 3rd Battalion, 14th Infantry, assembled.

The iron doors (three in number in each of the gateways) resisted the infantryman's efforts to crack them open, but Reilly's shells buckled them and a platoon of M Company, 14th Infantry, under a Lieutenant Murphy, went storming through, with their colonel, Aaron Daggett, and his staff. As the remainder of the battalion came pushing through into a courtyard beyond, Murphy's platoon came under heavy fire from the top of the second gate and the walls of the courtyard.

It was during this first clash that Captain Reilly was killed by a Chinese bullet as he directed his battery fire from the wall.

A Chinese counterattack into the courtyard was promptly thrown back by the Americans, now reinforced by the 3rd Battalion, 9th Infantry. While the doughboys' fire cleared the wall of Chinese sharpshooters, a platoon of Reilly's guns were manhandled into the courtyard to hammer at the second gate. Meanwhile some infantrymen had clambered up bamboo scaling ladders loaned by the British, found no live Chinese inside, and pulled the bolts. Beyond was still another broad courtyard.

The troops debouching into this were again met by heavy fire and the previous performance was repeated. This brought the Americans up against the third and last gate. It was here that Lieutenant Charles P. Summerall, commanding the artillery platoon accompanying the advance, calmly advanced under Chinese fire to chalk on the massive iron gate an aiming point for his guns. Chaffee's troops were knocking at the vestibule to the Forbidden City, just beyond.

And then the "Cease Fire" blew. To their amazement and rage the American troops were recalled. The *ad hoc* Allied Command Council, acting upon diplomatic requests—mysterious and frustrating to the fighting men, as always—had decided to give the Dowager Empress, the vindictive, bloodthirsty "old Buddha," opportunity to flee the city with her court, and take refuse in Sian.

Perhaps it was just as well. American soldiers, who had seen and heard of the atrocities, the mass murders, the tortures undergone by their nationals and by Chinese Christians alike, might have given short shrift to the "old Buddha's" Manchu dignitaries and her retinue of eunuchs.

As it was, Allied troops did not enter the Forbidden City for several days, when the entire expeditionary force paraded through it. In the meantime, and for some time afterwards, all concerned gleefully joined in the pursuit of loot.

The Boxer uprising was squashed. It remained for the great Chinese statesman Li Hung Chang to pick up the pieces and preserve what he could of his country's interests. But that is another story.

Field Marshal von Waldersee now arrived, with all Germanic pomp and panoply and a large force of German troops—a supreme commander without a war. Spurred by Emperor Wilhelm's sadistic admonition that he should so conduct himself and his forces as to impress the word "Hun" upon the Chinese nation in revenge for the murder of his Ambassador, von Waldersee did his best. That, too, is another story.

Insofar as American troops were concerned, the war was almost over. But before it was over, a flare-up in the vicinity of Tientsin on August 19 brought six troops of the 6th Cavalry into a smart brush with Boxers, and on September 4 a detachment of C Company, 9th Infantry, on railroad guard duty at Hashiwu, on the Tientsin line, engaged a wandering Chinese force. But to Troop L of the 6th came the honor of making the farthest penetration into China and firing the last American shots. On September 4 the troop, reconnoitering up the age-old caravan trail to Mongolia, clashed with wandering Chinese patrols at Chang Ping Chow in the Nankou Pass, thirty miles northwest of Peking.

By the end of October 1900, America's China Relief Expedition had melted away. Except for one regiment of infantry, a squadron of cavalry and Reilly's battery, guarding the legations, its components were back in the Philippines, engaged in bitter fighting with Filipino insurrectionists.

5

Mexican Interventions, 1914-1917

Tampico and Vera Cruz

In 1910 Mexico erupted in social revolution. The twenty-six-year-old prosperous but despotic rule of President Porfirio Díaz tumbled, Díaz abdicating, and revolution and counterrevolution swept over the land. Díaz's successor was assassinated; would-be "strong men" tussled with one another for power, and the tide of terror not only threatened the United States Rio Grande border but also trod on the toes of foreign governments.

Presidents Taft and Wilson in turn attempted without success to maintain a rigid neutrality in this internal squabble. United States troops patrolled the border,[1] and, as matters worsened, United States naval vessels in considerable force "showed the flag" in all major Mexican ports. The refusal of President Wilson in 1913 to recognize the government of General Victoriano Huerta, who had seized the presidency by force, brought about both injury to United States nationals in Mexico and loss of the mutual good will which had existed throughout the Díaz regime.

On April 9, 1914, a detachment of Huerta's troops touched a spark to this tinderbox at Tampico. A boat's crew of USS *Dolphin*, flagship of Rear Admiral Henry T. Mayo, then lying

[1] In 1911 a Maneuver Division, so called, was assembled at San Antonio; a pitiful skeleton of what it should have been. This extemporized unit was demobilized later, but the units—6700 strong—remained, scattered along the border. In 1913 another division was extemporized—mustering but 11,450 instead of its T/O strength of more than 22,000. In both cases, these numbers marked the maximum which could be scraped up in the United States.

in the harbor, was arrested at the lading pier. The Americans were unarmed and their boat flew the United States flag. They were peaceably engaged in loading supplies purchased ashore. The prisoners, including a commissioned officer, were marched publicly through the streets to jail.

Huerta, quickly releasing the sailors, admitted no wrongdoing; martial law had existed at the time, he stated. Admiral Mayo, enraged at what he considered, with justification, to be a flagrant national affront, demanded a formal disavowal of the act and as formal a twenty-one-gun salute to the United States flag by the Mexican commander on the spot. Huerta refused and the fat was in the fire.

Mayo had acted without consultation with Washington, but the President, supporting him, on April 20 asked and received congressional sanction to use force to uphold United States rights and secure redress for the insult. At this time reports had been received that a German cargo steamer *Ypiranga*, carrying arms and ammunition for Huerta's troops, was due in Vera Cruz. President Wilson ordered Rear Admiral Frank F. Fletcher, commanding the squadron then off Vera Cruz, to "take the Custom House immediately and prevent the delivery of arms and ammunition."

Fletcher, notifying the local Mexican commanders in the city and in the citadel of San Juan de Ulua of his intentions, proceeded to obey his orders. A marine detachment from the United States auxiliary cruiser *Prairie* tumbled ashore April 21—the first American invasion of Mexico since 1846. Landing without resistance, they seized the cable station, and nearby power plant. More marines and a battalion of bluejackets followed, from US battleships *Utah* and *Florida*.

The combined force, marines on the right, under Colonel W. C. Neville, USMC, and bluejackets on the left, under Captain W. R. Bush, USN, then took the custom house, post office, and railway station, before moving into the city. Small arms fire was received from windows and housetops, but was soon silenced by one-pounders in the landing craft and a few salvos from the *Prairie*. By the end of the day about one-half of Vera Cruz was in American hands. It is somewhat intriguing to note that the bluejackets wore their whites, hastily dyed brown in coffee grounds.

During the night USS *San Francisco* and *Chester* came into port, and deposited both seamen and marines. Early next morning Rear Admiral Charles J. Badger, Commander in Chief, U.S. Fleet, arrived with the battleships *Arkansas*, *New Hampshire*, *South Carolina*, and *New Jersey*. More reinforcements went ashore. On land now were the 1st and 2nd Marine regiments, brigaded under Colonel John A. Lejeune, USMC, and a naval brigade under Captain W. R. Bush, USN. Admiral Fletcher commanded the entire landing force.

On the twenty-second, fairly stiff resistance developed. This took the form of house-to-house fighting for the marines, and, briefly but dramatically, volley firing from the Mexican Naval Academy on one of the seaman regiments which was debouching onto a large plaza. This was abruptly halted by quick and intense fire from the five-inch guns of the cruisers *San Francisco*, *Chester*, and *Prairie*, which blew much of the second story off the offending building.

By April 24, Vera Cruz was pacified. In addition, a Marine battalion held an outpost at El Tejar, source of the city's water supply. The force ashore now numbered 7429 officers and men, of whom 2469 were marines.

Four days later, with peace restored, Army troops from the border—a reinforced brigade under Brigadier General Frederick Funston, USA—arrived and took over the town from the Navy. As the fleet weighed anchor, however, the Marine brigade, now 3141 strong, remained behind under Army command.

President Huerta, meanwhile, had broken off diplomatic relations with the United States, while the entire incident had done little more than to solidify his position in Mexican minds. But before actual war could break out President Wilson accepted an offer from the ABC Powers—Argentina, Brazil, and Chile—to mediate. At Niagara Falls, Ontario, June 30, the mediators proposed the retirement of Huerta, establishment of a Mexican provisional government pledged to agricultural and political reforms, and no indemnity to the United States for occupational costs at Vera Cruz. Huerta, refusing, was nevertheless eased out of office and Venustiano Carranza became President. American occupation forces were withdrawn on November 23, and on October 19, 1915, the United States and a number of Latin American nations recognized Carranza as *de facto* President of Mexico.

By this time a swarthy cutthroat called Pancho Villa had revolted against Carranza and was spreading fire and sword indiscriminately along the Rio Grande.

Villa

Francisco (Pancho) Villa, born Doreteo Arango, was a cattle thief and bandit, who first attached himself to Carranza then broke with him. He was but one of several revolutionary leaders fighting Carranza, but his geographical location in the northern provinces brought him and his brutal activities forcibly into the American limelight. President Wilson actually assisted the Carranza government to defeat him in 1915 by permitting Mexican troop movements over United States territory to the vicinity of Agua Prieta, opposite Douglas, Arizona.[2]

Villa, escaping entrapment by the government troops, moved farther along the border and began active guerrilla warfare. There American interests and Americans in our border towns had already been jeopardized by clashes between rebels and government troops. For instance, in October 1914, a pitched battle was fought in Naco, Sonora, separated from Naco, Arizona, only by a broad street. Across it, elements of the 9th and 10th U.S. Cavalry watched, under strict orders to refrain from returning the sporadic bullets which crossed the invisible border line.

Friction continued along the border during 1915. There were depredations and murders on American soil both by Mexican bandits and by Carranza's soldiers. American garrisons were harassed at night, American soldiers killed or wounded and their horses and equipment stolen. Flare-ups occurred at Browns-

[2]Under provisions of a treaty made in the 1870s, when Indian outrages were rampant on both sides of the border, movement of regular troops of either nation across the other's territory in close pursuit was permissible.

ville, Redhouse Ferry, Progreso Post Office, and Las Paladas.

In early January 1916, the United States requested Mexico to send troops to punish bands of outlaws who had looted the Cusi mining property eighty miles west of the city of Chihuahua, without effective response. At this time a group of Americans started by train from Chihuahua to visit the Cusi mines under assurances by the Carranza authorities that the country was safe. The party held safe-conduct passes issued by the government, but on January 10 the train was stopped by Mexican bandits and eighteen of the Americans were stripped of their clothing and shot in cold blood in what became known as the "Santa Ysabel Massacre."

General Carranza assured the Department of State that he had issued orders for the immediate pursuit, capture, and punishment of those responsible for this atrocious crime, but no one was ever brought to justice.

An Associated Press correspondent, George L. Seese, covering the story of the massacre, was approached by a personal emissary of Villa, who stated that Villa was not personally responsible for the massacre of the Americans, and that he, Villa, if his safety were guaranteed, planned to come to the United States at some future time, bring proof of his innocence in the massacre, and seek assistance from the United States in ousting the Carranza government. Seese was forbidden by the Associated Press to participate in the venture and informed Villa that he could not arrange his visit to Washington.

It may be that Villa fostered this ruse to cover his real future intentions. On March 3, General Gavira, Mexican commandant at Juárez, crossed the line to El Paso to place information that Villa's intention was to commit an act of violence that would compel the United States government to intervene in Mexico.

When this report came to Brigadier General John J. Pershing, commanding the Eighth Brigade at Fort Bliss, close to El Paso, the general said he was inclined to take it with a grain of salt. His view was shared by all concerned. It was so easy to be convinced that no Mexican force would dare an invasion.

American troops on the border at this time had but hearsay knowledge of any activities on the Mexican side beyond eyeshot.

Informers might or might not be reliable; in any case there was no means of verifying information, since patrolling or scouting across the line was strictly forbidden by Washington. On the other hand, Mexicans could come and go freely. All individual commanders in border town garrisons could do was to stand constantly on the alert.

On the night of March 9 Villa and his band raided the border town of Columbus, New Mexico, three miles north of the international boundary line.

Surprise in the Night

Columbus was a 'dobe-and-frame sun-baked little settlement squatting in mesquite plain at the junction of the El Paso & Southwestern Railway and the wagon road linking Deming, New Mexico, and Guzman, Mexico. It boasted neither electricity nor gas; its kerosene lamps were few. The settlement's importance, aside from being a port of entry and sporting a mud-shack customs house, was that it was headquarters for a border guard sector stretching 65 miles in air line from Noria to Hermanas, New Mexico.

Colonel Herbert J. Slocum, 13th Cavalry, the sector commander, had at Columbus the headquarters, machine gun, and four rifle troops of the 13th (twelve officers and 341 men less seventy-nine noncombatants). Two more troops (seven officers and 126 men, plus twenty-five added detachments from the Columbus garrison) under Major Elmer Lindsley lay at Gibson's Line Ranch, fourteen miles west, and one troop (two officers and sixty-five men) under Captain Jens E. Stedje was posted at the border gate itself, three miles down the road from Columbus.

Slocum's orders were to patrol the border; the details were, of course, left to him. He had established a routine of day and night patrols at irregular intervals, covering it as best he could. At Columbus itself the interior guard system consisted of three regular posts with their normal reliefs, a watchman, and—during the night—a patrol of one NCO and three privates, sometimes mounted, sometimes dismounted, covering the town and the camp, at the discretion of the officer of the day. In addition, some thirty men were on duty along the stable line.

The cantonment—flimsy barracks, brick mess shacks, stable sheds, a hospital, and a headquarters building—lay south of the railway line; the settlement itself was mainly to the north. Many of the officers lived in the settlement.

The Mexicans, numbering between five hundred and a thousand, sifted across the boundary line at a point three miles west of the border gate. Uniting at a place safe from observation they marched northeast until close to the American camp, when they split into two columns, one attacking from the southeast and the other from the west.

Private Fred Griffin, Troop K, on duty at Post # 3, at the headquarters, challenged a sudden movement in the night and was shot down, but killed three Mexicans before he died. The officer of the day, Lieutenant James P. Castleman, who had been up most of the night, about 4 A.M., heard firing and rushed out of his shack. As he turned the corner of the building he collided with a Mexican, whom he promptly shot. He ran to the barracks where he found his disciplined Troop F aroused and under arms. Castleman led them toward town; they crossed the railroad track on foot and approached Mexicans who were setting fire to the commercial hotel. The cavalrymen were at an advantage in a brisk firefight because they were in the dark while the blaze illuminated the Mexicans.

Lieutenant John P. Lucas,[3] commanding the machine gun troop, was awakened at 4:30 A.M. upon hearing someone riding by the open window of his room. He looked out and, although the night was quite dark, saw a man wearing a black sombrero riding toward camp. From the sounds it appeared that he had a number of companions and that the house was completely surrounded. Lucas recognized them as Villa's men.

His blazing .45 in hand, Lucas shot his way through scattered bandits to barracks, where he broke out the machine guns, kept always under lock and key. Posting one gun to command one of the railroad crossings, he then deployed the remainder of the

[3] He commanded the landings of VI Corps at Anzio, twenty-eight years later.

company to best advantage. Thus Troop F and the machine gun troop became nucleus of the American response, other outfits joining. Mexicans were everywhere, it seemed, burning and looting. For a time their scattered elements stood their ground, but discipline told as the 13th Cavalry shook itself together.

During the fighting, the kitchen detachment gave a good account of itself. The cook shacks of adobe construction were bulletproof. In the desert around Columbus there were many rabbits and quail, and it was customary for each troop to keep a shotgun with ammunition so that the mess detail could go out for game during the day. Attacking Mexicans now took shelter behind the bulletproof kitchen shacks. The kitchen crews, hearing them talking outside the windows, promptly opened fire with shotguns. One group of Mexicans did break into the door of a shack but recoiled when one cook doused them with boiling water, while another sailed into them with an axe.

In recounting experiences, a soldier of the stable crew told of killing a Mexican with a baseball bat. Captain Thomas F. Ryan, who occupied a house on the Guzman-Deming road near the camp headquarters, was away; his wife, alone in the house. As the Mexicans rushed the camp to the west, yelling and shooting, Mrs. Ryan got to her garage and stayed there until the fight was over. Captain Rudolph E. Smyser with his wife and two children left by a back window and took refuge in an outhouse when the Mexicans began battering on their front door. They heard the Mexicans talk of searching the place, so they abandoned the outhouse for the mesquite, picking up cactus thorns in the flight. Smyser then found his way back to his troop. Colonel Slocum, too, came in from the cactus, where he had hidden his wife. Mrs. Castleman and her two children crawled under a bed. It was reported that Lieutenant Castleman's butler, Carlson Jackson, contributed one of the most amazing achievements of the night by squeezing himself under a bathtub.

As a result of the action, seven American soldiers were killed and five wounded; with eight civilians killed and two wounded. The loss inflicted upon the Mexican is not known, though Villa later admitted 190; in town sixty-nine dead bandits were found.

As the early dawn revealed that the Mexican forces were withdrawn across the international boundary line, Major Frank Tompkins hastily mounted up Troop H in pursuit, mustering twenty-nine troopers, together with Captain Smyser and Captain George Williams, regimental adjutant. About three hundred yards south of the line, the American troops came upon a covering detachment of Mexicans holding a hill. The cavalry charged the position with drawn pistols; the Mexicans broke and ran, followed by the cavalrymen at a gallop.

A little later at a second position about a mile south of the border fence, Major Tompkins, dismounting the troop, accounted for thirty-two Mexicans. Here he was joined by Captain Stedje and Troop G, an additional twenty-seven soldiers. Once again the Mexican rear guard was driven back against the main body with many casualties on the Mexican side. On a third charge the troopers hit the Mexican rear guard and also attempted to turn the enemy's left flank at short rifle range. Major Tompkins was wounded in the knee, his hat was drilled with a bullet, and his horse was wounded in the head. Pursuing a mile south of the international boundary, Tompkins sent back word to Colonel Slocum asking for permission to further violate War Department orders about entering Mexican territory. Forty-five minutes later he received a reply telling him to use his own judgment.

The Mexican main column was now plainly visible only eight hundred yards away. The dismounted men of F Troop opened fire on the column while Troop H engaged the Mexican rear guard, who gave up and withdrew, leaving twelve of their dead on the field.

To prevent the Mexicans from again taking a defensive position, Major Tompkins moved Troop F to parallel and outflank the enemy while Troop H pressed the rear guard itself. The Mexicans, realizing that only twenty-nine men were in pursuit, attacked Troop H with an estimated three hundred men, forcing the Americans back four hundred yards to a stronger position. As ammunition was running low, and the troopers had been fighting without food or water now under blazing sun for several hours, Tompkins broke off action and got back to the post about noon. He had killed some seventy bandits and captured two machine guns as well as a quantity of rifles, pistols, ammunition, and other loot taken at Columbus. No casualties had been received other than one horse killed and another wounded.

Washington's reaction to Villa's raid was swift. Before March 10 had ended the War Department telegraphed Major General Frederick W. Funston, commanding the Southern Department: "President has directed that an armed force be sent into Mexico with the sole object of capturing Villa and preventing any further raids by his bands, and with scrupulous regard for sovereignty of Mexico."

As afterthought, the Department on March 13 wired Funston again, qualifying the original directive:

> The President desires your attention especially and earnestly called to his determination that the expedition into Mexico is limited to the purposes originally stated, namely the *pursuit and dispersion of the band or bands that attacked Columbus, N.M.* [emphasis added], and it is of the utmost importance that no color of any other possibility or intention be given, and, therefore, while the President desires the force to be adequate to disperse the bands in question and to protect communications, neither in size or otherwise should the expedition afford the slightest ground of suspicion of any other or larger object.

Across the Border

Two days later Brigadier General John J. Pershing rode into Mexico with some five thousand officers and men, officially designated as the Punitive Expedition, United States Army. This skeletonized division comprised four regiments of cavalry, two of infantry, two batteries of field artillery and engineer, medical, signal, and quartermaster detachments. New to the game was the 1st Aero Squadron, under Captain Benjamin D. Foulois; eight rickety biplanes, eleven officer pilots, eighty-four enlisted men, and one civilian mechanic. New to the game, too, was the motorized section of the quartermaster train.[4]

Pershing's orders were plain. They envisaged a movement into Mexico acquiesced in by reason of previous agreements. No towns were to be entered, nor were railway or telegraph communications to be used, without Mexican permission. Cantankerous Mexican President Carranza, however, took the attitude that this invasion was an act of war which he, his troops, and his people were free to resist.

As a result the expeditionary force found itself plunged into a terrain of high altitude, blistering hot by day and freezing by night; a roadless terrain of sand and rock and mesquite, where every man's hand was against it, it seemed. Its communications were almost nil, its march so rapid that no supply train could keep up, local supplies almost unobtainable. The few airplanes promptly broke down, quartermaster motor trucks foundered in mud, and motors burned out. Only the horse, the quartermaster four-line mule team, and man on foot could stand the gaff. And, of course, Villa and his men, unhampered, became will-o'-the-wisps in country where only the handful of elderly Apache Indian Scouts—last vestiges of a corps used in our frontier wars—were at home.

The expedition moved out in two columns. Colonel George A. Dodd's 7th and 10th Cavalry and a battery of artillery departed from Culberson's Ranch, sixty miles west of Columbus, with Pershing himself in the lead. From Columbus, which became the main base, went the remainder of the command, with Major Tompkins' squadron of the 13th Cavalry in the van, burning to avenge the Columbus outrage. The columns joined at Colonia Dublan, a deserted Mormon settlement, after a grueling march in which Battery B, 6th Artillery, covered the astounding distance of 145 miles in forty-six hours, without injury to horse or man, a tribute to Army horsemastership.

From that point on the expedition became a succession of fly-

[4] The line elements consisted of the 7th, 10th, 11th, and 13th Cavalry and the 8th and 16th Infantry regiments, all under strength. The artillery were Batteries B and C, 6th Artillery, eight guns in all. This force was doubled in number before the campaign ended, while in addition practically all Regular Army elements in the continental United States were mobilized along the border.

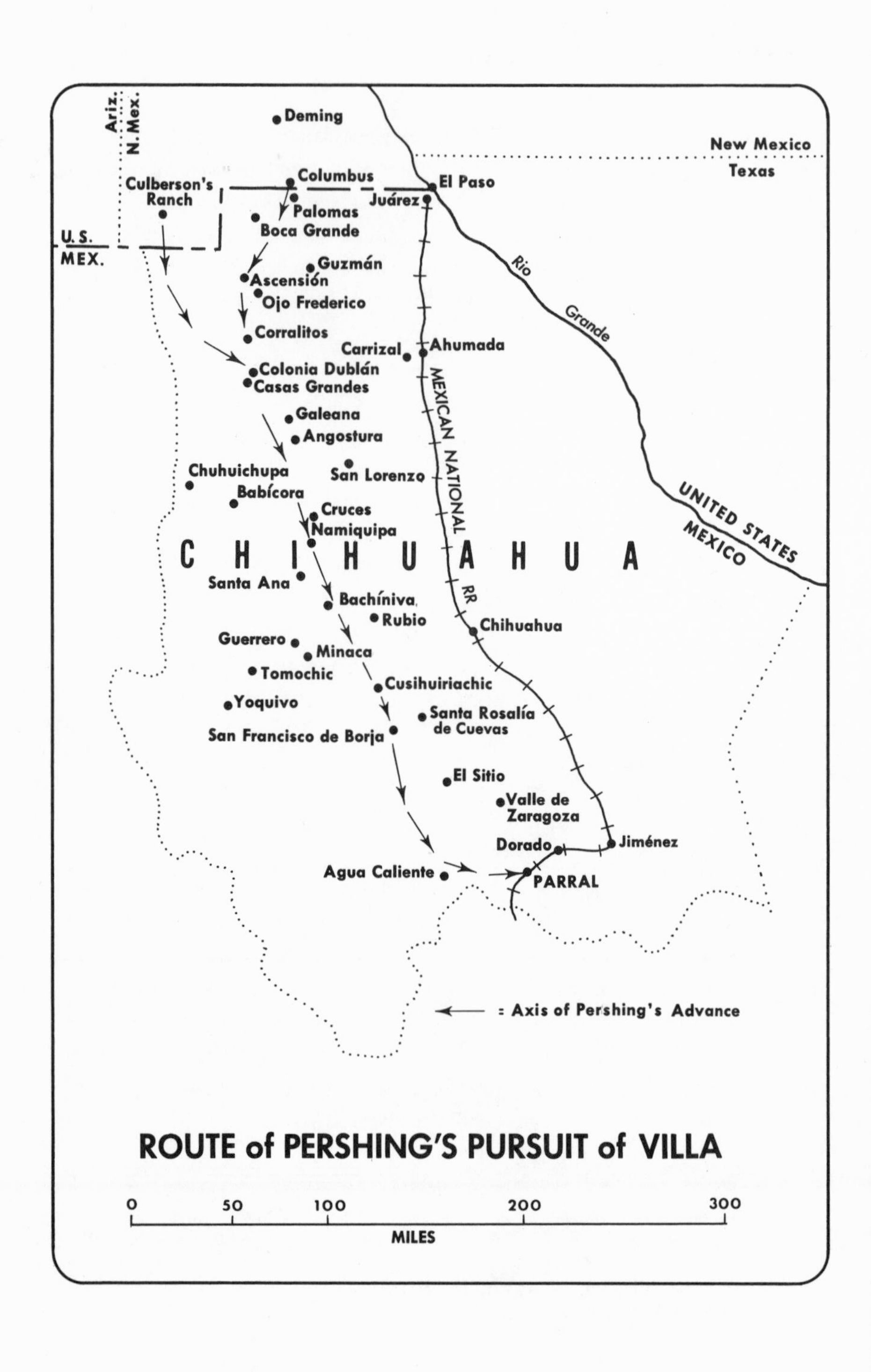

ROUTE of PERSHING'S PURSUIT of VILLA

ing columns groping for a fleeing enemy and hampered by scanty and usually unreliable information. The first real hostile contact came March 29, at Guerrero, 250 miles from the border by air-line, but practically twice that distance as marched.

Guerrero

It was the sixty-three-year-old Colonel Dodd, known throughout the Army of that day as the hardest of hard-riding horse soldiers, drove the 7th Cavalry (twenty-five officers and 345 men) through icy mountain weather, to find a Villista group in town, estimated at five hundred men. The bandits were preparing to mount up. Dodd swung one squadron wide to block retreat and plunged directly into the settlement. When the gunsmoke cleared, the Villista leader, a Colonel Hernández, and some sixty of his men were dead, the others scattered from hell to breakfast in the mountains beyond, safe from the jaded mounts of the cavalry. No prisoners were taken, but a number of machine guns and other materiel captured. The 7th Cavalry had five men wounded.

Dodd's savage blow so stirred Congress that his name was cheered on the House floor when news of the Guerrero fight came in to Washington, and he was speedily promoted to Brigadier General.

Unfortunately Villa himself was not at Guerrero. He had been wounded a few days previous in a clash with Mexican government troops, and was hustling south for refuge in the Chihuahua mountains.

During this time Pershing, who had established his advance headquarters at Namiquipa, 90 miles south of Colonia Dublan, was cruising the country in a battered automobile without escort except his two aides and the chauffeur. Crisscrossing the trails of his hard-riding detachments, he kept in as close personal touch as the circumstances permitted with the commanders to whom he had given their heads. Out of one of his cross-country dashes came the next real clash.

At Bachíniva, thirty miles northeast of Guerrero, Pershing and his mobile headquarters caught up with Major Tompkins and his squadron of the 13th Cavalry. Tompkins believed that Villa had holed up in his hiding-place of bandit days, the mountainous area around Parral, 140 miles to the south. He urged Pershing to let him make a stripped-saddle dash for Parral. Pershing gave Tompkins twelve pack mules from the nearby 11th Cavalry, five hundred silver pesos, five days' rations, and his blessing—"Go find Villa wherever you think he is." Within two hours Tompkins' thin squadron had moved out, Troops K and L, less than a hundred men strong.

Parral

Tompkins met with mixed reception in settlements he passed; some Carranzista troop commanders appeared to be helpful, others surly; all trigger fingers were itchy. The civilians, long pushed about by both Mexican government troops and by bandits were, to say the least, uncooperative. Tompkins accordingly adopted a rule of thumb relationship. When bivouacing near a settlement he warned the alcalde that his herd guard had orders to shoot at sight; he further warned that should any stray shots fall into his bivouac, the alcalde's house would go up in flames next morning. It worked. The fact that the *Americanos* actually paid in silver for what supplies they could purchase was also productive of good relationships.

At midday, April 12, Tompkins' command approached Parral, a town of some twenty thousand population where they had been promised food, a good campsite, and much-needed baths. As Tompkins has put it: "We were rapidly losing all outward resemblance to regular troops. We were ragged, shoes almost gone, and nearly everyone wore a beard. We certainly presented a hard-boiled, savage appearance."

To Tompkins' shock the Mexican Carranzista commander, a General Ismael Lozano, denied any knowledge of having invited the Americans into town and demanded they leave at once. The American acquiesced and the Mexican after some delay offered to lead the command out of town to a suitable campsite. However, as the ninety-odd troopers rode out mob violence flared.

Jeers and stones were followed by bullets. General Lozano and his staff disappeared and government troops threatened to envelop the squadron.

Tompkins' command was four-hundred miles in the heart of a hostile country; the Parral garrison amounted to some five-hundred men. Somewhere to the north Tompkin knew that another American column was presumably operating.

Covered by a rear guard of eight dismounted troopers and an officer, the little command moved north, its pack train leading. After a few Mexicans had been picked off by the sharp-shooting rear guard the hostile reception committee momentarily lost much of its élan and Tompkins made for the little hill village of Santa Cruz de Villegas where he felt he could safely make a stand. The Mexican troops followed in his rear and on his flanks.

From time to time during the ten-mile retreat each of the two troops in turn was dismounted to fight on foot as the Mexicans began to press in. A final charge by Mexican horsemen was met by rapid fire that, as later was found out, killed forty-two men including an officer, and wounded a larger number. That ended the pursuit.

Santa Cruz de Villegas was reached and fortified. When a Mexican was picked off at eight hundred yards by Captain Aubrey Lippincott, one of the best shots in the "old" Army, General Lozano called off his troops and sent a note to Major Tompkins urging that he leave.

Meanwhile several cavalrymen had been sent north, searching successfully for the other column; four rifle troops and the machine gun troop of the 10th Cavalry, under Colonel William C. Brown. At nightfall the welcome notes of "Officers Call," blown on a cavalry bugle, came to the ears of Tompkins' command and a little later Colonel Brown and his squadron came pounding in.[5]

American losses in the Parral fight were two men killed and seven (including Major Tompkins and another officer) wounded.

[5] "Officers Call" had been frequently blown during the Indian Plains wars, as an unmistakable recognition symbol.

Tomochic

The next conflict of any importance came at Tomochic, thirty miles southwest of Guerrero, on April 21. Colonel Dodd with fifteen officers and 175 men of the 7th Cavalry, hot on the trail of a Villista band some two hundred strong, under one Cervanza, surprised the Villistas in a deep canyon and in a sharp running fight completely dispersed them. Thirty bandits were killed or wounded, arms and horses were captured. Ten Americans were killed and three more wounded.

Pershing's estimate of the situation by mid-April was that Villa's bands had been so shattered and scattered that the Chihuahua area must now be combed. Accordingly the area was divided into five self-sustaining districts within which small detachments would operate. Pershing stressed again the necessity that cordial relations be maintained with government forces. But he cautioned all concerned that in case of unprovoked attack, from whatever source, "the officer in command will take the most vigorous measures to administer severe punishment, . . . bearing in mind that any other course is likely to be construed as a confession of weakness."

Cusi

Three Villista subordinates, Julio Acosta, Cruz Dominguez, and Ántonio Ángel, in early May, before American districting went into effect, joined forces, threatening the town of Cusi,[6] fifty miles southeast of Guerrero, and a small Carranzista force in the neighborhood. A plea from the townspeople of Cusi to General Pershing brought swift action. Major Robert L. Howze, with six rifle troops and a platoon of machine guns of the 11th Cavalry—fourteen officers and 319 men, with thirty Indian Scouts (Apache)—moved out of camp at San Antonio, made an all-night march, and at dawn, May 5, surprised the bandits—

[6] Cusi was a local abbreviation of Cusihulriachico.

less than 150 strong—at Ojos Azules ranch. The Villistas, from buildings and terrain accidents, put up a surprisingly stiff resistance, causing one of the Apache scouts to comment: "*Huli!* Damn fine fight!"

It was a typical cavalry fire fight, starting from a dismounted base and a mounted encirclement. A final charge using automatic pistols completed the job. There were no American casualties. Forty-four Villistas were killed; the number of wounded is unknown. A large number of prisoners was garnered, but since it was impossible to differentiate between peaceful villagers and bandits, these were all released. The action eliminated the Acosta-Dominguez-Ángel band.

Carrizal

Meanwhile relations between the two nations were worsening. A conference between Generals Hugh L. Scott, Chief of Staff, and Funston, representing the United States, and General Obregón, representing Mexico, was held at Juárez April 30. Obregón, amicable, was nevertheless insistent that all American troops be withdrawn, arguing that Villa, if not indeed dead, had been rendered harmless.

On May 8 Scott and Funston reported that the Mexican position was "redolent with bad faith" and recommended that at least 150,000 additional troops be mobilized. An immediate mobilization of Texas, New Mexico, and Arizona National Guard, they stressed, was essential to protect border points which were at that time being harassed by Mexican raiders. Pershing meanwhile had concentrated his force in the vicinity of Namiquipa. His attempt to iron out military differences with General Gabriel Gavira, Mexican commander in the area, came to nothing despite the apparent willingness of the Mexican to cooperate.

An ultimatum from Mexican General J. B. Trevina, commanding in the State of Chihuahua, on June 16, ordering that all movements of American troops, except to the north, cease immediately on pain of attack drew a sharp rejoinder from Pershing, who informed the Mexican he would move his forces wherever he wished; "if . . . the Mexican forces attack any of my columns the responsibility for the consequences will lie with the Mexican Government."

In consequence, reconnaissance of Mexican troops and movements was immediately initiated. Two troops of the 10th Cavalry, scouting along the Mexican National Railroad line suffered a severe defeat when their commander attempted to push through a considerable force of Mexican government troops barring their progress at Carrizal, ninety miles east of Colonia Dublan.

Captain Charles T. Boyd, with Troop C, 10th Cavalry, bivouacked at Santo Domingo Ranch, nine miles from Carrizal, on the night of June 20. His orders were to scout thoroughly in the direction of Ahumada, ten miles north of Carrizal, but was cautioned not to bring on a fight. Captain Lewis S. Morey, with Troop K of the 10th, on a similar mission, joined Boyd—the senior—that night. Early next day both troops, some ninety rifles, moved on Carrizal. Boyd's intention it seems was to pass through Carrizal and push north along the railroad line to Ahumada.

Outside of Carrizal the command was met by General Gómez, Mexican district commander, who told Boyd that he could not pass through the town. Boyd, insisting, dismounted his men and moved forward in line of skirmishers. A second and a third warning from General Gómez, who had a force of some four hundred men disposed in front of the town, were ignored. The Mexicans opened heavy fire. Boyd and Troop C dashed forward, while Troop K on the left took cover. Boyd and his only other officer, First Lieutenant Henry R. Adair, fell dead and after a brief fire fight Troop C panicked. The men of the other troop followed suit when Captain Morey went down, seriously wounded, and the entire American command disintegrated.

This defeat was a galling blow to American pride; scattered survivors of the little force wandered over the country for several days until picked up by relieving 11th Cavalry detachments under Major Robert L. Howze. American casualties were two officers and ten men killed, one officer and ten men wounded; while twenty-three other troopers were made prisoner (later released). On the Mexican side, General Gómez, eleven of his officers and thirty-three men were killed and fifty-three others wounded.

The incident probably brought the two nations closer to war than ever, but Pershing's cool head and tight rein prevented further clashes. Actually, not much of a case can be made for the unfortunate Boyd. His mission was reconnaissance, he had been cautioned not to start a fight, and passing through Carrizal itself was not necessary.

Pershing concentrated his command at Colonia Dublan, while a commission of three representatives of each government met at New London, Connecticut, to decide on withdrawal of American troops and joint but independent guarding of the border. Practically the entire National Guard of the United States—150,000 men—was called into Federal service and mobilized along the Rio Grande. Meanwhile the war in Europe was drawing ever increasing national attention. Carranza, on November 24, 1916, refused to accept the commission's proposal, but the American show of force brought some relief of tension. January 30, 1917, with war against Germany looming, the expeditionary force was ordered out of Mexico; the last man was across the border by February 5.

For the Record

An analysis of this little war, so completely limited in objective, is in order, since its results—politically, territorially, and militarily—were far greater than what on casual inspection may seem to have been but a bit of opera bouffe national frustration.

Its prelude, the Tampico incident and the occupation of Vera Cruz, gave evidence to the world that the dignity of the United States was not lightly to be imposed upon; a perfectly normal national reaction.

The expedition itself combined the interplay of domestic and foreign policy; of party politics intermingling with and affecting international relationships. President Wilson's campaign for a second term would, he hoped, be based upon the "he kept us out of war" theme. Yet he had to give service to the Monroe

Doctrine; anarchy in Mexico, unless suppressed by the United States, must in the long run bring foreign armed intervention. Villa's Columbus raid was beyond toleration, of course. It demanded retaliation. Yet an all-out war with Mexico might well wreck second-term ambitions. So Mr. Wilson's solution was to impose retaliation upon a strictly limited and legalistic basis. Villa was the villain; his bid for power must be dashed.

Did General Pershing attain the objectives laid down in his directive? Again, at first blush, one may say he failed. Villa was neither captured nor eliminated; he would remain an individual thorn in the flesh of Mexican good government until his assassination in 1923. But his troops—his outlaw bandits—were scattered, and many of his subordinate leaders were killed; they were no longer a force to be reckoned with. Villa's teeth had been drawn. And that was exactly what Pershing's directive from the War Department dictated: "the pursuit and dispersion of the band or bands that attacked Columbus, N.M."

Territorially, the affair emphasized the adamant policy of the United States to preserve the integrity of Mexico, and, by implication, of all the nations of the Western Hemisphere.

Militarily, the results were indirect but all important. Pershing's expedition could not have survived had it not been imbued—from the leader down to the rear ranks—with a remarkable discipline. This discipline rode triumphant over hardship and frustration. And the experience gained in solving problems of hurried mobilization, extemporized logistics, and kaleidoscopic situation changes was shortly to declare a dividend.

As William A. Ganoe, brilliant Army historian, has so well put it: "Few have ever regarded Pancho Villa as a benefactor. But his crossing of our border . . . had given our President the excuse of training a large proportion of the Regular Army and about 150,000 National Guardsmen on the Mexican border. The hardening, discipline and schooling in the field . . . made possible the later ability of the American forces, and particularly the 1st, 2nd, 26th and 42nd Divisions, to turn the tide in March, 1918, in France. There has been much speculation since as to what might have happened had not Mr. Villa done us this temporary or ultimate ill-turn or favor."

More specifically, the story of the Punitive Expedition is that of the last horse-cavalry campaign in the history of the United States Army. It should not be forgotten.

6

Caribbean Interventions, 1915-1934

Eenee, Meenee, Mainee, Mo!
Trouble starts when nations grow,
Some one has to stop it—so
Eenee, Meenee, Mainee, Mo!
Make—you—It!
—*From "A Counting-Out Song" by Rudyard Kipling*

Ever since the Holy Alliance—Russia, Austria, and Prussia—in 1823 threatened military molestation of the then newly born Latin American nations, the United States has exerted a paternalistic, if not always altruistic policy toward its Central and South American neighbors.

This first crystallized in the promulgation of the Monroe Doctrine, a definite "No Trespassing" sign to all Europe. As corollary, European nations being forbidden to meddle even in sustaining the legitimate rights of their nationals in the area, the policy perforce expanded to include United States intervention in Latin America whenever unrest there threatened the comity of nations.

Financial interests were also involved, since heavy investments of American and European capitalists were from time to time endangered by unrest and revolution in tottering nations. Out of this aspect of the Latin American situation grew the popular and frequently invidious characterization of United States armed stabilization efforts as "dollar diplomacy" or "gunboat diplomacy," directed against "banana republics."

As time went on, United States interventions were not few.

And with the advent of the twentieth century, United States national interest in the Caribbean-Central American regions bulged into a necessity of self-defense, to protect not only the Panama Canal but indeed the defense of the entire Western Hemisphere. Most of these interventions have been of short duration. However, three of them, in as many nations, assumed the dual character of both limited and guerrilla war.

This is the story of the trio, roughly concurrent for much of the time. Two of them were staged in the lush jungles, cane fields, and mountains of Hispaniola—Haiti, in popular parlance—most picturesque and most bloodstained of Caribbean islands; the third was waged in the low-lying, humid hinterland and the volcanic cliffs of Central America. All three were carried out by means of United States sea power, and all three were fought by the United States Marine Corps, with Navy support.

Haiti

On July 28, 1915, a howling mob of Haitians dragged their President, Vibrun Guillaume Sam, from hiding in the French Legation in Port au Prince and, quite literally, tore him to pieces. Ringleaders in the mob actually ate his heart. Within twenty-four hours American marines came tumbling ashore to snuff out, apparently, and certainly without opposition, the anarchy in the Haitian capital. But out through the hills the pulsing, haunting thump of the voodoo drums was sweeping and nineteen years would pass before the last leatherneck went home.

The 1915 outbreak was no spur-of-the-moment affair; it was the culmination of 110 years of independence and misrule in the Republic of Haiti, Negro nation occupying the western one-third of the island of Hispaniola. Up to this time Haiti had suffered under the despotic rule of twenty-six successive individuals—two emperors, one king, and twenty-three presidents—each of whom had kept himself in power by force of arms until overthrown or killed while in office.

Sam himself had come into office through revolution in early 1915, when Haiti's foreign debt had risen to approximately $24 million, the Banque Nationale had refused further advance (its remaining gold reserve of $500,000 had been hurriedly transferred to New York by the National City Bank, which controlled the Haitian institution), and Franco-German interests were clamoring for control of Haitian customs held under lien.

The United States State Department had tried without success to exert diplomatic pressure on the Haitian government to clean house, while United States Navy forces gathered in Haitian waters. Sam's seizure of power gave some promise, but that faded when another revolution broke out, headed by a Dr. Rosalvo Bobo. Sam imprisoned some two hundred leading citizens suspected of rebellious complicity, and ordered their immediate execution should revolutionists attack his palace in Port au Prince. It was attacked, Sam fled to the sanctuary of the French Legation, and his prison commandant put to death 167 of the hostages. The capital flared in an orgy of anarchy.

Even as the torso of Guillaume Sam was being dragged through the streets, the United States cruiser *Washington*, flagship of Rear Admiral William B. Caperton, USN, came hurrying under forced draft into Port au Prince from Cap Haïtien. Caperton put ashore three companies of bluejackets and two of marines under Captain George C. Van Orden, USN, and by nightfall had temporarily restored order.

The admiral then radioed Guantánamo for help, which arrived within twenty-four hours, in the form of the 24th Marine Company aboard the USS *Jason*. Five days later, the battleship *Connecticut*, which had completed a record run south, arrived with regimental headquarters and five companies of the 2nd Marine Regiment under Colonel Eli K. Cole.

It being evident that the Bobo revolution was gaining force in the northern part of the island, the 1st Marine Brigade, commanded by Colonel Littleton W. T. Waller,[1] arrived piecemeal from Guantánamo and the United States during late July and early August.

Admiral Caperton, under instructions from Washington, attempted to aid the establishment of law and order. Sudre Darti-

[1] Mentioned *supra* in both the Philippine Insurrection and the China Expeditionary Force, q.v.

HAITI and the DOMINICAN REPUBLIC

guenave was elected President by the Haitian Congress, with the blessing of the United States and Colonel Waller's Marine brigade, augmented by three batteries of Marine field artillery. The Marines took over operation of the principal Haitian customs houses and planned the organization of a constabulary and a program of public works, to be paid for from the customs receipts. Meanwhile the dissidence of Bobo and his adherents, augmented by an entirely new factor, broke into open revolt.

The Cacos

A substantial segment of the Haitian population consists of the so-called "cacos," descendants of the most warlike Negro slaves of the past, who had run away and established themselves in the mountains.

Accustomed to selling themselves to the highest bidder and thus controlling whatever government rose to power, the caco warriors resented the intrusion of a foreign element in their affairs. After making some tentative shakedown gestures to local Marine commanders and getting nowhere, the cacos went to war. A band, some two hundred strong, menaced the town of Gonaïves. Unfortunately for them, they also menaced a Marine major named Smedley D. Butler, who, with a company of marines, squelched them.

But the northern coast remained in uproar. Several minor clashes culminated in a brisk fight not far from Cap Haïtien, when two Marine patrols were surrounded. Colonel Cole, commanding in the region, called for bluejackets from USS *Connecticut* to take over routine duties at Cap Haïtien and with five companies of marines drove off the rebels. Six marines were wounded; the cacos left forty dead behind them.

Cole then drove the cacos from their principal settlement at Quartier Morin and for the moment pacified the neighborhood and restored the flow of food supplies into Cap Haïtien.

Colonel Waller, at Port au Prince, made a valiant attempt at total pacification of the northern region, by bribes to various leaders and by sweeping the area, garrisoning Ouanaminthe and Fort Liberté. He collected more than a thousand rifles, but, like quicksilver, the cacos slid out from control.

Waller, returning to Port au Prince, left the clean-up campaign to Cole. Its first phase was a series of reconnaissances through the mountainous areas generally south and southeast of Cap Haïtien. Of a number of resulting clashes the most important was that of Major Butler's patrol. With several officers and forty men, all mounted, Butler swept through the countryside on a six-day reconnaissance.

On October 24 the patrol was ambushed by an estimated four hundred cacos, while crossing a mountain stream after dark in search of a rebel stronghold. The patrol fought its way to a good position, established a perimeter and waited for daylight, while the cacos kept up a continuous but poorly aimed fire. At daybreak three squads of marines burst out in as many directions, surprising the cacos, who scattered in flight. The marines then found the strongpoint, Fort Dipitie, and overran it, killing eight cacos and wounding ten others. One marine received a slight flesh wound. Captain William P. Upshur, First Lieutenant Edward A. Ostermann, and Gunnery Sergeant Dan Daly,[2] the three squad leaders, won the Congressional Medal of Honor for their part in this action.

By November the constant sweeps through the area began to bear fruit; the cacos were gradually forced into their last stronghold, Fort Rivière. This was an old French work of solid masonry construction, some eight miles south of Grande Rivière; it was considered by the Haitians to be impregnable. Marine forces under Major Butler closed in on the place during the night of the 17th; the 13th Company from the east, the USS *Connecticut*'s Marine detachment on the south, and the 15th Company, with the ubiquitous Butler accompanying, on the west. Butler, with Sergeant Ross L. Iams, hunting for a weak spot in the defense, discovered a deep ditch leading from the undergrowth at the base of the wall. It led them into a drain about three feet in diameter. Butler, crawling into it, found it opened into the

2 This was Daly's second Congressional Medal of Honor; the first was won at Peking, during the relief of the legations; *vide* China Relief Expedition, *supra*.

center courtyard of the fortress. Satisfied, he wormed his way back and the pair returned to the troops.

At daylight the next morning, all units opened fire and began to advance toward the fort. Taken by surprise, some cacos attempted to escape over the walls only to be cut down by the accurate fire of the marines. Under cover of the confusion Butler led twenty-seven hand-picked men to the drain opening. Sergeant Iams and Private Samuel Gross volunteered to enter first. Butler crawled behind them.

Before the Cacos realized what was happening the handful of marines, wriggling through single file, were in their midst, and in a typical hand-to-hand battle tore into the enemy. Some seventy-two cacos were killed, including seven known bandit chiefs. The attacking marines suffered only a few slight wounds. Major Butler, Sergeant Iams, and Private Gross—the first three men through the opening into the courtyard—received the Medal of Honor for their heroic action. The marines now demolished the fortress, using a ton of dynamite, and ending the last vestiges of caco resistance. For the first time in over a century the turbulent political pot of Haiti simmered down to something resembling a state of peace.

As 1916 opened, the Marine occupation began to take the form of a quasi-military government, supporting civil power. Some sporadic clashes with bandit groups occurred, but the establishment of a native *gendarmerie* became a first priority. The problem was interesting, for it involved a constitutional violation. Marine officers and noncommissioned officers were perforce being encadred in the service of a foreign government. The hurdle was jumped by making such appointees in an "acting" capacity. Later, congressional approval was obtained.

Major Butler became chief of the Gendarmerie d' Haïti, with Haitian rank of major general, with ninety-five other Marine officers and noncoms under him. Administratively the Gendarmerie was divided into four geographical departments, and eighteen districts; these in turn were broken down into subdistricts, communes, and rural sections. Department commanders held the rank of colonel and districts were commanded by captains. Initially, all grades of captain and above were filled by

Marine commissioned officers; lieutenants were picked Marine noncoms. As time went on, qualified Haitians were commissioned, also, but for a number of years the Gendarmerie officer corps remained completely American.

For two years Haiti was peaceful, at least to outward appearance. But dissatsifaction with forced labor on the roads—a Haitian law for all who could not pay taxes—as well as the age-old caco banditry, brought about an explosion. Charlemagne Peraulte, caco chief, led the new revolt, which spread over the entire northern area of the republic. Terrorized peasants left their fields, food shortages developed, and the vicious circle grew to revolutionary proportion, beyond the Gendarmerie's capability. The Marine brigade—down to thirty-seven officers and 831 men now, through the exigencies of World War I—took the field in March, reinforced by four more companies from Guantánamo.

For three months marines and Gendarmerie fought the revolt, in some eighty indecisive skirmishes. Lack of coordination between the two forces was apparently to blame. Peraulte became so bold as to actually stage an assault on Port au Prince, October 7, which was promptly repelled.

And then came Hanneken; Marine Sergeant Hermann H. Hanneken, who wore the bars of a captain in the Gendarmerie d'Haïti, and commanded a district within Charlemagne Peraulte's sphere of action. Hanneken, convinced that the best way to end Charlemagne's revolt was to dispose of Charlemagne himself, set about doing just that. His plan was Machiavellian in concept and daring in execution. First he persuaded a native Haïtian civilian, in whom he put great trust, to organize a caco band of his own; then he had one of his own gendarmes "defect" to Peraulte's cacos, where he became a "secretary."

The fake caco chief, in some rather elaborately staged skirmishes with Hanneken's gendarmerie, speedily won a reputation in Charlemagne's eyes, particularly when Hanneken, "wounded" in one of the clashes, for several weeks sported a bandaged arm. News travels fast over the jungle drum telegraph. And, astoundingly, the gendarme "secretary"—by what means one is not sure, but probably because he could write—wormed his way into

Charlemagne's confidence, and actually became his adjutant!

Charlemagne was coaxed to attack the town of Grande Rivière, from which most of the government garrison had been openly withdrawn.

The caco attack came during the night of October 31, 1919, while Charlemagne waited the result of the action in a secret hide-out. But Hanneken, with his Gendarmerie lieutenant—Marine Corporal William R. Button—and twenty gendarmes, all masquerading in caco tatters, were being guided to the hideout by the "planted" gendarme; Hanneken and Button with faces and hands carefully stained. Charlemagne's force attacked Grande Rivière, was trapped between it and the returning garrison, and roundly trounced. But Charlemagne never knew it. Hanneken and his group passed the caco guards on plea of bringing news of victory, and Hanneken shot the caco chief as he stood beside a fire, while Button turned his automatic rifle on his guards.

Both Henneken and Button received the Congressional Medal of Honor for the coup, which resulted in the dispersal of Charlemagne's band, estimated to be twelve hundred strong. For the moment Haiti was again peaceful. But not for long.

Benoît Batraville, replacing Charlemagne, led a new burst of banditry in central Haiti. Benoît's own forces numbered some 2500, but he exercised a vague control over many more cacos, it seemed. Ambitious Benoît early staged a raid on Port au Prince, January 14-15, some three hundred bandits infiltrating the town. Marine and gendarmerie forces promptly crushed the affray and the cacos fled, leaving more than 150 of their number dead, wounded, or captured. Two marines were wounded.

A six-month campaign of active patrolling followed, during which more than three thousand cacos surrendered. But the remainder resisted savagely. A combined Marine-Gendarmerie patrol led by Lieutenant Lawrence Muth (Sergeant, USMC) was ambushed and surrounded by Benoît's cacos on Mount Michel. Muth was killed, but the patrol shot its way out, killing ten cacos. A retaliatory raid killed twenty-five more bandits.

Captain Jesse L. Perkins, USMC, ended the uprising during May. With one other officer and twenty-eight marines, Perkins ferreted out the location of Benoît's main camp. A caco outpost was flushed and fled. Perkins, sending his main force in pursuit, took three men and circled wide. He rushed the caco camp from the rear and nearly collided with Benoît himself, who attempted to shoot his way out but was immediately cut down by Marine Sergeant Passmore.

By the end of 1920 caco outrages had practically ceased and Haiti had become somewhat stabilized. The public works program of roadbuilding and sanitation was progressing. The Gendarmerie was reorganized and in 1928 was rechristened Garde d'Haiti. The Marine brigade was reduced to approximately five hundred in strength.

However, world-wide depression in the following year brought a series of strikes and disorders necessitating reestablishment of martial law in December. The Garde d'Haïti reverted to United States Marine command and several clashes with strikers occurred. The affair blew over shortly, and the appointment of a presidential Commission headed by W. Cameron Forbes initiated an era of stabilization. In October 1934 the Garde became completely Haitianized and on August 15 the United States Marine brigade evacuated Haiti.

Dominican Republic

The eastern two-thirds of Hispaniola are occupied by the Dominican Republic, sister nation to Haiti and, like her, the victim of bloody misrule since emancipation. Between 1844 and 1916, forty-three presidents, most of them military men, had passed in transient office. The people, customs, and educational *lacunae* of the country are quite similar to those of Haiti, as might be expected, but the negroid Dominican Republic differs in two vital though unconnected aspects: it is Spanish-oriented instead of French, and its citizens hold an abiding hatred for Haitians.

The United States first really bolstered the Dominican Republic in 1904, when on President Theodore Roosevelt's recommendation a receivership of sorts was organized and administered, to stabilize the finances of the then bankrupt nation. This receivership was to continue until Dominican bonded indebtedness to foreign interest should be fully repaid. Dominicans did not receive the situation with relish, and the country's chain of revolutions went on. In 1911, one of the many upheavals interrupted the customs service, and incoming revenues. Under United States pressure and threat of a Marine occupation, affairs were partly bettered, despite additional revolutions, during which it became necessary on several occasions to put small Marine forces ashore temporarily.

On May 5, 1916, fighting between the Dominican government forces of President Juan Isidro Jiménez and those of his rival, Desiderio Arias, flared in Santo Domingo City, while Jiménez himself rejected the United States demand that a financial advisor be appointed with its approval, and that a constabulary be established under American officers. So tense was the situation that two companies of marines, hurriedly detached from the forces then in Haiti, were landed to protect the American and Haitian legations, while a detachment of bluejackets from USS *Castine* seized and occupied nearby Fort Geronimo, to provide a base.

President Jiménez first asked, then rejected United States assistance to drive the rebels from his capital. More marines arrived from Guantánamo. Admiral Caperton, commanding in Caribbean waters, added the Dominican Republic to his Haitian chore, and after consultation with the United States Minister, W. W. Russell, on May 13, demanded immediate surrender of the rebels and disarmament of the city's inhabitants. Arias and his followers fled next day, but disorder continued.

Early on May 15, a battalion of marines, under Major Newt H. Hall,[3] entered Santo Domingo City and occupied strategic points, without direct opposition, but much to the resentment of the inhabitants. Jiménez resigned, his cabinet wrestled verbally with Admiral Caperton and Mr. Russell over the appointment of a provisional President, and Arias' rebel forces waxed stronger in other towns, particularly in the north.

Arias himself made his headquarters at Santiago. Marine

[3] We have met Hall before; *vide* the China Relief Expedition, *supra*.

detachments were put ashore at Puerto Plata and Monte Cristi, on the north shore, and after smart brushes occupied both places. However, the situation throughout the country had become quite serious, with the population generally hostile to the Americans. Accordingly the 4th Marine Regiment, a battalion of Marine field artillery, and several additional detachments were hurriedly sent in. The force officially became the 2nd Marine Brigade. Meanwhile, local Marine commanders were authorized to declare martial law should they deem it necessary.

Colonel Joseph H. (Uncle Joe) Pendleton, USMC, commanding the 4th Regiment, on June 18 assumed command of all troops ashore and advanced on Santiago, June 26, in two columns—the reinforced 4th, with thirty-three officers and eight hundred men, moving southeast from Monte Cristi and the 4th and 9th companies under Major Hiram I. (Hiking Hiram) Bearss, moving south along the railroad from Puerto Plata.

Pendleton's column next day found itself opposed by a heavily organized line of resistance on Las Trencheras Ridge, some twenty-odd miles from Monte Cristi. The position was considered by the rebels to be invulnerable. In the 1860s it had resisted several attempts by Spanish forces to take it away from the islanders. Pendleton advanced on a two-battalion front, covered by artillery fire, and after a brisk action overran it. The rebels, falling back to a second line of resistance, held briefly, but were driven off at the point of the bayonet. One marine was killed and four others wounded here.

Pendleton's column, after a clash at Guayacanas, July 3, reached the railway junction of Navarette, where it was joined by Bearss's command, which had had one clash with rebels on the way. The combined force moved on Santiago. A peace delegation met the advance July 5 and after some attempt at delay accepted the inevitable and Pendleton moved in, without opposition.

All organized resistance ceased temporarily while negotiations between the Dominican government and the United States dragged on. Losing patience, the United States Department of State then authorized establishment of military government throughout the nation. Captain Harry S. Knapp, USN, who had just succeeded Admiral Caperton, proclaimed it on November 29. Knapp became military governor. At San Francisco de Macorís, a provincial capital sixty miles east of Santiago, the governor, Juan Pérez, refused compliance with the new regime and prepared to defend the Forteleza, a Spanish work, with one hundred or more released criminal prisoners. Lieutenant E. C. Williams, USMC, whose small detachment had been billeted in the town, rushed the closing gate of the fort, with a dozen marines. Eight of his men were shot down, but Williams, reaching the gate with his four remaining marines, threw his body against it and rammed his way in. Williams' pistol jammed as a Dominican soldier raised his rifle to fire. Drummer Schovan grabbed the gun, Williams and his men killed two Dominicans, and seized the place. Meanwhile another detachment of Williams' men had captured the town police headquarters. A quick concentration of marines from nearby posts then pursued and dispersed Pérez' followers. Williams received the Congressional Medal of Honor.

Under military government administered by the Marines, with Colonel Pendleton and other officers, marines and Navy men, occupying key positions, the central government of the republic slowly took shape again. While the Dominican judiciary generally remained at their posts, a system of provost courts and a provost department also functioned, in close contact with the people. It was slow work, and delicate. One of its instrumentalities was the quickly organized Guardia Nacional Dominicana, a force analogous to the Garde d'Haïti. Its rank and file were Dominicans, its officers Marine officers and noncoms.

For eight long years the Marine occupation lasted; after the first campaign, it became an almost incessant succession of harassing patrol actions against groups of bandits. Most of these actions closed with Marine success, but a few had a different ending. One deserves mention. On August 13, 1918, a Marine patrol of a corporal and four men was ambushed at a stream crossing near Manchado by a gang of bandits who surrounded them. The marines, fighting on foot, were cut down until but one man, a Private Rushforth, still stood, although his right arm, slashed by a machete, was useless. Rushforth managed to run to his horse, scramble on him, and escape under a shower of bullets, two of them wounding both horse and man.

Marine occupation finally ended shortly after a constitutional government was established and inaugurated July 12, 1924.

The final report of Major General Harry Lee, USMC, the last military governor, sums up the results:

> The occupying force assumed control of a state rife with revolution, banditry, ungoverned and mismanaged. We left a state enjoying peace, and with a loyal and well-developed military force, with fine roads, many schools, a fine military hospital, and, in short, with every promise for a future of stable government under Dominican rule.

Fine words, and true words. They could apply also to Haiti when the Marines left it in 1935. Unfortunately, national character—or lack of character—in both nations on Hispaniola, together with the insidious proddings of infiltrating Marxist ideology, have combined to flout the promise.

Nicaragua

Nicaragua, stormy petrel of Central America, has been in sporadic conflict—externally with her neighbors and with foreign interests, internally in Liberal-Conservative clashes—ever since the dawning of her independence in 1811. North American fingers, official and private, first began dabbling in her muddied political waters when the California gold rush brought transportation tycoon "Commodore" Cornelius Vanderbilt into the picture in 1852. Vanderbilt's Accessory Transit Company shuttled prospectors across southern Nicaragua between San Juan del Norte on the Caribbean and San Juan del Sur on the Pacific. William Walker, Tennessee adventurer and filibusterer, popped into the Nicaraguan scene in 1855, at the invitation of a Liberal revolutionary clique, and by 1856 had fought his way to the presidency. But Walker had seized Vanderbilt ships and other Vanderbilt property. So Vanderbilt influence in Central America and in the United States froze him out in 1857.[4]

4 Trying to return in 1860, Walker was captured and shot.

All this rumpus attracted United States attention to the strategic, agricultural, and mineral potentialities of Nicaragua. American and foreign investors, first welcomed by successive Nicaraguan governments, sometimes found themselves pinched later by revolutions. American gunrunners did a lively business from time to time, supplying arms to revolutionaries. All in all, by 1909, when Nicaraguan President José Zelaya shot two United States citizens who had been filibustering, relations between Uncle Sam and Nicaragua could not be considered cordial.

The United States, breaking off diplomatic relations with the Zelaya government, openly fostered a revolution. Zelaya resigned but the revolution continued against his successor, Dr. José Madríz. Still taking the side of the revolutionaries, the United States gunboat *Paducah* prevented a Nicaraguan government gunboat from attacking a rebel force at Bluefields and a landing party was sent ashore on May 19 to protect American interests.

A new President, Adolfo Díaz, was elected in May and the Nicaraguan government staggered along, bolstered by a $1,500,000 loan from American bankers, secured by control of the National Bank of Nicaragua and the government-controlled Pacific coastal railway as well as by customs receipts. However, rebellion, headed by Generals Mena and Zeladón, soon threatened complete disruption of the entire Pacific coastal area.

Two companies of marines, under Major Smedley D. Butler, were hurried in from the Canal Zone to bolster the United States legation guard on May 30, 1912, but the situation worsened and President Taft, pressured by the American financial interests involved, authorized armed intervention in support of the Díaz government.

Butler's Marine battalion, reinforced, had its hands full trying to keep the railroad open between the port of Corinto and Managua, the capital. Another Marine force, some eight hundred strong, under Colonel Joseph H. (Uncle Joe) Pendleton, moved in. Rear Admiral W. H. H. Sutherland, USN, in the battleship *California*, accompanied by the cruiser *Denver*, arrived at Corinto August 28 and assumed command. A combined bluejacket-Marine force began control of the entire railroad line running through populous and developed Pacific coastal zone. Pendleton's 1st Marine Battalion occupied Leon, while he and the remainder of his command pushed on to Managua.

Cleanup of rebel forces opposing lackadaisical government troops south of Managua followed. A stiff brush with rebels at Masaya, September 19, enabled Butler's battalion to occupy Grenada on the twenty-second bringing Red Cross supplies to the relief of its citizens.

However, a strong rebel force still occupied Coyotepe Hill, overlooking the railway line near Masaya, and threatened further communications. Nicaraguan government troops being unable—or unwilling—to make progress against the rebel stronghold, Pendleton attacked, early October 4, breaking through barbed-wire entanglements, and overrunning the position in an assault that lasted but thirty-seven minutes. Four Americans were killed and fourteen wounded; known rebel losses were sixty dead.

Rebel forces lost all heart after this, and after a few further skirmishings were broken up and scattered. General amnesty to all rebels who would give up their arms by October 12 was announced. A gratified Nicaraguan government also expressed its thanks, and the American intervention came to an end. By January 16, 1913, only a legation guard of four officers and 101 men remained on Nicaraguan soil.

Sandino

Some twelve years of quasi peace in Nicaragua followed, with political differences being settled at the polls, while the nucleus of a constabulary was being organized, under Marine supervision, similar to the establishments so successful in Haiti and the Dominican Republic. However, here the organization was still in its swaddling clothes when an optimistic State Department brought about the windrawal of the Marine legation guard in August 1925. This coincided with the inauguration of a coalition Nicaraguan government, under President Carlos Solorzano. Disappointed at the polls, former President Emilio Chamorro Vargas launched a *coup d'état* in October, seized La Loma, a fortification

NICARAGUA
0
100
200
300
400
MILES
Cabo Gracias
Puerto Cabezas
Coco R.
Poteca
El Chipote
Garrabo
Honduras
Ocotal
Quilalí
Santa Cruz
Jinotega
El Source
NICARAGUA
CARIBBEAN
SEA
Corinto
León
Lago de Managua
Managua
Masaya
Granada
Bluefields
Lago de Nicaragua
PACIFIC
OCEAN
San Juan del Sur
San Juan del Norte
Costa Rica

dominating Managua, and overturned the government. This time the entire country flamed, while the United States refused him recognition. Marine landings at Bluefields followed, to maintain a neutral zone, while United States naval vessels in Nicaraguan waters watched developments.

A conference between Chamarro and rival political leaders gathered at Corinto, guarded by marines—at the request of all parties. Chamarro withdrew from the picture and former President Adolfo Díaz was reelected in 1926, again as a compromise. It wouldn't work; Juan Bautista Sacasa and Generals José María Moncada and César Augusto Sandino headed an uncompromising rebellion against Díaz despite his recognition by the United States.

Establishment of additional neutral zones under Marine supervision followed, but, although western Nicaragua remained under government control, the uprising in the east gathered force and in January 1927 Moncada moved west, with a strong rebel force. Still maintaining neutrality, the United States sold the Díaz government a quantity of arms and ammunition, while additional Marine ground reinforcements and a Marine aviation squadron arrived, bringing United States strength to some two thousand men, under Brigadier General Logan Feland, USMC.

An American mission, headed by former Secretary of War Henry L. Stimson, was rushed to Nicaragua by the State Department, in an endeavor to end the conflict. After thorough investigation, Stimson decided that the military situation was a stalemate. A tripartite conference between Díaz, Moncada, and Stimson, agreed to a general disarmament, the reorganization of a Marine-trained and supervised constabulary, and new general elections, to be carried out under United States supervision. Until the constabulary—the Guardia Nacional—could be organized and trained, the Marines—now more than three thousand strong—would maintain order.

Major General Frank R. McCoy, USA, personally picked by President Coolidge to supervise the coming elections, now picked up the ball and by his diplomatic acumen succeeded in bringing about political harmony. Moncada's nephew, Anastasio Somoza, who also had political ambitions, was for a time a thorn in the flesh to the American mission, but McCoy won him over.

One standout remained, however: Sandino. His operations changed the entire situation from that of a somewhat haphazard bickering to a real civil war, with Communistic overtones. Posing as a patriot, refusing all offers of compromise, Sandino, operating in the mountainous area of northern Nicaragua, antagonized not only the occupation forces but also the more temperate elements of the nation itself.

Sandino's operations were felt first in the gold-mining area west of Puerto Cabezas on the eastern coast. Then he shifted to the state of Nuevo Segovia in the northwest. With six hundred men he fell upon a newly established garrison at the village of Ocotal, where Captains G. D. Hatfield, with a score of marines, and G. C. Darnell, with forty-eight guardsmen, had just moved into two stone buildings.

The Sandino mob swirled in during the night of July 15-16, 1927, but was repulsed in two separate engagements; the Marines in one house, the Guardia in another, were able to assist one another only by firepower. Gathering in the dawn for another assault, the rebels were spotted by two Marine reconnaissance planes out of Managua, eighty miles away, who immediately carried the word back.

Five planes, under the aviation detachment commander, Major Ross F. Roswell, USMC, at once took off. At Ocotal, where the Sandino force was now attempting to smother the Marine-Guardia garrison in a heavy fire fight, Roswell's antiquated de Havillands came screaming down. The attackers, who had never seen a plane before, stood gaping until a hail of machine gun bullets and light extemporized bombs swept them. Then the survivors melted away, leaving more than fifty dead behind them. One marine was killed, another wounded.

But Sandino was still potent in Nuevo Segovia. Marine air reconnaissance spotted his fortified camp at El Chipote and Captain Richard Livingston with 150 marines and a handful of Guardia moved through the jungle to attack it. Near Quilalí, Livingston's long column was ambushed, his pack train scattered. The attackers were driven off, at cost of five Marine dead and twenty-three wounded. Some five miles away a smaller detachment—some sixty-odd marines and members of the Guardia under First Lieutenant M. A. Richal—moving to join Livingston, was also ambushed that same day, and was extricated only with Livingston's aid. The combined force dug in at Quilalí, while by strenuous efforts an airstrip was extemporized. Here First Lieutenant C. F. Schilt, USMC, in a series of daring shuttling flights which won him the Medal of Honor, brought off the wounded to Managua.

It was quite evident by now that the pacification problem had become a major task. So while diplomats and marines worked hand in hand with the preparations for the election next year, the main objective became the elimination of Sandino. Government troops were useless, the Guardia still in swaddling clothes. The burden of a guerrilla war had fallen squarely on the shoulders of the Marines—with, of course, Navy support.

The plan proposed was simple; its execution almost impossible: containment of Sandino in the northern mountain hinterland by a combination of garrison posts strung across the country, and of combat patrolling to pin down an elusive enemy who knew the terrain, as the French have it, like his pocket.

It was a fantastic jungle war; an almost incessant series of skirmishes and bickerings, in squad, platoon and—sometimes—company or greater strength. It was in theory a pincer movement. The Marine forces operating simultaneously from bases on the Pacific and the Caribbean coast, would link and push Sandino against the Honduran border on the north. But the fallacy was that Honduras was a Sandino haven, not a barrier, across which he moved at will.

In the northwest, still in Nuevo Segovia, a probing force of three hundred men under Major Archibald Young, USMC, based on Ocotal, by the end of the year arrived within striking distance of Sandino's own stronghold at El Chipote, north of Chihili, which had been spotted by Marine aviation. On January 14, 1928, Young closed in, but met strong resistance. And when the leathernecks finally rushed the place, on January 26, the bird had flown across the Honduran border. Sandino himself was on the way to Mexico. For the moment the rebellion seemed dead although banditry was still rife. One exception developed in a thrust by Captain Robert Hunter, USMC, from Quilalí. After several days' march Hunter's patrol, on May 13, 1928, fell in with a large bandit group who showed fight. They were driven off, but Hunter himself was mortally wounded, one marine was killed, and another wounded.

The Caribbean arm of encirclement during all this time was most active, with Puerto Cabezas its base. Incessant patrols pushed westward, while garrisons were established in key border villages. The most important of these probings was the so-called Cacos Patrol, which brought fame to Captain Merritt A. (Red Mike) Edson, USMC.

Edson pushed up the Coco River to Poteca—140 miles in air line from Puerto Cabezas—where a Marine reconnaissance plane had reported a rebel headquarters. With one hundred men, traveling by dugout and supplied by air, Edson reached Poteca August 17, 1928, only to find it deserted.

The Coco River, with headwaters in north-central Nicaragua, takes a winding course to the sea at Cabo Gracias a Dios, marking the Honduran border. Edson actually went as far west as Santa Cruz, linking with patrol activities of the Northern Zone. Meanwhile other patrols had made similarly fantastic sweeps. Captain William W. Walker, USMC, had reached as far as Garrabo, at the headwaters of the Bocay River, a twenty-six day trip from Cabo Gracias.

The national elections went off smoothly in November 1928, under Marine supervision. Moncada was reelected, heading a temperate regime which promised Nicaraguan stabilization. But it was only a promise which whirlwind Sandino, with the help of do-gooders and bleeding hearts in the United States, was soon to dissipate.

Propaganda fostered by the Communist Party excited liberals and pacifists in America and abroad to lend not only their voices but, more to the point, financial support to the man whom Henri Barbusse hailed as the "George Washington of Central America." Henry Garrison Villard's *Nation* staunchly supported his "patriotic" struggle against American "imperialism." So

Sandino came back in 1930, fortified spiritually and physically, and Nicaragua flared again.

Three more years of ferment were to follow. The Marines and the growingly efficient Guardia Nacional, now commanded by Colonel Douglas C. McDougal, USMC, in combination snubbed but could not completely eliminate Sandino. However, they did reduce his stature from that of a national menace to one of a mere bandit leader.

During this time Captain Lewis B. (Chesty) Puller, USMC, came into the limelight. A glance at his operations will give not only some picture of the Nicaraguan campaigning of the period but also a vignette of a coming Marine "character."

Puller, transferred from Haiti to Nicaragua, was at first detailed to administrative duties, but was sent in March 1929 to Corinto, where a street mob had shot and wounded a Marine lieutenant. His orders were to take command and restore order. Puller boarded a train, carrying a suitcase containing a Thompson submachine gun and ammunition. When he arrived, he found Corinto quiet. Alone, he took his suitcase to the waterfront and within sight of a sullen crowd of longshoremen opened it, took out the weapon, and with a few bursts sank several cans in the water. He then put away the gun, called in his Guardia detachment, and arrested a dozen ringleaders in the mob.

Puller was then sent into the field in the northeastern area, in a combined Marine-Guardia force. On one of his first excursions, Puller's patrol of about thirty men was in single file along a wooded trail when from a ridge to their left came a hail of fire from rifles and automatic weapons. Puller called for one blast from the bugler, and the men took cover. Puller led a flanking movement and turned the half-seen bandits from their position. In the action the Guardia had had three men wounded, but nine bandits had been killed. During the attack there had been some mysterious heavy explosions. Puller, investigating the bandit positions, found crude bombs—bags of rawhide which had been sewn around several sticks of dynamite, the interior of each bag being packed with fragments of stone and iron to act as shrapnel.

Meanwhile, the Marine occupation force gradually became a reserve to bolster up Guardia activities. All was not well, however, as a Guardia mutiny at Telpaneca in the northwestern section of the country showed. On October 5, 1929, the entire Guardia garrison mutinied, murdering its commander, Second Lieutenant Lewis H. Trogler, a Marine Corps sergeant. The mutineers reported his death as being the result of a bandit attack and Second Lieutenant Charles J. Levonski, another Marine sergeant, was sent to take command. Again the garrison mutinied, this time marching off for the Honduran border with Levonski and another officer as prisoners. Loyal guardsmen freed them from the column and with them reached safety. Again, in 1930, two Guardia officers were murdered; however, these incidents were exceptions to the rule.

Nature took a hand in Nicaraguan troubles next year. On March 31, 1931, an earthquake wracked the capital city of Managua, causing heavy casualties; more than a thousand persons were killed. The Marine occupation force, now under Brigadier General F. L. Bradman, promptly assumed control, assisting the Guardia to enforce martial law, and prevent looting, while first-aid and emergency food centers were set up.

With heavy political pressure mounting at home for the withdrawal of the Marines, and Latin American propaganda campaigns blaming "*yanqui* imperialism" for Nicaragua's ills, President Hoover now determined to get the Marines out as soon as the general elections of 1932 were safely over.

Sandino, his banditti slowly beaten back into the northeastern mountain Honduran border, had disappeared in early 1931, only to come back once more as the pre-election activities waxed during the autumn of that year. President Moncada took the field in person, with government troops, and as the fighting stiffened "Chesty" Puller once more rocketed in.

Puller had been engaged in heavy fighting, out of Jinotega, in the province of that name, situated in the north-central area of Nicaragua, some eighty miles northeast of León. President Moncada's train, moving up an extension of the coastal railway from León, came into Puller's territory. The bush telegraph rumored that Sandino himself would blast the new line to atoms, and Moncada with it.

"Chesty," with seven marines and sixty-four of the Guardia, took personal charge of the chief executive's train as it moved to the end of construction, nor far from El Source, forty miles west of Jinotega. One of Sandino's lieutenants, a bandit named Juan Umanzor, had chosen that time to attack the construction camp and the train chugged in to meet a burst of machine gun fire.

Puller's detachment came boiling out of their cars and a ninety-minute fire fight followed, terminated when a detachment of the Guardia outflanked the outlaws, and Umanzor's mob fled, leaving thirty of their dead behind them.

Shortly after this Sandino once more faded away across the Honduran border. On January 1, 1933, Dr. Juan Sacasa was sworn in as President, and his nephew Anastasio (Tacho) Somoza assumed the command of the Guardia Nacional, whose officer corps was now entirely Nicaraguan, the Marine Corps officers having all returned to Managua. The organization was now 2650 men strong, Marine-trained, and complete with medical and legal departments, a military academy, and a communications system linking all its stations.

The Marines were ready to leave. Since the beginning of this intervention the Corps had engaged in some 150 clashes and had lost thirty-two men killed in action while fifteen more died of wounds. Accidental deaths, including air crashes, totaled forty-one, and twenty-four more leathernecks had died of other causes. The Guardia Nacional while under Marine leadership had approximately 510 engagements, with losses of about two hundred men killed or wounded. Rebel losses approximated more than a thousand.

Before the year had ended all marines had left the country. The last bayonet of American "gunboat diplomacy" had been sheathed.

There is a postscript to this. "Tacho" Somoza, with the Marine-trained Guardia Nacional his instrumentality, not long afterward assumed the presidency of Nicaragua, to become a dictator. But before that he had accomplished by treachery what the United States Marines had been unable to do in battle.

Sandino was lured into governmental clutches in Managua and assassinated by members of the Guardia in February 1934.

All this is another story. What we are interested in is what was accomplished by the intervention of 1927. In the broadest sense, it foiled the first attempt of Communism to infiltrate Latin America. From the military viewpoint, the intervention furnished a most valuable blueprint in the isolation of the guerrilla. But it did more than that, for from its operations developed the doctrine of air-ground close support for combat, supply, and evacuation, as well as the theory of small-unit fire power—groups of riflemen utilizing fire and movement around a machine gun base.

7

Interventions in Russia, 1918-1920

Here we sit in a branchy row,
Thinking of beautiful things we know;
Dreaming of deeds that we mean to do,
All complete, in a minute or two—
Something noble and grand and good,
Won by merely wishing we could.
Now we're going to—never mind,
Brother, thy tail hangs down behind!
—*"Road-Song of the Bander-Log" by Rudyard Kipling*

Prologue

The Treaty of Brest-Litovsk, March 3, 1918, ending hostilities between revolution-wracked Russia and the Central Powers, dissolved World War I's Eastern Front, and triggered off two simultaneous side shows. Allied forces invaded both North Russia and Siberia. President Wilson permitted American participation. The North Russian adventure, which should never have occurred, was a futile tragedy; the Siberian expedition might be termed, insofar as United States objectives were concerned, a limited success—very limited, indeed.

As one historian has summed up the entire mess: "Never, surely, in the history of American diplomacy has so much been paid for so little."[1]

[1] George F. Kennan, *The Decision to Intervene,* Princeton University Press, Princeton, N.J., 1958, *q.v.* for the best and most detailed exposition of the amazingly complicated background of our Russian undertaking. See also R. Ernest Dupuy, *Perish by the Sword,* Military Service Publishing Co., Harrisburg, Pa., 1939, for a military analysis of operations in both North Russia and Siberia.

The cold fact was that Allied diplomats sold Mr. Wilson a bill of goods in order to bring the United States militarily into the effort to reestablish an Eastern Front.

It was argued in Allied chancellories and in the Supreme War Council that (a) vast quantities of munitions shipped to the aid of Imperial Russia still rested in depots there and must be preserved from falling into German hands; (b) that ice-free Murmansk must not become a German submarine base; (c) that given help, the restoration of the empire or at least a pro-Ally government was feasible; and (d) that Allied action was necessary to ensure that forty thousand or more well-trained Czechoslovakian troops now trying to get out of Russia get back to their homeland.

The fate of these Czechs had indeed attracted much attention, particularly in the United States, instrumental in obtaining recognition of a Czechoslovakian nation freed from Austro-Hungarian vassalage. Deserters from the Austro-Hungarian armies for the most part, these Czechs had long been fighting for Russia. Now they wanted nothing to do with Bolshevism, but demanded free transit to the west to take up the cudgels for their country—and for the Allies. Their proposed route was via Archangel, whence they would be shipped around to Western Europe, and the Bolshevik government had at first put no obstacles in their way. The German-Bolshevik peace pact of Brest-Litovsk changed all that.

Mr. Wilson, at first definitely opposed to any armed intervention in Russian affairs, was dependent upon his diplomatic representatives in Russia for clear-cut, logical intelligence. What he did get, instead, was both faulty and biased. As a result, on July 17, in an *aide-mémoire* drafted on his own typewriter, the President, gingerly surrendering to the Allied pressure, laid down the rigidly limited conditions under which American military intervention in Russia would be sanctioned. This document, handed at once to Allied embassies in Washington, became later the one and only directive for our military commanders.

Its basic points must be noted:

> . . . It is the clear and fixed judgment of the Government of the United States . . . that military intervention there would add to the present sad confusion in Russia rather than cure it, injure her rather than help her, and that it would be of no advantage in the prosecution of our main design, to win the war against Germany. . . . Military action is admissible in Russia . . . only to help the Czecho-Slovaks consolidate their forces and get into successful cooperation with their Slavic kinsmen and to steady any efforts at self-government or self-defense in which the Russians themselves may be willing to accept assistance. Whether from Vladivostok or from Murmansk and Archangel, the only legitimate object for which American or Allied troops can be employed . . . is to guard military stores which may subsequently be needed *by Russian forces* [italics supplied] and to render such aid as may be acceptable to the Russians in the organization of their own self-defense. For helping the Czecho-Slovaks there is immediate necessity and sufficient justification. Recent developments have made it evident that that is in the interest of what the Russian people themselves desire, and the Government of the United States is glad to contribute the small force at its disposal for that purpose. . . .

The *aide-mémoire* then stressed that the United States had no desire to interfere in the actions or policies of the other Allied governments, but hoped that they would unite in assuring the Russian people that no "interference of any kind with the sovereignty of Russia, intervention in internal affairs or any impairment of her territorial integrity" was contemplated. The only complaint from the Allies to the dictum came from Japan, who read in it—correctly—opposition to her designs on the Asian mainland.[2]

In actuality, once American troops did arrive in North Russia and Siberia, Great Britain, France, and Japan bent every effort

[2] See *Foreign Relations, 1918, Russia,* Washington, D.C., 1931-1932, Vol. 2, pp. 287-290, for complete text of the *aide-mémoire*. It may also be found in Kennan, *op. cit.,* pp. 482-485.

to use them in furtherance of their own political objectives; objectives definitely at cross-purposes to Mr. Wilson's *aide-mémoire*. And shocking as it may seem, these Allied efforts were aided and abetted by representatives of our own State Department and by other American civilians officially on the scene.

In particular, David R. Francis, United States Ambassador to Imperial Russia, lived in a dreamworld of his own. Raymond Robins, chief of the American Red Cross Commission to Russia, brashly tried to usurp ambassadorial power—and nearly got away with it. Francis dreamed of restoring the Tsar's empire; Robins was convinced of the integrity of the Bolsheviks. Neither, it would appear, had the faintest concept either of the objectives or the latent power of the Bolshevik movement.

One young American diplomat alone, Felix Cole, Vice Consel at Archangel, saw the situation with remarkable clarity and warned against any military offensive. But his was a minor voice and went unheeded.

In the United States, War Secretary Newton D. Baker and Major General Peyton C. March, Army Chief of Staff, looked askance at the use of United States troops in Russia, but were overruled by the President. In France, General Pershing was too busy, it seems, to take much interest in side shows not under his command so long as they presented no appreciable diminution of his gathering strength in the American Expeditionary Force. Major General Tasker H. Bliss, Mr. Wilson's representative on the Allied Supreme War Council, appears to have been hoodwinked; at least, he put up no strong opposition.

Robert Lansing, Secretary of State, while attempting to uphold loyally the hands of his President, nevertheless supported his own subordinates in their attempts to hamper our military commanders in the field—particularly Major General William S. Graves in Siberia. Interesting is the remark of Secretary of War Newton D. Baker, later: "I cannot even guess at the explanation of the apparent conflict between the War Department and the State Department of the United States with regard to the Siberian adventure, nor can I understand why the State Department undertook to convey its ideas on Siberian policy, as it seems occasionally to have done, directly to General Graves. Perhaps the State Department was more impressed than I was with some of the Allied views as to the desirability of cooperation beyond the scope of the *aide-mémoire.*"

In August 1918, when American troops first set foot on Russian soil, the situation had become one of frenzied frustration. On the ruins of Imperial Russia, the Bolsheviks had erected a new political scaffolding, still flimsy, and strained by counterrevolutions. The Allies, catching their breath as the last of the Ludendorff offensives faded in France, still hoped against hope to restore an Eastern Front and relieve further pressure on the West.

Per contra, the Central Powers sought the grain of the Ukraine and the complete elimination of Russian military capability. German troops were on the move again in the East, and Finnish White Guards, German-led, were menacing the Murmansk peninsula.

The United States was pouring its tremendous manpower into France. Japan was watchfully waiting for opportunity to grasp Manchuria and the Maritime Province of Siberia. Allied forces had already been landed in small strength in North Russia and Siberia, with the grudging assent of the Bolsheviks; an assent soon withdrawn.

In the midst of the commotion the Czech Legion was now spread out along the trans-Siberian Railway from the Urals to Vladivostok, combatting both German and Bolshevik forces. Actually, this force, postponing its journey home, was becoming nucleus, with Allied blessing and guidance, for a great White Russian counterrevolution based in Siberia.

In short, the objectives laid down in Mr. Wilson's *aide-mémoire* no longer existed. The Czech Legion, over whose fate both Mr. Wilson and the American people worried, needed no help; the accumulation of military matériel and supplies in Russian ports had already been liquidated by the Bolsheviks. Only the presidential prohibition of interference in Russian internal affairs remained. This prohibition was clear-cut on its face, but our commanders in the field, like Alice in Wonderland, found that things became "curiouser and curiouser" when dumped into the Allied-Russian maelstrom. In North Russia the *aide-mémoire* would become but a scrap of paper. In Siberia, thanks to forceful, stubborn, and loyal American leadership, its principles were preserved, as we shall see.

North Russia, 1918-1919

On September 4, 1918, the British transports *Somali*, *Tydeus*, and *Nagoya* arrived in Archangel harbor, to debark the 339th Infantry Regiment, 1st Battalion, 310th Engineers, 337th Field Hospital, and 337th Ambulance Company, all detached from the U.S. 85th Division, lately arrived in England. These were National Army troops, drafted from Wisconsin and Michigan. Lieutenant Colonel (shortly to become Colonel) George Evans Stewart, a Regular, commanded. The global strength of the little force, when swelled shortly by some five hundred reinforcements from the 85th Division, was 162 officers and 4946 men.

These troops were not in a particularly happy mood. They had been drafted, they thought, to fight Germans; not to be thrust into some mysterious adventure in the Arctic under British command. The British had seen to it—on the mythical premise that enormous quantities of Russian ammunition still remained stored in Archangel—that the small arms and machine guns these men had trained on were stripped from them, and Russian-type ordnance substituted: long, clumsy Russian "three-ligne" rifles, whose range scales were marked not in yards but in paces. They were to have, also, both Lewis and Colt machine guns of Russian type, air-cooled. Instead, they had been furnished with Vickers water-cooled guns chambered for Russian ammunition. Would these guns freeze in Arctic temperature? (They would, indeed.)

Winter clothing, also of British issue, was in the form of the British "Shackleton kit," so-called; articles based on the recommendations of the famed British Arctic explorer of that name. There seems to have been grave doubt as to the efficacy of this clothing, when compared to the American Alaskan winter issue.

Worse still, from the viewpoint of the American doughboys, was the fact that they had been put on British rations when in camp at Aldershot, with lime juice substituting for fresh vege-

NORTH RUSSIA
0 20 40 60 80 100
MILES
Road
Archangel-Vologda RR
DVINA GULF
ONEGA GULF
Pinega
Archangel
Isakagorka
Butinskaya
Koskogurskuga
Pinega R.
Onega
Kholmogorskaya
Onega R.
Siskue
Chunovskaya
Chekuevo
Obozer-skaya
Yemetskoe
Kaska
Bolchie Ozerkie
Selet-skoye
Prilutskoe
Yemtsa
Yemtsa R.
Kodish
Dvina R.
Tarasovo
Mekrenga R.
Plesetskaya
Beresniki
Chamova
Toulgas
Zastrova
Kitskaya
Lipovets
Petrupavlovski
Shenkursk
Ust Padenga
Vaga R.
Ust-Puskoi

tables, and tea for coffee. Now, as they at once found out, they would have more of the same.

Colonel Stewart, reporting on arrival to British Major General Frederick C. Poole, G.O.C. Archangel, found an amazing situation, in which, it appeared, he would be but a figurehead. Two of his battalions were marked for field duty under British command—this was a British show—while he and the remainder would stay in Archangel, now in the throes of an anti-Bolshevik coup engineered by Poole.

The small Allied forces in North Russia, at Murmansk and Archangel, Stewart learned, were not only already in active conflict with Bolshevik forces, but Poole was about to launch an offensive move through the heart of the country to meet the Czechs, then at Ekaterinburg (now Sverdlovsk) in the Urals.

This grandiose scheme was the brain child of two young assistant military attachés in the foreign diplomatic corps accredited to Imperial Russia and now nestled in Archangel under Allied shelter. American Major E. Francis Riggs and French Commandant Lelong had recommended an Allied offensive based on Archangel and amounting to fifteen battalions of infantry and five of field artillery—approximately fifteen thousand men and sixty guns. Poole, approving, had sent them to lay the scheme before the Supreme Allied War Council (it would be turned down September 27) and meanwhile was about to start his move with the forces now available. In sum, he proposed to accomplish with a handful of troops what Napoleon with a *Grande Armée* of 360,000 men and hundreds of guns could not do.

Poole's was a force remarkable for neither its strength nor its components. There was British infantry in the approximate strength of one wartime American battalion—detachments from the Royal Scots, King's Liverpool, Durham Light Infantry, and Green Howards; but most of the men were classified as unfit for combat on the Western Front. There was a battalion of French colonial infantry, trained for tropical service; a detachment of French field artillery and machine guns, and a rag, tag, and bobtail assortment of White Russians, Poles, Lithuanians, Finns, Estonians, and some Chinese, about four thousand strong and mostly unreliable. Half of this last melting-pot assortment was organized into an Anglo-Slav Legion, British-led. But Poole did have the 16th Brigade (battalion), Royal Canadian Field Artillery, two splendid batteries of tough, hardfisted fighting veterans, and a mixed detachment (twenty-five men) of blue-jackets and marines from the United States cruiser *Olympia*. Several river steamers, partly armored, were manned by heterogeneous crews, supplemented by British tars and *Olympia* blue-jackets. There was also an armored train, carrying one 77-mm. and one 155-mm. gun.

And now Poole had the reinforced U.S. 339th Infantry, which he proceeded to break up into detachments, spearheading his fantastic multiple-pronged offensive. All in all, subtracting a strong garrison at Archangel—a necessity even if a seemingly sympathetic anti-Bolshevik local government remained—Poole could dispose of perhaps eleven thousand men of widely varying capabilities, training, and loyalties for his venture.

The task was to penetrate a desolate countryside, sparsely populated and incapable of supporting the expedition. It was a wilderness of coniferous forests, dotted with bogs and lakes. Through it, straight south, cut a single-track railroad from Archangel to Vologda on the trans-Siberian line, some 330 miles away.

East of the railroad flowed the broad Dvina River, which empties into the White Sea at Archangel, after meandering generally northwest from Kotlas, 220 miles south in central Russia. The Dvina was open to navigation only between May and November. Into it drained the Yemtsa and Vaga rivers from the west and the Penega, far north, from the east; all also navigable only during the ice-free season.

West of the railroad the Onega River, generally paralleling it, swerved sharply to empty into the Gulf of Onega at the town of the same name, about one hundred miles west of Archangel. Onega was important in that through it ran the only trail linking Archangel by land with Murmansk to the northwest, where British Major General Charles C. W. Maynard, with a small but efficient expedition, had organized a Russo-British groupment. He had cleared German-Finnish White Guards from the Murmansk-Petrograd railroad and eliminated any threat to establish a German submarine base on the peninsula.

General Poole's knowledge of the enemy was vague and inaccurate. Actually there were by this time some twenty-thousand-odd Red Guards loosely ringing the Archangel area and also Murmansk. This force was gathering strength; Leon Trotsky, then engaged in the colossal task of building a Red Army, would soon give the area his personal attention. All Poole knew, in essence, was that there were Bolshevik forces there. He had already received a bloody nose when he sent a composite force—one hundred French troops; twenty-five bluejackets from USS *Olympia*, commanded by an Ensign Hicks; and some fifty White Russians, all under command of a British Colonel Hazelton—to outflank a Bolshevik detachment at Obozerskaya, seventy miles south of Archangel on the railroad. On September 2 the detachment, called "B" Force, was ambushed and driven in disorder into the woods; the survivors turned up a week later.

On the assumption that the Czechs were able to move west along the trans-Siberian Railway from Ekaterinburg to Viatka (now Kirov), there were alternative routes for Poole's offensive; the rail line to Vologda, the Dvina River line to Kotlas, thence a rail line to Viatka.

Neither of these routes would present serious logistical problems, given a temperate climate and no opposition. But this was war-torn North Russia in September, and the Dvina would be open for but two more scant months. After that, Arctic winter would close the river; sleighs, horse- or reindeer-drawn, over frozen apologies for roads would be the only means of transportation, while Archangel itself would be sealed tight from the sea by ice. And to make matters worse, Poole had split his forces between the rail and river lines.

"A" Force on the right moved down the Vologda rail line, with a side show on the Onega-Murmansk trail; "B" Force had already been eliminated at Obozerskaya; "C" Force was on the Dvina-Vaga River line while "D" Force, up the Yemtsa River, was apparently to provide interior flank protection to both "A" and "C" forces. Spearheading each of these thrusts were elements of the U.S. 339th Infantry team. Colonel Stewart was left in Archangel, with regimental headquarters, supply, most of the 2nd Battalion (Major J. Brooks Nichols), and some five hundred cases of flu. Northeast of Archangel, another mongrel element, labeled Pinega Force, constituted a wide-flung flank protection to Archangel; several detachments of 339th Infantry troops served here from time to time.

On the Onega flank of "A" Force, commanded by a British Colonel Sutherland, H Co., 339th, with detachments of White Russians and Cossacks, occupied Chekuevo on the Murmansk trail line September 15; it was then hit by two successive Bolshevik attacks. Repulsing them, it pushed ten miles upriver to Kaska, where it was pinned down by additional Bolo forces. The White Russians on the west bank, commanded by a Captain Barton, Royal Marines, fled, but Barton, and two squads of H Company, cut their way back. The remainder of the American company, on the east bank, finally extricated themselves and fell back on Chekuevo. On October 19 the Bolos at Kaska withdrew, and H Company began probing south upriver.

Along the railway at Obozerskaya the main body of "A" Force, a French Colonel Lucas commanding, included the 3rd Battalion, 339th, with machine gun and trench mortar detachments, under Major C. G. Young. Bolo attacks on September 11 and 16 were driven off, but a Bolo armored train kept up continued harassing fire. On September 28 the Americans attacked, in conjunction with a detachment of French Colonial Infantry. I and M companies with the light weapons detachments drove south while K and L, under Captain Michael Donoghue, attempted a flanking movement from the east. Faulty reconnaissance and, it was alleged, the blundering of Colonel Sutherland, brought the flanking force up against an impassable swamp, while both holding force and flankers were pinned down by enemy fire from three sides. At nightfall I and M companies and the small French component fell back on Obozerskaya.

It was all a very nasty, discouraging mess, as are all complicated movements with green troops. Donoghue's two-company flanking force, cut off, wandered twenty miles east to Yemetskoe on the Dvina, 110 miles from Archangel, where they joined with "D" Force, commanded by British Colonel Knowles. K Company was put on outpost duty a few miles up the Yemtsa, at Seletskoe. On September 14 a Bolshevik attack in force drove in the outpost—K Company, a detachment of Royal Scots and Royal Marines. Reinforced by L Company, the force retook Seletskoe and attacked a Bolo strongpoint at Kodish, fifteen miles upriver. Repulsed at first, a second attack, led by Donoghue, on October 15 overran the Red position and dug in. An exasperating sidelight to all this was that neither of these two American companies ever received their barrack bags, so during all this fighting and marching they were without overcoats, extra shoes, and underwear. "Fighting Mike" Donoghue's report on this British laxness is a gem of mixed metaphors and Hibernian bitterness.

Over on the railroad, meanwhile, the remainder of "A" Force, Companies I and M, on October 14 moved out of its entrenched position in an attempt to nab a Bolo armored train whose fire had been particularly harassing. A flanking attempt by a demolition detachment of the 310th Engineers attempted to blow up a railway bridge behind the enemy train but failed to reach it in time. However, the main attack under Major J. Brooks Nichols (succeeding Young) drove down the line for some twenty miles. Then the force dug in, at Verst 444 on October 17.

Over on the Dvina all this while, "C" Force, commanded by British Colonel John Josselyn, and including the entire 1st Battalion, 339th, Lieutenant Colonel John B. Corbly commanding, was steeped in an active amphibious campaign launched from Beresniki, confluence with the Vaga. Corbly's men, in barges, had been towed from Archangel by side-wheel steamers of the Allied flotilla, commanded by Captain Altham, RN.

At Beresniki the Americans were split into small detachments, and Corbly was relegated to a fifth-wheel status. While the flotilla skirmished with and dominated Bolo flotillas on both rivers, the troops pushed along.

On the Vaga, Captain Otto A. Odjard, piling his Company A—some two hundred strong—on the side-wheel steamer *Tolstoy* went paddling upriver to capture, on September 18, without a shot, Shenkursk, one of the few populated towns in the area. Shenkursk, two hundred miles from Archangel, strategically situated on a high bluff, had been a highly popular summer resort. Its Bolo garrison had now fled, and its people received the Americans with acclaim.

Odjard, not content, broke off communications and pushed boldly upriver for an additional fifty miles, pointing for Kotlas, before Bolshevik opposition stiffened. By the end of the first week in October, Odjard's little band was in the village of Puya. A large detachment of Soviet troops blocked their advance, and scouting reports indicated that another detachment had closed in behind the American force, blocking their retreat down the river. Odjard decided to attack southward against the main Russian group and, with a good deal of luck, his audacity paid off. In the attack about fifty of the enemy were killed as compared to three wounded for the Yanks. Also, at the same time the Bolshevik detachment which was cutting off the retreat route interpreted the attack as a prelude to heavy American reinforcements from Shenkursk and withdrew into the forest. The Allied force quickly moved back from the river to Ust Padenga, thirty miles from Shenkursk, which offered good cover and an advantageous position for holding off counterattacks.

Odjard didn't know it at the time, but his audacious thrust had made the deepest penetration of the entire expedition. We shall hear more of this fighting Norseman.

Up the Dvina, all this while, action was very heavy both on land and water. Altham's flotilla sunk four Bolo steamers and captured many prisoners, while B Company and a detachment of Royal Scots stormed in succession the villages of Chamova, Toulgas, Zastrova, and Lipovets. A White Russian field battery gave strong support.

Later, a determined Bolo counterattack, supported by gunboats, resulted in a night evacuation, October 4, and "C" Force recoiled to Toulgas, which would become a strongpoint.

Meanwhile, on the Vaga, most of the remainder of the 1st Battalion, 339th. had consolidated positions at Shenkursk behind A Company. D Company fanned out to the west along the Yemtsa in an attempt to link with "A" Force on the railway;

one of its platoons became lost, joined up with a White Russian detachment and was not reunited with the company for more than a month.

Came November and winter snows; ice was forming in the rivers. Poole's offensive came to a grinding halt, while the 310th Engineers worked like mad to put up log blockhouses and string barbed wire on all parts of the front.

On the Dvina, B Company, Captain Robert Boyd, was at Toulgas; on the Vaga, A and C companies at Ust Padenga and Shenkursk. K and L companies were clinging to Kodish on the Yemtsa. On the railway, where the bulk of the 3rd Battalion was located, Verst 444 had been fortified, while over on the Onega, H Company was at Prelutskoe and patrolling the Murmansk trail between Bolchie Ozerkie and the railroad.

Someone higher up had begun to realize that the problem in North Russia was now not how to make contact with the Czechs but how to avert complete disaster. So on November 8 in came Major General Sir William Edmond Ironside, a six-foot-four specimen of competent, fighting British soldier, to relieve Poole and pick up the pieces. Ironside at once announced a complete reversal of policy; the Archangel force would go on the defensive.

It was about time that, as Captain J. C. Hall, Medical Reserve Corps, reported to Colonel Stewart on October 21, "an efficient Hell-raiser" take charge of the expedition. The American soldiers had no socks, shoes were gone, and tea leaves, straw, hay, and moss were substituting for tobacco. Under Ironside's pressure coffee was added to the American ration; supply speeded up, despite the difficulties of snowbound trails; new British field commanders came in; Brigadier General R. G. Finlayson, Poole's chief of staff, relieving Josselyn on the Dvina front, and Brigadier General Graham commanding on the Vaga.

Came November 11 and the Armistice. World War I had ended. But the North Russian war was about to move on to greater intensity. For Trotsky had completed formation of his 6th Army—34,700 strong, with ninety-four field guns and 378 machine guns, and was on the way from Moscow to lead them against the invaders. The first inkling came on Armistice Day itself.

On the Dvina at Toulgas came a storm of fire from Bolo artillery and small arms as gray-coated Bolos charged the settlement in complete surprise. Over on the river, enemy gunboats crept through the still-fragile ice to add to the fire falling on B Company, 339th, a company of Royal Scots and one section of Canadian field artillery (one gun).

It turned out to be a four-day assault, with the Bolsheviks braving the defenders' fire time and time again. Fortunately there was plenty of ammunition and Yank and Scot doughboys kept mowing them down, while the one Canadian gun spewed shrapnel fuzed to muzzle burst. Once a group crashed through, led by a black-bearded giant who stormed into the dressing station, shouting that he would kill the wounded. But a quick-witted corpsman shoved a jug of rum before him and the giant stopped to drink, and a slim boyish companion, pleading with him to spare the wounded, coaxed him back into the fighting.

The giant, whose name it seems was Melochovski, received a mortal wound. His companion dragged him back to the dressing station and when he died *she* stayed and nursed the Allied wounded. "The Lady Olga" they called her in the official report.

The seemingly hopeless situation was corrected by a daring dawn counterattack on November 14. Lieutenant John Cudahy,[3] B Company, led a platoon into the snow-packed woods and jumped the sleepy enemy. A log building overrun turned out to be an ammunition dump which, promptly set afire, exploded to create panic in the Bolo ranks. Some thirty prisoners were taken, while the remainder of the enemy force disintegrated. The garrison had lost twenty-eight killed and seventy wounded, but some three hundred dead Bolos were scattered in the snow. For the time being Toulgas was safe; but not for long.

All along the North Russian front now came a month of quiet before the storm; chilling monotony, with men huddling in their hovels, wondering why they could not go home; growl-

Cudahy, surviving the campaign, later wrote an impassioned book about it: *Archangel: The American War with Russia.* (A.C. McClu g & Co., Chicago, 1924). Later still, he would become in turn United States Ambassador to Poland (1933), Minister to Eire (1937), and Ambassador to Belgium (1939). In this last post Cudahy would witness war again, on another scale and in a far different setting.

ing as they sat in the flickering of their only light—rags floating on bacon grease in bully-beef cans. They froze on lonely vigils. Patrols were sniped at in the woods, and timber wolves nosed along barbed-wire entanglements. One day, some of B Company's soreheads on the Dvina actually threatened to strike; they were civilians in spirit still, it seems, despite their growing combat ability. Cooler heads disabused them, but much would be made of this back home as well as of a later attempt to "strike" at Archangel.

On the Yemtsa River front, where E and L companies, 339th, had entrenched themselves December 31 at Kodish after a stubborn fight, the Bolo offensive struck early, but without too much force. They Americans were forced back to Seletskoe, where they anchored themselves, and the Bolos had neither the strength nor the will to force the issue further.

Instead, on the Yemtsa River bridge carrying the road between Seletskoe and Yemetskoe, Red speechmakers from their outposts bombarded the air nightly with propaganda in English. Donoghue's men listened and cheered derisively, punctuating their protest at particularly boring passages by taking potshots at the unseen speakers. Nobody was hurt, it seems, but it was a diversion which the Yanks welcomed. Not everyone in the expeditionary force was so lucky.

Then, in January, at Toulgas on the Dvina, came another attack and another repulse. In February an elite Bolo outfit, the 82nd Tarasovo Regiment, came piling up to the barbed wire. They wore white smocks, they had wire cutters. Some got through, but died. The remainder, checked by the wire, were caught by the garrison's sortie and they too died. And that was the last big fight at Toulgas, though not until the spring came and the ice went out would the boats come up the Dvina and bring B Company back to Archangel.

Over on the far right flank, along the Onega, we left H Company, 339th, with British and Polish detachments, pushing slowly south from Kaska, despite the winter weather. They got as far as Prilutskoe, 40 miles beyond Chekuevo, where the Murmansk trail from the east met the river, on December 31. On New Year's Day, while consolidating the position, a hurried message from C.O. "A" Force ordered evacuation within two hours.

Actually Trotsky's 6th Army was moving in to cut communication between Murmansk and Archangel. H Company, leaving its impedimenta behind, escaped annihilation by a narrow margin; Bolo advance elements harried the retreat back to Chekuevo.

The Bolsheviks made no further move on this front until March 16, when freezing temperatures hardened the wide marshy area between the railroad and the Onega. A Bolo detachment cut the Murmansk trail west of Bolchie Ozerkie, preventing the return of an H Company patrol—a corporal and five men—from Chekuevo.

A thirty-man detachment of H Company, under Lieutenant Collins, with a Lewis gun and four days' rations, went hunting for the patrol, picking up the commander of "A" Force, French Colonel Lucas, on the trail. Lucas ordered Collins to escort him back to his headquarters at Obozerskaya on the railroad. Just west of Bolchie Ozerkie the detachment was ambushed; horses bolted under heavy machine gun fire and sleighs upset. Fortunately the fire was too high and Collins and his men wriggled away in the snow, to take cover in a hamlet, while Colonel Lucas, his dignity upset and one hand frozen, caught one of the sleighs and scurried west to Chekuevo.

By one of the coincidences that sometimes mean the difference between life or death, a three-company detachment of the Green Howards—6th Yorks—pounding east from Murmansk to reinforce Ironside's "A" Force, popped out of the woods into Collins' perimeter. Major Mundy, commanding the Britishers, combined with the Americans, who were also reinforced by a half-platoon of H Company, and the joint command moved on Bolchie Ozerkie.

What they didn't know was that Trotsky's 6th Army was knocking at "A" Force, assaulting straight down the railroad. The American thrust was parried, Collins was mortally wounded. They tried again on April 1, this time reinforced by the rest of H Company, under Captain Richard W. Ballaesinger, and a Polish battalion.

But the Poles refused to join the firing line, unlimbering their machine guns to open a long-range, useless fire over the heads of the Americans. Then a cry that the enemy had broken through in rear brought a mass Polish stampede which Ballaesinger, despite his drawn pistol, was unable to check. An enemy counter-attack was blocked by Lieutenant Philips' platoon of H Company and a company of the Yorks, while the main body rallied and the medical detachment snaked out the wounded to the sleigh park. Then came a fighting retreat back to the Onega. The Murmansk trail was cut for good.

Meanwhile Bolchie Ozerkie itself—fortified by a complex of blockhouses—was the scene of heavy fighting. E and M companies, 339th, with detachments of White Russians, Poles, and Yorks were assaulted there March 31. Three battalions of the Bolo 2nd Moscow Regiment crunched past the right and attempted to turn the rear. But two White Russian three-inch guns softened them up and the Americans pushed them back.

Next day the Bolos tried again, this time with the 97th Saratov and Kazan regiments heading the assault. The village itself was occupied but the blockhouse line held. Beaten back from Blockhouse No. 1 by M Company's fourth platoon and a handful of Yorks, they made another try April 2, but were again repulsed; M Company's second platoon taking the brunt of this assault. Then the Bolo offensive gradually died away. On April 18 the enemy evacuated Bolchie Ozerkie. There would be no further Bolo assaults along the railroad line.

Meanwhile the Vaga River front had been the scene of the most extensive and most complicated swirl of fire and movement of the entire campaign. British Brigadier General Graham's command at Shenkursk and its outpost at Ust Padenga consisted of Companies A and C, 339th, a detachment of the 310th Engineers and detachments of British infantry, Canadian field artillery, and units of the Anglo-Slav Legion—in all some two thousand men.

The outpost at Ust Padenga, as we know, was garrisoned by Odjard's A Company. Odjard held the fortified village with the bulk of his command, while entrenched on a bluff-fronted hillock to the south, called Nijni Gora, was Lieutenant Harry J. Mead's forty-seven-man platoon.

The Bolo assault struck Nijni Gora in broad daylight on January 19—a wave of infantry that almost engulfed it. Mead and five of his men cut their way out and Odjard led a rescue party to aid the wounded doughboys sprawling in the snow. Not only was he able to rescue all fifteen of the wounded but—wonder of wonders—the Bolshevik fire ceased until the last man had been dragged away; a very gallant and courteous gesture. Then the assault moved down on Ust Padenga and its chain of log blockhouses.

Four days of fighting followed. Then the Bolos brought up artillery over the hard-packed snow and incendiary shells began falling. On orders from Graham, Odjard pulled out in a quick withdrawal before the entire village flamed, and the survivors of A Company, heads up and still full of fight, reached Shenkursk's shelter forty-eight hours later. Odjard had lost ten men dead and seventeen more missing in his defense.[4]

While the Bolos surrounded Shenkursk and began to open fire from several field batteries and a group of heavy artillery—one nine-inch, two six-inch and four 4.7-inch pieces—Graham felt he could hold out indefinitely. He had almost two thousand men and thirteen guns, mostly eighteen-pounders, behind well-constructed blockhouses and entrenchments. Ammunition was plentiful and supply ample. But Ironside, at Archangel, thought differently, Peremptorily, by plane, he ordered immediate evacuation.

Graham received the order on January 24. His own order was issued at 10:30 PM the same day and at 1:30 AM the twenty-fifth—three hours later—the entire command was on the road, in —30° temperature.

Lady Luck divided her favors that night. The competent Graham was dependent on a Russian guide to detour around a Bolo company planted squarely on the river road, and the guide made good. The leading element, ninety-eight sick or wounded men, tucked in horse-drawn sledges and convoyed by the detachment of the 310th Engineers, got safely past and then the rest of the column pushed behind them.

But canny Graham's flanking screen, a detachment of the

[4] All the missing men, whose bodies were later recovered, had been killed in action or froze to death after being wounded.

Anglo-Slav Legion, failed him. They panicked or deserted, or both, *en masse*, warning the Bolos, who took up immediate pursuit. However, the pursuit was never serious, though all the artillery had to be tumbled into the snow to keep the column moving. Not one of the sick and wounded was lost and casualties in rearguard actions were few. D Company, 339th, came up from Beresniki to assist the sleepless troops and in forty-eight hours Graham's command had reached Kitskaya, where they stood until spring, despite two serious Bolo attacks, March 5 and 9. These were repelled, but necessitated the withdrawal of the outpost at Vistafka. In this fighting A Company, 339th, apparently took the brunt of the assaults.

The winter dragged on, with gloomy outlook for all the Allied troops in North Russia. General Ironside, well aware that he faced a possible second Gallipoli, strained every effort at building up a White Russian force which could take care of itself should Allied evacuation be ordered. He also did his best for his commands in the field, certainly gained the admiration of every American soldier by his frequent informal but thorough field visits.

It wasn't enough. As Ironside would later write: ". . . We were drawing terribly near the end of our tether as an efficient fighting force."

The dry rot of falling morale had infected Russians, French, and British. The Slavo-British Legion, in Archangel, pulled and tugged both by Bolshevik propaganda and the ineptness of the local White Russian government, revolted December 11; the mutiny was quelled by Headquarters Company, 339th, with two rounds of mortar shells. A battalion of the Yorks, lately arrived, when ordered to march from their billets at Seletskoe, February 26, to take over the Kodish front, refused to turn out. The prompt, efficient leadership of their commander saved the situation. Their spokesmen, two sergeants, were arrested and the battalion moved out obediently next day.

Wild rumors of the British mutiny reached French troops at Archangel, marked for a move to the railroad front to relieve American elements. They, too, refused to march, even when Ironside himself came to their barracks on the run. French marines from a cruiser in harbor settled that; recalcitrant leaders were hurried away, and the French turned to again.

Then came the Americans' turn. I Company, 339th, resting in Archangel, grumbled when ordered back to the front. It was only a murmur, and it ended when a forceful lieutenant ordered the men to load the waiting sleds. But Colonel Stewart read them a lecture, then asked for questions, which came with startling unanimity: "Why are we here?" Stewart had the sense to say bluntly that he didn't know himself, but if they wouldn't fight to protect themselves, they might all be wiped out. That made sense. Next day I Company was on the front.

Unfortunately, news of this episode reaching the United States was exaggerated, to add to the uproar now rising at home.

To unprejudiced eyes it had become evident that this entire North Russia intervention was a dismal failure. Yet both the Peace Commission in Paris and the Allied Supreme War Council closed their ears. They heeded neither the cackling of Ambassador Francis, now on leave, for a 150,000-man Allied army to sweep into Russia, occupy Petrograd and Moscow, and erase the Bolsheviks, nor Mr. Churchill's somewhat oblique arguments along the same lines. But the War Council couldn't bring themselves to a clean break-away.

There was no denying the facts. The Bolshevik position had solidified throughout Russia, despite counterrevolution. In Siberia the Kolchak insurrection, at first promising, was beginning to wane. In the United States public opinion took the bit in its teeth. In Wisconsin and Michigan, whence the majority of the Americans in North Russia had been drafted, the home folks' demands that the troops come home were read by the administration loud and clear. Politicians fulminated in Senate and House. The war was over—Mr. Wilson's war to make democracy safe. Bring the boys home! The administration bowed.

The first step was to send out Brigadier General Wilds P. Richardson, Alaskan expert, to take command of the little American force. Richardson arrived in Archangel April 9, to find the city seething; Bolshevik influence was spreading and the White Russian local government tottering.

Between Ironside and Richardson a comprehensive schedule

was worked out; White Russian and British replacements began to move into the front-line defensive sectors and with the thawing of the rivers the Americans slowly withdrew to Archangel. By the end of May the American force was together once again—for the first time since the original debarkation. A Memorial Day parade, also participated in by Allied troops, was the last official formation of the American North Russian Expeditionary Force. The troops moved into British transports for the long trip home, via Brest; the last ship, bearing the 310th Engineers, clearing Archangel June 27, 1919.

How did they feel? Perhaps the remark of Lieutenant John Cudahy of the 339th best sums it up:

> When the last battalion set sail from Archangel, not a soldier knew, no, not even vaguely, why he had fought or why he was going now, and why his comrades were left behind—so many of them beneath the wooden crosses.[5]

A few statistics are in order. The expedition lost 109 men, four of them officers, killed in action; two officers and thirty-three men died of wounds, eight-one men died of disease, nineteen others as a result of accidents, for a total of 244. Wounded numbered 305, twelve of them officers. Four men were made prisoner (all returned).

Without making invidious comparison, it should be noted that Americans predominated other nationalities in each major combat formation in this campaign. The British were a not-so-close second.

Postscript

The end in North Russia followed close on the departure of the American North Russian Expedition. Ironside's efforts to produce an efficient White Russian force to replace the Allied troops as they were withdrawn failed. However, the White Rus-

[5] A Chronicler (John Cudahy), *Archangel: the American War with Russia,* (A. C. McClurg & Co., Chicago, 1924.

sian did not collapse until the Allied evacuation from both Archangel and Murmansk, a well-planned affair, was completed September 25, 1919. On February 21 the first Red troops entered Archangel and the dream of a revamped White Russia had ended.

What is sometimes forgotten, however, is that American troops unconnected with the Archangel force played an important part in assisting its evacuation: the North Russia Transportation Corps Expeditionary Force. In April 1919 the 167th (Operations) and 168th (Maintenance) companies, U.S. Railway Engineers, under Major Edward H. MacMorland, CAC, landed at Murmansk to join General Maynard's Murmansk force. This aggregation, 720 strong, were competent American railroad men, all volunteers.[6]

The efficient Maynard mounted a thrust down the Murmansk-Petrograd line to relieve pressure on the Archangel evacuation. The Americans repaired, reorganized, and maintained in combat the railroad from Soroka south to Petrozavosk, near Lake Onega,[7] only two hundred miles in air line from Petrograd. They were, in fact, the backbone of Maynard's successful operation. Their losses were but two men killed in action and two more wounded, in a series of minor engagements against the Bolo 7th Army, including operation of an armored train. On July 28 the railroad was turned over to the British and the Americans came home.

"Every man . . . ," writes General Maynard in his *The Murmansk Adventure*, "was a volunteer, full of enthusiasm and the love of adventure, and I pay ungrudging tribute to the excellent service they rendered."

[6] This was a detachment of the Russian Railway Service Corps, commanded by Colonel John F. Stevens. Composed of competent, trained American railroad men, all volunteers, it had been organized in 1917 at the request of the Kerensky regime to reorganize the war-torn Russian railway system. The Bolshevik revolution interrupted this scheme, and most of its personnel cooled their heels in Japan until the spring of 1919, when they took over supervision of the operation of the Trans-Siberian Railway.

[7] Despite the similarity of names, Lake Onega and the Onega River have no connection whatsoever.

Siberia, 1918 -1920

". . . Going to Siberia"

"You are going to Siberia. . . . This contains the policy of the United States in Russia, which you are to follow. Watch your step; you will be walking on eggs loaded with dynamite. God bless you and goodbye."

The speaker was Newton D. Baker, Secretary of War of the United States, and "this" was a sealed enveloped handed to Major General William S. Graves, USA, at the termination of a brief clandestine rendezvous in the railroad station at Kansas City, Missouri, on August 3, 1918.

Graves, at Camp Frémont, Palo Alto, California, had been summoned by a msteriously worded top secret War Department wire "to take the first train out of San Francisco and proceed to Kansas City" to meet the War Secretary.

Baker now stepped aboard his waiting Washington-bound train and Graves, going back to his hotel room, opened the envelope and began reading the Wilsonian *aide-mémoire.*[8]

In such fashion the newly made commander of the 8th Division, then preparing to embark for France, found that he would, instead, on the other side of the globe lead one of the most fantastic overseas operations even launched by the United States.

He would indeed walk on eggs loaded with dynamite. Before the task was completed his troops would clash with both Red and White Russians. His relations with the Japanese, maintained on a hair-trigger basis, constituted a magnificant example of what a later generation would call "brinkmanship." He would find himself at loggerheads with most Allied commanders on the scene and with representatives of the United States Department of State. He gained the enmity of Allied chiefs of state abroad. And through it all he was the target of slanderous whispering campaigns both in Siberia and the United States.

But imperturbable Graves, West Pointer of the Class of 1889,

[8] *Vide,* p. 171, *supra.*

adhering steadfastly to the role laid down in the *aide-mémoire*, accomplished his mission. He would satisfy his Commander in Chief, President Woodrow Wilson, and gain the admiration and support of both Newton D. Baker and the steely-eyed General Peyton C. March, Army Chief of Staff. March—when the going really got tough—would cable him: "Keep a stiff upper lip, I am going to stand by you until Hell freezes over."

The saga of the American Expeditionary Force in Siberia, then, is primarily one not of battle but of leadership. There were no major combats, although such skirmishes and armed bickerings as did occur were sanguinary; the fact that a round score of Distinguished Service Crosses were awarded for acts of individual heroism attests to that fact.

Siberia, in August 1918, from the Urals to the Pacific Ocean fermented in a mish-mash of revolution and counterrevolution.[9] In the west, White Russian forces nominally controlled by a rump government at Omsk, were battling the Red Guards of Bolshevism in the foothills of the Urals. The principal component of this White Russian force was the capable Czech Legion, three divisions strong and mustering now more than 65,000 men.

The White Russian army had but one line of communications: 3500 miles of thin rails—the Trans-Siberian Railway—threading from the front to the Pacific Ocean. Near Chita, five hundred miles east of Lake Baikal, the rail line branched. The Chinese Eastern Railway cut east through Harbin in Manchuria to debouch at Vladivostok, three hundred miles away. The main Trans-Siberian line followed the winding Amur River to Khabarovsk, then jutted south down the Ussuri Valley to Vladivostok, a stretch of twelve hundred miles in all.

Vladivostok—sole gateway to the Allied world—was the supply base for all White Russian operations and also headquarters for the Allied missions of Japan, France, Great Britain, China, and Italy, representatives of the Allied Supreme War Council in Europe. All these missions were actively and openly supporting the White Russian movement, but also wrangling and plotting among themselves in a conflict of diverse interests.

[9] See George Stewart, *The White Armies of Russia,* the Macmillan Co., New York, 1933, for a lucid military survey of the entire anti-Bolshevist counterrevolution.

Britain and France were definitely backing the Whites, hoping to reconstitute an Eastern Front against Germany. Their military forces were minimal—one infantry battalion each—but they were using the Czechs as pawns. Great Britain's Sir Charles N. E. Eliot, High Commissioner—he wore two hats, being also Britain's Ambassador to Japan—and Major General Alfred W. F. Knox, who had been his nation's representative on the old Imperial Russian General Staff, were ardently anti-Bolshevik. So, too, was French General Maurice Janin, who would soon take over, at Allied nod, nominal command of the Czech Legion.

Japan's General Kikuso Otani, senior Allied officer present, with an army of 74,000 men already in East Siberia, was playing another game. Japan's eventual objective was possession of Eastern Siberia; her policy, to keep both White Russians and Bolsheviks in a state of mutual weakness against future seizure. In consequence Otani, while giving lip service to the other Allies' support of the White Russian counterrevolution, was freely distributing Japanese gold to subvert White Russian commanders in East Siberia and they willingly danced to the strings he pulled.

We will have more to relate concerning these White Russian leaders. For the moment it is sufficient to say that the anti-Bolshevist counterrevolution had unfortunately attracted to its banners all that was evil of the old Imperial regime. These self-seeking autocratic individuals, unbelievably cruel to the marrow, would of themselves constitute the best recruiting agents the Bolsheviks could wish for; their sadistic excesses and atrocities were gradually turning the East Siberian peasantry from its original support of the White Russian cause.

> Systematic drives were made by the local White commanders . . . in guise of requisitioning supplies and contributions. The flimsy pretext that a Bolshevist unit had been operating in the vicinity of a village was sufficient. An armed party would march in, corral men, women and children and demand indemnity. The usual procedure was first to gather in the important persons of the community. If money and supplies were not instantly forthcoming, these

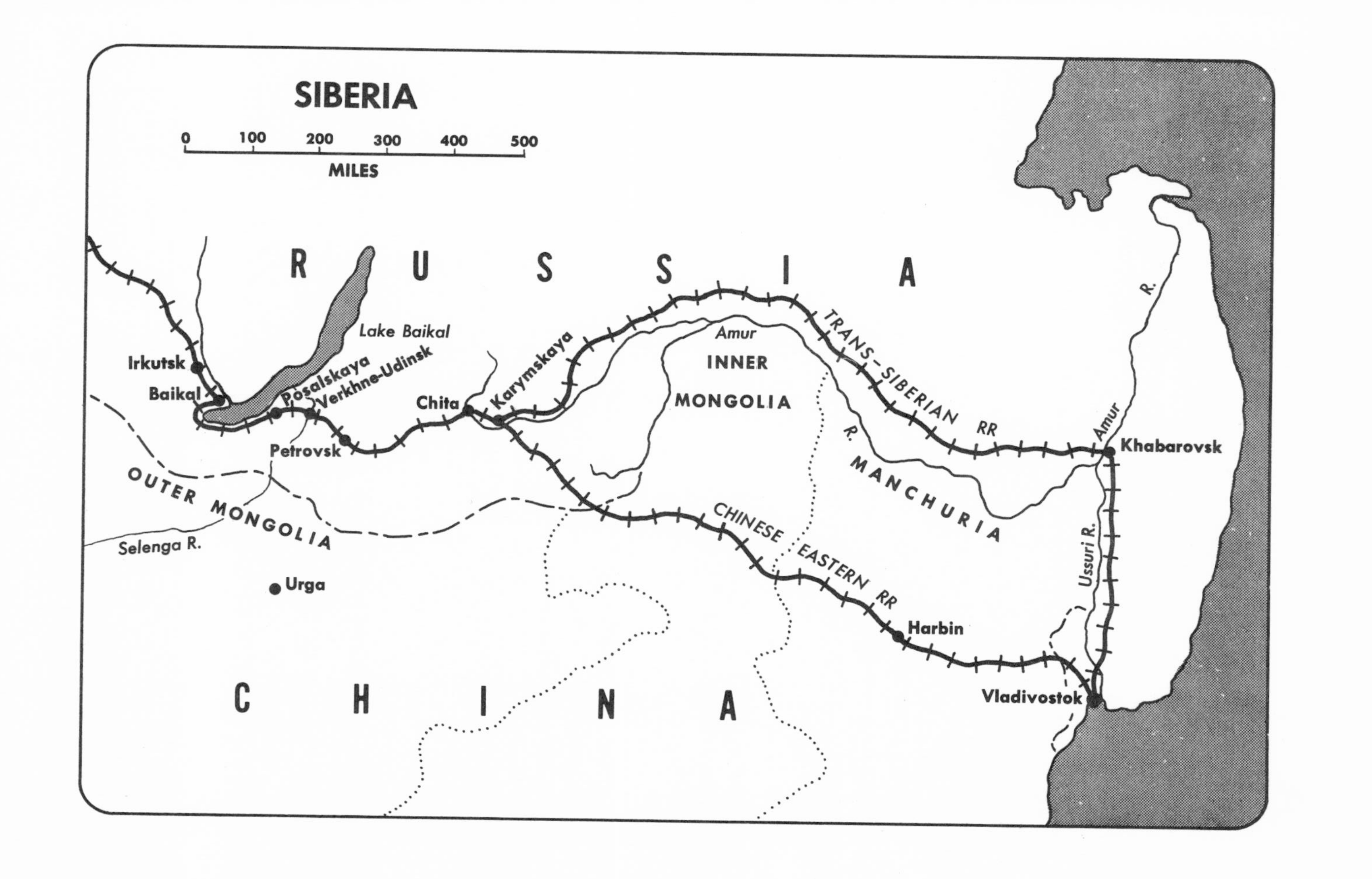
SIBERIA
0
100
200
300
400
500
MILES
RUSSIA
Lake Baikal
Irkutsk
Baikal
Posalskaya
Verkhne-Udinsk
Petrovsk
Chita
Karymskaya
Amur
INNER
MONGOLIA
TRANS-SIBERIAN RR
R.
MANCHURIA
Amur
R.
Khabarovsk
Ussuri R.
CHINESE EASTERN RR
Harbin
Vladivostok
OUTER MONGOLIA
Selenga R.
Urga
CHINA

people would be executed out of hand, being shot, burned, tortured. In winter-time a favorite method was to cut a hole in the ice of a near-by stream or pond, dip the victims in several times until they were ice-coated and then leave them as frozen monuments. Men and women were strung up by the ears to the fronts of their houses, loot was collected by wagon-load and car-load, taken to Khabarovsk and Chita, and later sold across the Chinese border for the enrichment of the local commanders.

Naturally such excesses aroused the populace to fury. Homeless villagers gathered in bands, resisted where they could and waylaid White stragglers. It was the Jacquerie of Middle Age France in a modern setting. These partisan bands, sometimes definitely Red, sometimes White, sometimes neither, roamed the woods like human wolves. The Allied missions, intent at first upon the preservation of the Eastern Front, and later upon the demolition of Bolshevism, could see no wrong in this regime of Kolchak, who, it must be admitted, had little real authority over his subordinates. To the Allies, then, as to the Whites, all Russians who were not heart and soul for Kolchak must be Bolshevists. So the vicious circle widened slowly, drawing into its slimy whirlpool Graves and his men.[10]

So, to these individuals as well as to all the Allied military commanders and chiefs of mission, the interjection in their three-ring circus of a johnny-come-lately American commander and troops, openly proclaiming neutrality in Russian affairs, was most embarrassing. When this commander followed up by seeking information from all sources, including representatives of the *zemstvos*—Siberian local government councils—it became intolerable, as Graves soon found out.

Graves' force consisted of the 27th and 31st Infantry regiments, 4th Field Hospital and 4th Ambulance Company, 17th Evacuation Hospital, and adequate quartermaster, ordnance, and signal detachments. He even had a bakery company. Neither cavalry

[10] R. Ernest Dupuy, *Perish by the Sword,* Military Service Publishing Co., Harrisburg, Pa., 1939, p. 225ff.

nor field artillery were provided, since the War Department considered the job would be one of occupation and guard duty only. As finally assembled in Siberia the American force numbered 338 officers, 8050 enlisted men, and seventeen female nurses.

Key members of Graves's command and staff structure were Regulars like himself; men who had served together and who knew one another. The troops were Regulars—not a few of them veterans of combat in France—supplemented by a hand-picked reinforcement of 8th Division personnel. And prior to his departure Graves had made specific logistical arrangements; his supply was by direct requisition from the Depot Quartermaster, San Francisco, whose vessels, the Army Transport Service, already shuttling regularly to the Philippines, simply included Vladivostok as a scheduled port of call.

The American Expeditionary Forces, Siberia, thus constituted an independent command; a self-reliant, self-sufficient miniature of Pershing's A.E.F. in Europe; far cry indeed from poor Colonel Stewart's handful in North Russia, living a hand-to-mouth existence and dependent entirely on alien supply.

The 27th Infantry, Colonel Henry D. Styer, rushed from Manila, landed at Vladivostok August 15-16; the 31st Infantry, Colonel Frederic H. Sargent, also from the Philippines, arrived the twenty-second. Graves, with his staff and a contingent of replacements, debarked September 3. He was in for a shock; some of his troops were already in combat under Japanese command, fighting Bolshevik forces.

Japanese General Otani, springing rank as commander of Allied forces in Siberia—which was true—had taken two companies of the 27th immediately on their arrival, to spearhead a Japanese column advancing up the Ussuri Valley to Khabarovsk against a Bolshevik force alleged to consist of German ex-prisoners of war.

Graves on arrival at once informed Otani that while willing to cooperate he had no intention of permitting his troops to operate under foreign command. However, since the force was already committed, and the war with Germany still on, he sanctioned the detachment temporarily. Companies E and G, reaching Khabarovsk, then continued west with the Japanese column to

Blagovischensk on the Amur, its objective, taking light casualties. They were then returned, in late September, with Otani's commendation: "I admire the astonishing rapidity of the operations along the railway." And that was that; but Graves had given the *ad hoc* Allied command its first shock.

Meanwhile he settled down to business falling within the limitations of the *aide-mémoire*. Since the Suchan coal mines not far north of Vladivostok were essential to the operation of the railway, he agreed to take over guard of the Vladivostok-Khabarovsk line in the Ussuri Valley and its narrow-gauge shuttle to the mines. He also settled amicably a strike of the mineworkers.

The 31st Infantry, garrisoned at Vladivostok, sent E Company to the mine area, F and G to Spasskoe (now Spass), L to Razdolnoe, and patrolled the railroad up to Khabarovsk, where the 27th Infantry settled. The 27th, at Khabarovsk, took control of a prisoner of war camp at nearby Krasnaya Rechka, and its three thousand German and Magyar inmates. A.E.F. headquarters were in Vladivostok, where several warehouses were taken over, while the troops occupied existing Russian barracks. In all this house-hunting and housekeeping Graves and his staff had to cope not only with a certain amount of reluctance and slipshod foot-dragging on the part of the White Russian military representatives, but also the definite opposition of the Japanese, who had spread themselves wide and were most reluctant to give up space. However, by November, when the cold weather set in, the American troops were fairly comfortably quartered.

Then came the Armistice of November 11, 1918, in Europe. Close on its heels Siberia's pot really boiled over. Admiral Aleksandr Vasilievich Kolchak, with Allied consent and at British instigation, on November 18 overthrew the shaky White Russian government at Omsk. Entitling himself Supreme Ruler of Russia, Kolchak assumed command of all anti-Bolshevik forces.

The Admiral, a sincere patriot, who was regarded as one of the very few capable naval officers of the old Imperial regime, nevertheless inherited all the limitations and weaknesses of his autocratic background. His unsavory subordinate commanders, whom he would not or could not control, instituted a reign of terror, particularly in East Siberia, from Lake Baikal to the Pacific.

Foremost of these gentry was Gregorie Mikailovich Semenov, Ataman of the Trans-Baikal Cossacks, who ravaged the Selenga River Valley from his strategic position at Chita, astride the Trans-Siberian at its junction with the Chinese Eastern line. Semenov, originally a commisar of the short-lived Kerensky regime, had been ousted from the Trans-Baikal by the first wave of Bolshevik violence and fled over the Chinese border. Then he returned with an aggregation of former Tsarist officers and men—Cossacks, Mongols, and Buriats. Under Japanese control—he was well paid by them—he alternately supported and opposed Kolchak and played hob at will with the supply flow from Vladivostok to the White Russian front. He counted his victims in thousands. On one occasion, August 19, 1919, his "Savage Division," commanded by a General Levitsky, rounded up some sixteen hundred men, women, and children, loaded them in fifty-two railway cars and carried them to one of his three killing grounds, where they were machine-gunned *en masse*.

Over at Khabarovsk on the Amur was Ivan Pablovich Kalmykov, Ataman of the Ussuri Cossacks; a young man in his early thirties, whose timid air disguised a diabolic character. Describing Kalmykov as "the worst scoundrel I ever saw or heard of," Graves reported that "Kalmykov murdered with his own hands, where Semenov ordered others to kill." Kalmykov was not only in Japanese pay, but his troops were armed and supplied by the Japanese. Credited with more fifteen hundred murders, he boasted that he changed his methods of killing daily.

Kolchak's overall commander in East Siberia was at first General Pavel Pavlovich Ivanov-Rinov, former officer of the old Imperial regime, who sat at Vladivostok, and directed periodic searches for recruits and weapons in the countryside. His excesses of torture and looting were fantastic. He would be relieved in May 1919 and replaced by Baron General Sergei Rozanov, another former officer of the old Imperial school, who continued wholesale looting, torture, and murder. He, too, was in Japanese pay.

Under these conditions, Graves, mindful of the admonition of the *aide-mémoire* that United States troops were in Russia "to steady any efforts at self-government or self-defense in which the Russians themselves may be willing to accept assistance," was at once faced with an interesting conundrum: What Russians? Reds, Whites, or the prowling partisan bands of peasantry savagely resisting the ravages of both sides?

Seeking information, a task in which his G-2, a brilliant young lieutenant colonel named Robert L. Eichelberger plunged with vim, Graves shortly received a formal visit from Ivanov-Rinov's deputy. The Russian, filled with the importance of his "cease and desist" mission, had the temerity to inform the American commander that White Russian headquarters would provide him with "all the information it was necessary for him to have." Unimpressed, Graves had the man shown the door. And that brought him into conflict with the Kolchak regime.

Everybody, it seemed, was getting into the game of baiting Graves. Dr. Maurice Teusler (a relative of Mrs. Woodrow Wilson) in charge of Red Cross activities in Siberia, actually told the General that should the Czechs call on him for help in their battling for White Russia, he would not "dare refuse." The Red Cross, quite properly, was rendering every assistance possible to the Russian people. But Dr. Teusler, perhaps through ignorance, chose to ignore the fact that his people were turning over trainloads of supply to Semenov, who as promptly sold them to Chinese and Japanese agents. It must be noted that the Y.M.C.A. representatives, who did a major job of assisting American troops, played no part in this finagling.

Worse still, from Graves's viewpoint, was the callousness with which the Allied commanders received his protests against White Russian atrocities. At one inter-Allied council meeting British General Knox blandly told him that the Russian people were "swine" who didn't know what they wanted. Later, Knox would publicly characterize both Graves and Vice Admiral Austin M. Knight, United States Naval commander at Vladivostok, as "stupid and stubborn," because they refused to take active military part in the civil war on the anti-Bolshevist side.

In late January 1919, up at Khabarovsk, some seven hundred of Kalmykov's troops, fed up with mass murder and the cruelty with which he treated his own men, deserted. A good half of them, 398 men with their animals and arms, including four fieldpieces and three machine guns, sought sanctuary in the 27th Infantry's compound. Colonel Styer granted it, disarmed them, and kept them under armed protection.

Graves, approving the action, was at once deluged by official protests from Japanese headquarters, demanding the return of the mutineers. Knowing full well that a massacre would result were the men to fall in Kalmykov's clutches, Graves refused and the 27th Infantry prepared to fight. General Otani, while disclaiming any responsibility for Kalmykov, then made formal request for the surrender of the deserters' arms, on the ground that they belonged to Japan!

To this Graves consented:

> I told the Japanese Chief of Staff that if Japan would make written acknowledgement that she had armed this murderer, that the property had not been paid for . . . and if they would identify the property and sign a receipt for it, I would let them have it.

Amazingly enough, Otani complied. The arms were identified, turned over to Otani's representatives on April 8, and the Japanese receipt filed in U.S. War Department records. As for the mutineers, they were permitted to filter freely to their homes. But from that day on, Kalmykov's reduced forces, when they carried out their looting raids, were always accompanied by Japanese detachments to protect them.

With the spring came major changes in the Siberian situation, vitally affecting the A.E.F. The Allies, recognizing Kolchak, determined to bolster his forces. The United States, while refraining from recognition, joined "to assist it with munitions and food." By Allied agreement Colonel John F. Stevens' Russian Railway Service Corps[11] came into action to restore the Trans-Siberian rail system, now sadly deteriorating. At the same time the inter-Allied command at Vladivostok reshuffled the railway guard allocations. To this, of course, Graves gave willing consent, though reinterating his intention of remaining militarily neutral

[11] *Vide,* p. 196 *supra.* Protection of these American railway men automatically fell to Graves.

in Russian internal affirs.

Accordingly a task force of the 27th Infantry, two battalions under Colonel Charles H. (Judge) Morrow, moved from Khabarovsk to Verkhne-Udinsk (now Ulan Ude) and assumed control of the rail line from that point west to Mysova (now Babuskin), where the Czechs assumed the line guard all the way west to the fighting front.

The rest of the 27th, with the 31st Infantry, remained in the coastal area, maintaining order in Vladivostok and guarding the Amur division of the Trans-Siberian north to Spasskoe, as well as the Suchan mine area. One detached company of the 31st was stationed at Harbin, Manchuria, on the Chinese Eastern line, guard of which was assumed by the Chinese. The remainder of the rail system was controlled by the Japanese.

One notes that Graves not only made no objection to this fourteen-hundred-mile gap now dividing the principal elements of his force, but apparently welcomed it. There is no doubt that it favored accomplishment of his concept of responsibility—ensuring that American supply bound for Kolchak actually reached its destination.

Graves at this time was feeling increased pro-Kolchak pressure from all sides, including U.S. State Department representatives, whose policy definitely clashed with the provisions of the Wilsonian *aide-mémoire*. Roland Morris, Ambassador to Japan, who also assumed the role of a quasi-high commissioner in Siberia, made no bones about it.

"You will now have to support Kolchak," he told Graves; ". . . The State Department is running this, not the War Department." And then and there Graves drew the line. "The State Department is not running me." As it turned out, the State Department had just begun to fight.

British General Knox tried another tack, by recommending that since the Japanese would guard most of the rail system east of Lake Baikal, overall command be given to General Otani. This of course would incidentally put Graves's troops under Allied command and draw them officially into the civil war. Graves torpedoed that proposition by the announcement that he would guard his sectors of the line in his own way, which was nobody else's business unless and if it failed.

What to do with this American commander, who could neither be bullied nor mousetrapped? The British and the French brought their complaints right up to President Wilson at the Versailles Treaty conference, without success; the White Russians and the Japanese instituted a major propaganda campaign in Siberia, Japan, and the United States.

Meanwhile Graves's troops ran into action, as the spring thaws, opening up the country, brought increased partisan activity, particularly in the Ussuri Valley between Vladivostok and Khabarovsk, and in the adjoining Suchan mine area.

In June a partisan force menaced squads of C Company, 27th Infantry, in the Spasskoe area. Reinforced by a platoon of F Company, they were then attacked by a strong partisan force, which was repelled. That same afternoon, the remainder of F Company was ambushed while marching from Shmakova to Uspenka, but drove the attackers off.

An officer and four men of the Suchan mine detachment were captured June 20 by partisans wearing red hearts pinned to their clothing to indicate their Bolshevist allegiance, and dragged to the village of Novitskaya. H Company, 31st Infantry, stormed the place, losing an officer and three men killed. Sergeant Delbert Farrington, taking command of his platoon when its commander was killed, won the D.S.C. for his daring leadership in this action.

The prisoners were carried away by the retreating partisans to a neighboring village. Lieutenant Colonel Eichelberger, Graves's G-2, on the twenty-eighth daringly stalked into the partisan camp alone, and persuaded the band to give up their prisoners, who were unharmed. For this deed he received the D.S.C.

At Romanovka, June 25, a platoon of A Company, 31st Infantry, attacked by an overwhelming partisan band, lost nineteen men killed, and twenty-five wounded out of a strength of seventy-two. The survivors, rallied by Lieutenant Laurence D. Butler, held out until reinforcements arrived.

At Sitaz, June 26, a platoon of C Company, 31st Infantry, successfully defended a railway bridge against a heavy attack, while Corporal Arthur H. Vogel deliberately ran a locomotive back and forth under a bluff to draw enemy fire and disclose their position.

A succession of platoon and squad actions in the lower Suchan Valley followed, through the summer, as the 31st Infantry successfully defended the railroad line from partisan raids. American losses were small, but most of the bickering was hard-fought. And when the Americans were not themselves fighting they had time to glower at the frowsy Cossacks leering from the Kalmykov *bronivik* (armored train), which ever so often rumbled past, bound, as the soldiers well knew, on some murderous plundering foray. Itchy American trigger fingers were restrained only by discipline.

Up in the Baikal area, Colonel Morrow's 27th Infantry was having troubles of its own, beginning with its arrival at Verkhne-Udinsk. Although barracks accommodations had been promised by the White Russians command at Vladivostok, no housing was available. So the 27th remained under canvas until the middle of September, when a warehouse nearby would be available. Then the local commander, a General Majack, received orders from Vladivostok that under no circumstances would any buildings be turned over to the Americans; they were to be used by another Russian command.

Majack, evidently a Russian of honor and courtesy rarely found in Siberian White Russian ranks, informed Morrow that he would delay transmitting the order until ten next morning. "I think you will know what to do," he told Morrow. The "Bull of the Woods," as Morrow was known affectionately by his own men, did know. Two companies of the 27th moved immediately, took over the warehouse complex, and that ended that argument.

The White Russian attitude in the neighborhood, however, became most intolerable. A Russian officer in one instance who shot and killed an American soldier because the man stood in his way, was exonerated by a local Russian court. Morrow took steps. When a drunken party of Semenov Cossacks attacked a group of Americans on pass in Verkhne-Udinsk, an American military policeman quite properly shot and killed the ringleader out of hand.

Semenov's armored trains—he had seven of them—kept up at

first a reign of terror along the 27th Infantry sector. Railway employees were molested, normal train movements were retarded, and even the passage of White Russian reinforcements to the front was challenged by Semenov's men.

Morrow, once more taking matters in hand, gave Semenov twenty-four hours to remove any and all of his trains from the American sector, and put teeth in his threat with 37-mm. guns. The *broniviki* and their sullen crews, under Japanese guard, decamped. When they returned, six months later, they came in a definitely hostile move.

Matters in Siberia were now going from bad to worse. Kolchak's troops were being pushed back while the bloody tantrums of his East Siberian leaders increased. Over on the Amur, September 5, a Kalmykov raiding party triggered off another incident, which rolled to snowball proportions; an American captain and a corporal were arrested at Imam, allegedly because they had no passports. Major Charles A. Shamotulski, 27th Infantry (born, be it noted, in Tennessee), hotfooted with a 150-man detachment to Imam and captured a detachment of Cossacks as reprisal. A Japanese detachment guarding the Kalmykov force threatened to open fire unless the Cossacks were surrendered. Announcement that the captured Americans had been removed to Khabarovsk prevented an immediate open Japanese-American clash, but Shamotulski held his own hostages until both Americans were returned, two days later. In the interim, it appears, the corporal had actually been whipped savagely by Cossack *knouts*.

Down in Vladivostok, General Graves told Rozanov—Ivanov-Rinov had been relieved—that if Kalmykov's men ever again touched an American soldier he would capture the brigand leader at once. Kalmykov then broadcast an appeal to the Cossacks to drive the Americans out of Siberia, and Graves lowered the boom. A shipment of American rifles consigned to Kolchak was about to move from Vladivostok west to the front. Graves help up the shipment, informing Kolchak that military supplies from the United States would cease so long as White Russian agents threatened military force against American troops. Meanwhile his Vladivostok-Amur force concentrated at Spasskoe prepared to repulse any White Russian attack.

Graves, who had cabled a report of his action, requesting approval, was informed by the War Department that the shipment must go through; it had been paid for in gold. So the arms moved, in two trains, for delivery at Irkutsk, west of Lake Baikal. The first train went through; the second was halted in the Chita yard, a *bronivik* ran alongside and Semenov demanded that fifteen thousand of the fifty thousand rifles be turned over to him.

Lieutenant Patrick A. Ryan, train guard commander, refused and mustered his fifty-man detachment, with loaded rifles, against Semenov's ragings, while Japanese officers watched complaisantly. Graves wired Ryan to stand pat, gambling that since Chita was within the Japanese sector they could not permit Semenov to make an actual assault on the American train. He was right. After forty hours of tension, the train was permitted to move on and Ryan delivered his rifles.

Parenthetically, these rifles, or some of them, popped up again, not long before the A.E.F. was ordered home. Graves, tipped off that four railroad cars carrying original cargoes of small arms were sidetracked within the Japanese sector, bluffed the Japanese into acknowledging the fact and surrendering the cargo—5900 rifles in original packing cases, which had never gotten beyond Irkutsk.

All this while Graves was bearing the brunt of vocative criticism in the United States and abroad. There was, for instance, Acting Secretary of State Frank Lyon Polk, who, playing the British tune, at Versailles reported to the Commission to Negotiate Peace that Graves was "tactless, at least," because "he announced categorically he is responsible to his Government and no one else, and will not consider orders from the Japanese commander."

By this time, at Vladivostok, General Rozanov had instituted a virulent anti-American propaganda campaign in the local press, which was promptly picked up in Japan. He dubbed the A.E.F. "Bolshevik." Graves's protests against inflammatory and false articles in the Rozanov-controlled press were followed by a visit from a Rozanov staff officer. If $20,000 per month were guaranteed to Rozanov, he explained, all anti-American ropaganda would cease immediately!

By October 1919 the entire Kolchak regime came apart at the seams. The Czechs, disgusted, withdrew from the active front and began to move back for Vladivostok and shipment home. The remainder of the White Russian forces disintegrated under increased Red pressure, despite the efforts of General Radula Gaida, a disgruntled Czech to whom Kolchak had given field command.

The end of White Russian hopes was nearing. On November 14 Kolchak and his staff, together with Allied mission personnel, fled Omsk for Irkutsk, one day ahead of the Reds, and the remnants of his forces rolled back against the steady Red advance.

That same day General Gaida, who had broken with Kolchak, came to Vladivostok. Two days later, conspiring with a Social-Revolutionary group, Gaida attempted to seize Vladivostok and proclaim a liberal White government. For forty-eight hours Rozanov's and Gaida's two White Russian-factions fought it out in the streets, while Allied and American troops stood by. Then Gaida's supporters, outnumbered—the Czech elements in the city refused any support—took refuge in the railway station and most of them were shot down. Gaida, escaping, sought and obtained refuge at Czech headquarters.

This flurry is of interest because American troops turned out to protect the railway station from both Rozanov and Japanese occupation. M Company, 31st Infantry, hurriedly piled into trucks, raced a Japanese motorized detachment through Vladivostok's streets and arrived split seconds ahead of it. The doughboys piled out with bayonets fixed and lined up in front of the building. The Japanese convoy did not even detruck; it rolled away.

Graves, well advised of the situation through his efficient intelligence reports, and his own personal visit to Omsk in July 1919, now cabled the War Department his estimate that the Kolchak government was dissolving, and arbitrarily refused to forward any more arms shipments, which he felt would only fall into either Bolshevik or—more probably—into Semenov's hands for the brigand's own use. In this move he was again castigated by State Department consular officials.

To add to General Graves's annoyance at this time, an officer of War Department G-2, Lieutenant Colonel Benjamin B. McCroskey, Inf., appeared in Vladivostok, under special orders to report directly to Ernest L. Harris, U.S. Consul General at Irkutsk, who throughout the life of the expedition had been one of the most vocative antagonists to Graves's neutral stand. In theory, Graves would have no control over McCroskey. This officer carried a monograph issued by Brigadier General Marlborough Churchill, War Department Assistant Chief of Staff for Intelligence, one paragraph of which contained an amazing contradiction to the *aide-mémoire*:

> The American troops are in Siberia *primarily to support Kolchak against Bolsheviks* (emphasis added) by keeping his line of communications open along the Trans-Siberian railroad.

Graves, who believed—probably correctly—that General March had no knowledge of this officer's mission, cabled Washington and received permission from March to force the officer to extract this statement from the document and burn it in his presence, which was done. Then McCroskey was permitted to go on to Iskutsk. We shall hear more of him later.

In early December Kolchak was persuaded by General Janin to accept the protection of the Czechs, who were recoiling unhurriedly and efficiently along the rail line. He and his entourage, together with his gold treasure—Tsarist gold which he had been loyally safeguarding—rolled into Irkutsk December 14 under Czech protection to find the city controlled by a liberal Social-Revolutionary (anti-Bolshevik) faction who demanded Kolchak's surrender. Janin and the Czech commander, General Jan Syrovy, acceded on the ground of self-defense, an act of apparent treachery which has never been fully explained. The Bolsheviks took Irkutsk a few days later and on February 6 the ill-fated Admiral was taken out and shot.

Kolchak's last official act before surrender was to transfer supreme White Russian military and civil power in East Siberia to Semenov, whose rage now fell on the 27th US Infantry in the Lake Baikal region, pursuing its legitimate line guard task for the protection of the Czechs still passing through.

To understand what now happened we must remember that Colonel Morrow's task force occupied the railroad stations in its sector in platoon force, with the main body in reserve at Verkhne-Udinsk. The line guard detachments had made themselves comfortable in railroad cars on sidings, banked with earth and protected from the cold by outer wooden walls and tops. Wood was of course plentiful and roaring stoves kept the quarters snug and warm. An elaborate "Alert Plan" including wire communication had been inaugurated and the troops were thoroughly exercised in it. The appearance of a Semenov *bronivik* within any block was the signal for the detachment to stand to arms—at night, out of their bunks, fully dressed and prone on the car floor, arms in hand. S.O.P. was to have one man always awake in each car.

On January 9, 1920, Semenov asked and received permission to send four armored trains west through Morrow's sector, to relieve the situation at Irkutsk. A fifth *bronivik*, labeled the "Destroyer," came into the Verkhne-Udinsk station early that evening and under the eyes of American sentinels seized the stationmaster and started looting his house. Colonel Morrow immediately double-timed from his office to the station and demanded an explanation from the Russian commander, "General" Nicolai Bogomoletz, who calmly responded that he had arrested the stationmaster and was about to shoot him. To Morrow's demand for the man's immediate release Bogomoletz retorted that he was not responsible to the Americans, that he would do as he pleased, and that the conversation was closed.

The "Bull of the Woods' " report of the incident is an understatement: "I informed General Bogomoletz that the conversation was just beginning, and that if he did not release the stationmaster I would forcibly take him away with American troops."

With a ring of American bayonets around his train, and a 37-mm. gun close-focused on his car, Bogomoletz saw the point. The man was released and the "Destroyer" chugged westward into the night.

Sixty miles up the line at Posolskaya station the "Destroyer" came to a halt late that night beside the darkened row of boxcars housing Second Lieutenant Paul Kendall, 27th Infantry, and thirty-eight men of M Company. Not even a sentinel was visible. Actually, one of Kendall's men that evening had been warned by a Russian girl that the Semenov train was in the area, and the "Alert" plan was in effect.

The *bronivik* lay still for twenty minutes, with locomotive simmering. Then gunports clicked open and Kendall's boxcars shivered under an avalanche of fire from a three-inch gun, one-pounders, machine guns, and small arms.

The splintering cars disgorged Kendall and his men. Circling the *bronivik*, they poured fire into it through the gunports on its unmanned side. Sergeant Carl Robbins, from Concord, Tennessee, climbed into the engine cab through a hail of machine gun and rifle fire to toss a hand grenade, which cut a steampipe but also killed him. The Russian train started. The Americans, running alongside, blazed at loopholes until it gathered speed. But Robbins' grenade had done its work well. Leaking steam in a dozen places, the locomotive died four miles up the line and Bogomoletz, fearing reprisal from the peasantry, wired back to Posolskaya, offering surrender.

Another detachment of M Company, moving from the next post, picked up the *bronivik*'s crew and brought them in to Kendall—Bogomoletz, six other officers, and forty-nine men. Five other Russians were dead, and twelve more had decamped. The American loss was two men killed and another man wounded.

"I am sorry that Lieutenant Kendall did not hang Bogomoletz to a telegraph pole," commented General Graves later. "But he acted within the law and really exhibited better soldierly qualities in acting as he did."

The Russian train and the prisoners were towed into Verkhne-Udinsk, where they were held until the 27th Infantry evacuated its sector January 15. Morrow, expecting that Semenov might block the rail line at Chita, had prepared to march his task force overland on the Gobi Desert caravan trail through Urga to Kalgan and Peking. But the "Ogre of Chita" had had enough; Morrow's trains were not molested. Before departing

Morrow obtained a Russian receipt for the train, the prisoners, and the "Destroyer's" harvest of loot—177 pocketbooks and a half-million rubles. Also, full statements had been obtained from the prisoners regarding their depredations.

But Morrow did not leave Semenov's domain without incident. As his train halted at Chita, he observed that attached to one of Semenov's *broniviki* was Lieutenant Colonel McCroskey's car, and it developed that McCroskey had been attached to Semenov's headquarters by Consul General Harris, who had left Irkutsk to seek shelter from the advancing Reds. Morrow, no man to quibble, ordered McCroskey's car to be attached to his own train and McCroskey stuck his neck out.

"You have nothing to do with me," he told the "Bull of the Woods," "and General Graves has nothing to do with me. . . . Semenov is the only thing standing between civilization and Bolshevism, and I do not intend to listen to anything against Semenov."

Despite his protests and the angry remonstrance of Harris, McCroskey was hustled aboard Morrow's train under arrest, and carried to Vladivostok, where Graves, after a thorough investigation and report, received orders from General March to ship him home.[12]

The A.E.F. was going home, its task completed. The Czech Legion, concentrating at Vladivostok, where an anti-Bolshevist Socialist-Revolutionary government had ousted Rozanov, was awaiting water transport home. Morrow's force began embarkation January 17; on April 1 General Graves, his headquarters, and the last remaining units left.

General Graves's departure was marked by an interesting—if transitory—exhibition of international good will. General Otani held an official review of Japanese troops in his honor, and as the *Great Northern*, with the American commander and his staff aboard, cast loose from her pier in Vladivostok Otani's band

[12] An aura of cloak and dagger surrounds this McCroskey affair. A medical board, convened by Graves, found him mentally competent but "of a nervous temperament." On return to the States, McCroskey demanded court-martial or a court of inquiry, neither of which were granted. He remained in service, was retired in 1930 for disability, and died in Louisiana in 1948. It should be noted, too, that General Churchill's seemingly extracurricular link with the State Department in opposition to General Graves has never been publicly explained.

struck up an American tune—"Hard Times Come Again No More."

Epilogue

Manifestly, this narration of the adventures of the American Expeditionary Forces in Siberia gives only fragmentary consideration to the whole painful picture. The Allied effort to restore a White Russian government to Russia ended with the collapse of the Kolchak government. All nations but Japan withdrew their missions and forces. Japan, remaining until 1922, finally gave up—temporarily, as it turned out—her efforts to gobble the Maritime Province.

The Czech Legion was repatriated by water, mostly in American transports. Some went via the Suez Canal to Italian ports, others via Japan, the Philippines, and thence to the United States; transported across the continent, they took ship again to Europe. The American Red Cross played a prominent part in this mass transfer. By August 1920 these stubborn fighters were back in their newborn nation.

The White Russian villains of the piece decamped; most of them to meet violent death in Asia. Two men—Semenov and his subordinate Bogomoletz—first sought shelter in the United States. Semenov, who came in openly, was deported in 1922 after his case had been thrashed out in the Congress of the United States. He was executed by the Bolsheviks in 1945. Bogomoletz, sneaking in, was discovered in Hollywood, in 1937, when he attempted to take out first citizenship papers. In July 1938 he was deported by Federal Court order, on grounds not of murdering American soldiers, but of moral turpitude. Fighting deportation to the U.S.S.R., he was shipped to Latvia. His fate is not known.

In his annual report as Chief of Staff, United States Army, June 30, 1920, General March summed up America's Siberian adventure:

> The expedition affords one of the finest examples in history of honorable, unselfish dealings with an unfortunate people

and of a dignified and sincere attempt under very difficult circumstances to be helpful to a people struggling to achieve a new liberty and a self-government. The situation which confronted the commanding general, his subordinate commanders and troops was a peculiarly difficult and hazardous one. The manner in which this difficult and arduous task was performed is worthy of the best traditions of the Army.

Regulars could ask no more.

Bibliography

Chapter I

Frost, Holloway H. *We Build a Navy*. U.S. Naval Institute, Annapolis, Md., 1929.

Knox, Dudley W. *A History of the United States Navy*. G.P. Putnam's Sons, New York, 1936.

Morris, Richard B., ed. *Encyclopedia of American History*. Rev. ed. Harper & Row, New York, 1965.

United States Navy. *Naval Documents Related to the Quasi War Between the United States and France, 1797-1801*. U.S. Government Printing Office, Washington, D.C., 1935-1938. 7 vols.

Chapter II

Allen, Gardner W. *Our Navy and the Barbary Corsairs*. Houghton Mifflin Co., Boston, 1905.

Frost, Holloway H. *We Build a Navy*. U.S. Naval Institute, Annapolis, Md., 1929.

Knox, Dudley W. *A History of the United States Navy*. G. P. Putnam's Sons, New York, 1936.

Morris, Richard B., ed. *Encyclopedia of American History*. Rev. ed. Harper & Row, New York, 1965.

Tucker, Glenn. *Dawn Like Thunder*. Bobbs-Merrill Co., Indianapolis, Ind., 1963.

United States Navy. *Naval Documents Related to the United States Wars with the Barbary Pirates*. U. S. Government Printing Office, Washington, D.C., 1939-1944. 6 vols.

Chapter III

Dupuy, R. Ernest. *The Reserve Story*. Unpublished ms. Washington, D.C., 1967.

Fiske, Bradley A. *War Time in Manila*. The Gorham Press, Boston, 1913.

Ganoe, William A. *The History of the United States Army*. Rev. ed. D. Appleton-Century Co., New York., 1942.

Hobbs, Horace P. *Kris and Krag*. Privately published, Washington, D.C., 1962.

Sexton, William Thaddeus. *Soldiers in the Sun*. Military Service Publishing Co., Harrisburg, Pa., 1939.

Spaulding, Oliver L. *The United States Army in War and Peace*. G. P. Putnam's Sons, New York, 1937.

Chapter IV

Dupuy, R. Ernest. *The Compact History of the United States Army*. Rev. ed., Hawthorn Books, New York, 1961.

Fleming, Peter. *The Siege at Peking*. Harper & Bros., New York, 1959.

Ganoe, William A. *The History of the United States Army*. D. Appleton-Century Co., New York, 1942.

Henry, Léon. *Le Siège du Pe-Tang*. Lazarist Print Shop, Peking, 1921.

Knox, Dudley W. *A History of the United States Navy*. G. P. Putnam's Sons, New York, 1936.

Landon, A. H. S. *China and the Allies*. Charles Scribner's Sons, New York, 2 vols., 1901.

Metcalf, Clyde H. *A History of the United States Marine Corps*. G. P. Putnam's Sons, New York, 1939.

Spaulding, Oliver L. *The United States Army in War and Peace.* G. P. Putnam's Sons, New York, 1937.

United States War Department. *Reports of Commanding General, 1900 and 1901.* U. S. Government Printing Office, Washington, D.C.

Chapter V

Dupuy, R. Ernest. *The Compact History of the United States Army.* Rev. ed. Hawthorn Books, New York, 1961.

Ganoe, William A. *The History of the United States Army.* Rev. ed. D. Appleton-Century Co., New York, 1942.

Spaulding, Oliver L. *The United States Army in War and Peace.* G. P. Putnam's Sons, New York, 1937.

Tompkins, Frank. *Chasing Villa.* Military Service Publishing Co., Harrisburg, Pa., 1934.

Toulmin, Harry A. *With Pershing in Mexico.* Military Service Publishing Co., Harrisburg, Pa., 1935.

United States War Department. *Reports of the Chief of Staff, United States Army, 1913, 1914, 1915, 1916.* U. S. Government Printing Office, Washington, D.C.

Chapter VI

Metcalf, Clyde H. *A History of the United States Marine Corps.* G. P. Putnam's Sons, New York, 1939.

Morison, Samuel Eliot. *The Oxford History of the American People.* Oxford University Press, New York, 1965.

Morris, Richard B., ed. *Encyclopedia of American History.* Rev. ed. Harper & Row, New York, 1965.

Pierce, Philip N., and Hough, Frank O. *The Compact History of the United States Marine Corps.* Hawthorn Books, New York, 1964.

Chapter VII

General

Dupuy, R. Ernest. *Perish by the Sword.* Military Service Publishing Co., Harrisburg, Pa., 1939.

Halliday, Ernest M. *The Ignorant Armies.* Harper & Bros., New York, 1960.

Kennan, George F. *Soviet-American Relations, 1917-1920, Vol. II, The Decision to Intervene.* Princeton University Press, Princeton, New Jersey, 1958.

McEntee, Girard L. *Military History of the World War.* Charles Scribner's Sons, New York, 1937.

Stewart, George. *The White Armies of Russia.* The Macmillan Co., New York, 1933.

U.S. Department of State. *Foreign Relations of the United States, Russia, 1918.* Washington, D.C., 1931-1932.

_______. *Foreign Relations of the United States, Russia, 1919.* Washington, D.C., 1937.

U.S. War Department. *Report of the Secretary of War, 1919.* Washington, D.C., 1919.

_______. *Report of the Secretary of War, 1920.* Washington, D.C., 1920.

Walsh, Edmund A. *Fall of the Russian Empire.* Little, Brown & Co., Boston, 1928.

Wrangel, P. N., *Memoirs.* Duffield & Green, New York, 1930.

North Russia

Becvar, Gustav. *The Lost Legion.* Stanley Paul & Co., London, 1939.

Chronicler, A (John Cudahy). *Archangel: the American War with Russia.* A. C. McClurg & Co., Chicago, 1924.

Dupuy, R. Ernest. "The Archangel Adventure," In *American Mercury*. March 1930.

Ironside, William Edmund (Lord Ironside). *Archangel, 1918-1919*. Constable & Co., London, 1953.

Strakhovsky, Leonid I. *The Origins of American Intervention in North Russia*. Princeton University Press, Princeton, New Jersey, 1937.

Siberia

Ackerman, Carl W. *Trailing the Bolsheviki*. Charles Scribner's Sons, New York, 1919.

Graves, William S. *America's Siberian Adventure, 1918-1920*. Peter Smith, New York, 1931.

Janin, Maurice. *Ma Mission en Sibérie*. Payot, Paris, 1933.

Manning, Clarence A. *The Siberian Fiasco*. Library Publishers, New York, 1952.

U.S. Senate. "Deportation of Gregorie Semenoff," In *Hearings, Committee on Education and Labor, 67th Congress, 2nd Session, Part 1*. Washington, D.C., 1922.

White, John Albert. *The Siberian Intervention*. Princeton University Press, Princeton, New Jersey, 1950.

Index